Communicate!

John Foster, Pat O'Shea and Andrew Carter

Based on the TV series *Communicate!*
produced by Andrée Molyneux

Published by arrangement with
BBC School Television

Macmillan Education

First published 1981
Reprinted 1982, 1983, 1985, 1986

Published by
MACMILLAN EDUCATION LTD
Houndmills, Basingstoke, Hampshire RG21 2XS
and London
Companies and representatives
throughout the world

Printed in Hong Kong

British Library Cataloguing in Publication Data
Communicate!
1. Communication
I. Foster, John L   II. Carter, Andrew
III. O'Shea, Pat
001.51   P 90
ISBN 0–333–30562–0

Contents

Unit 1 Journalism

How do you set about writing a newspaper report? David Emery is a sports journalist working on the *Daily Star*. In this article he describes how he sets about his work.

No branch of journalism has taken such immense strides forward in the past 20 years as the art and projection of sports reporting.

The whole of life is there, on the playing fields of the world, and the sports reporter is in the first trench bringing the drama and excitement to an increasingly hungry public. He is expected to write with a flourish, to bring the full colour and vigour of the event to his readers.

In that, he has more poetic licence than in any other section of the newspaper because serious and money-laden as sport may be, it is still essentially a diversion, an entertainment, a shield from the harsh everyday realities found in the other sections of the paper.

Perhaps the 'Come with me to the cauldron that was Wembley last night' approach now appears over-dramatic. But the reporter's prime task is still to make the reader feel he was actually there.

Inside that framework of informing and entertaining lies the golden rule — be accurate. Apart from checking facts before you write them a good knowledge of sport is essential both for minimising mistakes and being able to recognise a story when it comes along.

An understanding of the game through having played helps but is not vital.

Armed with your knowledge and a handy reference book, you are ready to cover, say a tennis tournament.

Background Read about the players taking part so you know their age, nationality, particular idiosyncracies (e.g. champagne-drinking, woman-hating, Ferrari-driving), their past results (especially against other players in the tournament), physical attributes (tall, short, overweight, bald, or, in Buster Mottram's case, size 13 feet). Any of these little gems can be dropped into your story.

Live play Take your seat in the Press box before the match starts with a notebook and at least two pens. Take down the basic details: weather, condition of court, players' attire, umpire's name, time of each set, score. Make a note of each player's strength and weakness (serve, backhand, crosscourt passing shots). Watch for flashpoints which will add tremendous colour to your article: rows with umpire and/or linesmen, reaction of crowd (size of crowd?) players' behaviour towards each other.

Post-match interviews Sometimes these are lined up as a matter of course, in a room with a table and a microphone. Other times you have to grab the players as they come off court, or else hang around in the cold outside dressing rooms while they change.

But after-match quotes can breathe life into the most ordinary story: 'I felt my neck click in the third set, but it wasn't until I saw the doctor I realised it was broken. . .'

'That guy cheats. I'm reporting him to the Association . . .', etc.

How much you write will depend on your next task: the phone call to the office. Tell them what's happened, what's been said and they will evaluate it and give you a length, say 400 words.

Now it is you against the clock. You need a good opening paragraph to grab the readers' attention, some vivid imagery and, mainly, short, punchy words. The story is supposed to be understood and enjoyed by everybody from the age of 15 upwards so don't blind them with science or unnecessary long words.

And remember: if in doubt, leave it out. Then maybe one day people will be saying: 'Of course, you can believe almost everything you read in the newspapers.'

On Friday 15 June 1979, David Emery went to Chichester to report the quarter-finals of the Crossley Carpets tennis tournament. He saw Britain's Sue Barker beat the American Kate Latham. After the match, David Emery and the other journalists reporting the tournament interviewed Sue Barker. David Emery then wrote this report, which appeared in the *Daily Star* the following day.

Catwoman!

BARKER CLAWS WAY THROUGH
by DAVID EMERY

ALL the alleycat instincts that carried Sue Barker to the top of world tennis were on show again at Chichester yesterday.

The 23-year-old Paignton blonde who seemed to have forgotten how to fight, scratched and clawed her way into the semi-finals of the Crossley Carpets £30,000 tournament.

She beat Californian Kate Latham 6–3, 6–4 in swirling wind and on a treacherous rain-swept grass, then she told me:

"You have to battle and fight in these conditions. It's no good worrying about the quality of your tennis — you're bound to make mistakes."

"I had a long talk with my coach Arthur Roberts last night and he told me it was just a case of getting stuck in. That's what I did . . . and I can feel my confidence building all the time."

Sue, seeded four, began brilliantly, taking the first four games in a row.

"I didn't miss a ball," she said. "That's as well as I've played all year. But I knew I couldn't keep it up in these conditions."

Miss Latham, a distant relative of Mark Twain, provided moments of resistance — mainly in the first set when she forced her way back from 4–0 to 4–3 thanks to two service breaks from Sue.

"I had trouble with my serve again in the wind," said Sue. "But I'm still working on it and it's improving all the time."

In today's semi-final she meets Tanya Harford, the 20-year-old South African who knocked out British No. 1 Virginia Wade in the second round.

Miss Harford, ranked 119 in the world, beat the No. 6 seed Pam Shriver 6–4, 5–7, 7–5.

Sue Barker . . . determined

The most important thing for any journalist to do, before he writes his report, is to collect as much background information about his subject as he can. Sometimes, the only way he can collect this information is by asking people questions and either tape-recording or making notes of their answers. But there are often books, or other printed sources, such as files of press cuttings in a newspaper library, which can provide him with information.

When he went to the tournament at Chichester, David Emery took with him the *1979 Media Guide to Women's Tennis*. It contained this information on Sue Barker. (It would tell him about her opponents too.)

Sue Barker

Born: April 19, 1956, Paignton, England

Home: Paignton, England

Height/weight: 5-5, 117

Plays: righthanded

School: Marist Convent

Computer: (Jan 1): 26

CAREER HIGHLIGHTS

Wimbledon—semifinalist 1977, quarterfinalist 1976
Wimbledon Doubles—semifinalist 1978
French Open—1976
Australian Open—semifinalist 1975, 1978 (Jan.), quarterfinalist 1979 (Jan.)
Italian Open—quarterfinalist 1976
Italian Open Doubles—finalist 1975
German Open—1976
Canadian Open Doubles—finalist 1976
U.S. Indoor Doubles—semifinalist 1978
Virginia Slims Championships—finalist 1977, 5th, 1976
Virginia Slims of San Francisco—1977

Virginia Slims of Dallas—1977
Family Circle Cup—semifinalist 1976
Toray Sillook (Tokyo)—semifinalist 1977
Toyota Classic (Melbourne)—finalist 1976, semifinalist 1977
New South Wales Open—finalist 1975, 1977
Swedish Open—1974-75
Swedish Open Doubles—1974
Head Cup Austria—1975
Head Cup Austria Doubles—1975
Wightman Cup team—1974-78
Federation Cup team—1974-78
Avon Florida—quarterfinalist 1979
Avon Chicago—quarterfinalist 1979
Avon Seattle Doubles—finalist 1979
Avon Detroit Doubles—finalist 1979
Avon Dallas—quarterfinalist 1979
Avon Dallas Doubles—semifinalist 1979
Avon Philadelphia—semifinalist 1979
Avon Boston—finalist 1979
Avon Boston Doubles—finalist 1979
Avon Championships—3rd 1979
Avon Championships Doubles—2nd 1979

CAREER BACKGROUND: Reached top five on international computer rankings after a fabulous Virginia Slims season in 1977. She won events at San Francisco and Dallas, had three other runner-up finishes and then went on to upset Martina Navratilova to gain the finals of the Virginia Slims Championships . . . Illness and injury kept her off the tour for part of the late spring and fall, but when she was able to play, Sue was always a title threat. Took Betty Stove to three sets in the semifinals at Wimbledon and also reached semis of Toray Sillook, Toyota Classic and Australian Open in 1977 . . . Finished with 55-16 match record (.775), figures inferior only to Evert and Navratilova . . . Rookie of the Year on 1976 Virginia Slims tour as she finished sixth in the Silver Ginny point standings and won the Tennis Magazine Most Improved Player award when she followed her Slims successes by winning the German and French Opens . . . Made first big breakthrough by advancing to semifinals of 1975 Australian Open before losing to Goolagong . . . Made quarterfinals of Australian Open this year . . . On 1979 Avon tour Barker made singles quarterfinals or better five times and was three times a doubles finalist . . . Finished third in Avon Championships singles and teamed with Ann Klyomura to finish second in doubles.

PERSONAL: Introduced to tennis by her elder sister at age 10, started taking lessons from Arthur Roberts the next year and still works with him . . . Nearly quit the sport a few years ago to study home economics in college, but Roberts convinced her to keep at it . . . Enjoys swimming and horseback riding . . . Father is a retired brewery manager . . . Nicknamed "the Blonde Kitten" by the German press.

■ 1 Imagine you were going to interview Sue Barker. Use the information from the *Media Guide* to prepare a number of questions to ask her, then decide the order in which you would ask them.
2 Use the information from the *Media Guide* to write either a pen-portrait of Sue Barker to go into a programme for a tennis tournament, or a brief summary of her career to be broadcast as part of a radio sports programme.

Study the article David Emery wrote in the *Daily Star*.
1 Which details included in the *Media Guide* has he used in his article?
2 One thing a journalist must do is to try to capture his reader's interest. How does David Emery try to do this in the first sentence of his report? Do you think he is successful? Why?
3 Why does David Emery use the words 'scratched' and 'clawed' in his second sentence?
4 How does David Emery describe the weather conditions in which the match was played? Why is it important for him to make the reader realise how difficult the conditions were?

5 Why does the photograph of Sue Barker have the caption 'determined'? Can you suggest any other appropriate words, which the caption-writer could have chosen to fit in with what David Emery wrote?
6 Discuss the headline. Do you think it is suitable? Can you suggest any alternatives? □

Here is how another journalist, writing in the *Guardian* newspaper, described the same match between Sue Barker and Kate Latham.

Miss Barker was clearly relieved to come through a difficult and scrappy match interrupted by rain for almost an hour. The No. 4 seed began well, taking a 4—0 lead for the loss of just two points, but then became bogged down in a mutual exchange of errors that turned a simple task into a tricky manoeuvre.

However, seven consecutive points after the enforced break put her into an unassailable position. "I warmed up on some hard courts before the match and got a rhythm going," said Miss Barker, "but then I lost it after passing and hitting the ball so well."

Compare the *Guardian* piece with David Emery's report.
■ 1 Does the *Guardian* report include any facts which are not in David Emery's report?
2 How does the *Guardian* reporter present Sue Barker's victory differently from David Emery?
3 Choose a headline for the *Guardian* report.
4 If there had been a picture of Sue Barker in the *Guardian*, what word would you have chosen to use as a caption?
5 Sum up what you have learned from this exercise about how two reports of the same incident can differ. □

Here is the way another journalist got ready for an interview and used her notes to write it up afterwards.

Jill Eckersley writes for a teenage magazine called *Look Now*. In May 1979, she heard from a film company that the American actor Kurt Russell was coming to Britain to promote a film of the life of Elvis Presley, in which he played Elvis.

Jill Eckersley decided that an article about Kurt Russell — and the film — would be interesting for the readers of *Look Now*. So she arranged to interview him. Before the interview, she found out as much as she could about the actor and the film — and, of course, about Elvis himself.

The makers of the film helped journalists like Jill Eckersley by compiling information that they would find useful. Their *press release* contained a synopsis of the film; facts about how the film was made; details of the cast and some facts about the life of Elvis Presley.

Here is the page from the press release that contained the facts about Elvis.

■ Compile a press release like this one, that could be used by a journalist. Your subject could be a pop star or a sports personality that you admire. Or you could assemble facts and figures about yourself or one of your friends.

Remember, you are aiming to gather together information that a journalist would find useful. But you want to encourage the journalist to write an article that would show your subject in a good light! □

Jill Eckersley used the press release and other material to prepare for her interview. She could then go to her meeting with Kurt Russell confident that she knew what she was going to ask him.

It isn't easy for a journalist to carry on the interview and at the same time note down what is said. Jill Eckersley overcame this difficulty by making a tape recording of her interview. That way she didn't have to take notes while talking to Kurt Russell. She could take the recording away and make her notes later when she had plenty of time.

Here is an extract from the notes she made as she listened to the tape.

This part of Jill Eckersley's notes formed the basis of part of her article, which is printed opposite.

Find which part of the article is based on the extract from Jill Eckersley's notes. Then compare the two versions. Look carefully at the way she has turned her notes into clear, interesting English.

ELVIS PRESLEY: FACTS AND FIGURES

August 16, 1977: King of rock and roll Elvis Presley dies in Memphis Tennessee, at 42... To date, over 500,000,000 copies of Elvis' records have been sold worldwide... Presley's RCA recording "Hound Dog" has sold over 7,000,000 copies... There have been 33 movies starring Elvis released to date... His first was "Love Me Tender" on November 16, 1956... His first appearance was on Tommy and Jimmy Dorsey's show... 32 of Elvis' albums have been Gold Records, 2 Platinum... Elvis' "Aloha From Hawaii" TV special was the first TV entertainment show transmitted worldwide by satellite, reaching over one billion viewers... His first job out of school was as a $35-a-week truck driver for Crown Electric Company in Memphis... At birth, he was the surviving member of a set of twins named Jesse Garon and Elvis Aron... He made his first recording in 1953 for Sun Records... His first professional recording for Sun came a year later ("That's All Right Mama")... RCA bought out Elvis' contract from Sun for $35,000, a record figure for an untried artist... Elvis had a seven year movie contract with Hal Wallis (making such films as "King Creole", "G.I. Blues", "Blue Hawaii", "Girls! Girls! Girls!", "Fun In Acapulco", "Roustabout", "Paradise Hawaiian Style" and "Easy Come Easy Go")... Presley was drafted into the U.S. Army on March 24, 1958, and discharged two years later (March 5, 1960)... He married Priscilla in May 1967, and they had a child (Lisa Marie) February 1st 1968.....................

My opinion is he was a nice guy with an incredible talent — that just my opinion. New things in ev part you play. Don't know B Holly story v well but sure it was well researched. Sft aspects of a char come out that people don't expect. I wasn't EP fan, didn't know much abt him, learned a lot like he was painfully shy for most of his life. On stage he was... Elvis — but offstage v. shy guy. I been at this for 18 yrs. If I was to try perf. all time I'd get tired. Some stars do that, others only work when cameras roll or when they are on stage, really enjoy perf. for an audience. But when perf. is done, live own life.
Elv so incred. pop. that he lived life isolated. Kind of sad if can't do what want to do but it goes with job.
Sth you have to live with and do best you can. E took it to extreme point — dealt with it only way could.

- 1 What has she left out?
- 2 What has she added to what Kurt Russell said?
- 3 Has she rearranged the order of things very much? □

When you read Jill Eckersley's complete article, notice how she puts together information from various sources: there is information she learnt from Kurt Russell (some — but not all — of this takes the form of quotations from what he actually said); there are also facts from the press release and other sources.

- Are there any special features of Jill Eckersley's article which show that it was written for a teenage magazine?
  Think about:
  the subject matter;
  the length;
  how easy it is to understand.
  As a teenager, do you think the article appeals to your age group? □

Meet Kurt Russell the new ELVIS!

To play the part of Elvis, the King of rock 'n' roll, must be one of the hardest roles Kurt Russell will ever have to tackle . . . but, through it, he's gained so much more than just acting experience!

When I was introduced to Kurt Russell, my first thought was that he didn't look a bit like Elvis Presley! In the film *Elvis — The Movie*, Kurt plays the part of the King of rock 'n' roll. It must be a daunting prospect for any actor to play someone like Elvis, who was the idol of millions. I asked Kurt how he felt about this.

"I tried not to worry too much about it," he said. "I wanted to do a good job, though, both for my own sake as an actor and for Elvis's

sake. I was chosen to play the part by the casting director, who had seen my work in the past. They wanted someone who could handle the part and be made-up to look like Elvis, rather than just an Elvis look-alike!"

Kurt is well aware that if this film biography of Elvis isn't a success, both he and the rest of the team will come in for a lot of criticism from Elvis fans.

"There was always the possibility I might either do something awful or something that people could look at and learn something about a guy who meant a lot to many people."

Kurt is certainly no newcomer to films, he told me that this is his eighteenth year in the business! By an astonishing coincidence, as a boy actor, he got his very first film part in an Elvis Presley movie, *It Happened At The World's Fair*, where he played a small boy who kicked Elvis on the shins!

"I don't remember much about it, except that it was a lot of fun to make and that Elvis was very nice to me," he said.

Kurt's Father — a professional baseball-player-turned-actor — actually plays Elvis's late Father in the film and it was he who brought the family from Kurt's birthplace on the East Coast of the USA, to Hollywood. Kurt appeared in several

Walt Disney films and in TV series like *The Quest*, before being chosen to star as Elvis. In order to make the film as authentic as possible, Elvis's own family and friends helped the actors and production team to get the details absolutely right.

"Priscilla Presley, Elvis's ex-wife, was involved in writing the scenes between Elvis and his wife, and Charlie Hodge, who played in Elvis's backing band, was our technical adviser," said Kurt.

Perhaps surprisingly, Kurt says that he wasn't a particular fan of Elvis before he made the film.

"You learn new things about every character you play," he told me. "My opinion is now that he was a nice guy with an incredible talent, but I didn't realise that, in fact, he was painfully shy for most of his life. On-stage, he was always Elvis the star, but off-stage he was a very shy guy!"

Of course, it wasn't possible for Elvis Presley to live the sort of life that most of us consider 'normal', and most fans must have heard at least some of the stories of his strange existence at his Memphis, Tennessee home.

"Elvis was so incredibly popular that he lived a very isolated life," Kurt pointed out. "It's kind of sad that he couldn't do what he wanted to do, but I'm afraid that inevitably it goes with the job!

"Making the film was a happy experience for me. Elvis's family were very positive and easy-going with me. They seemed to know and appreciate what I was trying to do. Afterwards, I had a telegram from Elvis's Father and his manager, Col Tom

Parker, thanking me personally. What with Kurt's Father playing Elvis's Father and his brother-in-law and his best friend in the production team, it was a family affair from the start! As if that wasn't enough, romance soon blossomed between Kurt and his co-star, the pretty young actress, Season Hubley, who plays Elvis's wife in the film.

"I guess it was quite romantic," Kurt admitted, shyly. "We are very different people, but we liked each other from the start and we spent lots of time together when we weren't actually working."

Kurt and Season subsequently got married and, from now on, plan to share their time between his house up in the mountains of Colorado

and Season's house in Los Angeles. "It's nice to have two homes and to be able to get away from the film business when we want to," smiled Kurt. "We don't party too much, anyway. Even when we are in Los Angeles, we usually like to stay home."

Life is very different for the Russells when they are in their Colorado home, however. Kurt was a professional baseball player for a time, himself, and he still enjoys sport, especially soccer.

"I play for Aspen Men's Soccer Club, and we came fifth in the State Championship last year!" he told me. "I ski in the winter and ride the rapids in my canoe! I go hunting and fishing, too. . . ."

Since the Elvis film came out, Kurt has been kept busy going on promotional trips, so he's had a chance to see some of the other parts of the world.

"England seems very different!" he said. "It's all a matter of scale. People think nothing of driving three hundred miles to see a football game, then home again over here! In California, we don't know what's going on in New York and, in Colorado, we don't know what's going on any place else in the world!"

Kurt's hoping that his next movie role will be something completely different from Elvis.

"I don't mind being known as the guy who played Elvis," he said, "but I want to be Kurt Russell, too!"

JILL ECKERSLEY

ELVIS
THE MAN AND THE MOVIE

Did you guess? Our front cover photo isn't of Elvis at all — it's Kurt Russell!

(Top) Kurt as Elvis — and how he looks in every life. Quite a transformation!

It may be hard to believe, but it's two years since the death of Elvis Presley. A timely occasion for the release this week of the film that pin-points the amazing rise of the King of rock 'n' roll: **Elvis The Movie.**

It's a film that looks closely at the man who gave youthful music its first great fling in the fifties. His records, including **Jailhouse Rock, Wooden Heart, Heartbreak Hotel, Love Me Tender, Hounddog,** and **Crying In The Chapel**, have sold, over 500,000,000 copies (yes, that's right, five hundred million!) so far, and continue to sell. He's had over 30 gold albums, 2 platinum, and he made 33 feature films. In the first 24 hours following his tragic death, American record stores sold a staggering twenty million copies of his albums alone, while TV showings of his films and concerts, and constant radio play keeps his voice regularly in the ears of listening millions.

The tragedy of Elvis' twin brother — who was born dead — meant that the future hero to a generation grew up an only child on whom his parents showered much love and affection. This helped him to promote his rare talent; although he was never able to read music, he certainly showed his unique singing and performing style at high school concerts.

When Sun Records heard a cheap disc he'd made for his mother at the age of 17, Elvis was whisked to stardom — and from then on never left the heady heights. Since 1956, he's had over 1,000 weeks of residence in the British charts, over 90 hits in all, over 50 Top Ten hits and 16 number ones!

A phenomenal success story, and the basis of the exciting new Elvis film . . .

Starring as Presley is 28-year-old Kurt Russell, who literally looks the part, as you can see from our photograph. In fact, the film makes it difficult to believe that we are not actually watching Elvis himself!

To highlight this, when Kurt started to perform on stage for the movie, girls really began to swoon. *"It was remarkable,"* says Kurt, *"but when I was playing the role, people behaved as if they really wanted me to be Elvis — as if they really wanted him to still be alive."*

What is even more amazing is the fact that Kurt, former Disney child actor and star of the TV western series **The Quest**, is playing Elvis at all. And he admits: *"I look nothing like him."* Yet in the film — which was premiered on American TV — he manages to capture the magic and the mood of The King.

"They tested everyone before they finally got round to me," says Kurt. *"They even tried out the Elvis clones, the people who have had themselves altered by plastic surgery to look like Elvis."*

But finally they decided that they wanted an actor, *"which is where I came in. My job is to try to get the audience thinking about the film and not about how much the make-up men may or may not have got me up to look like him."*

The film follows Elvis's life from his childhood on the poverty line in America's deep South, through his first success and onto his marriage and eventual divorce from Priscilla. It ends up neatly in 1969, before the declining years that led up to Elvis's death in '77.

It certainly gives Kurt a chance to go through his acting paces. *"I knew about the 700 or so at the auditions who wanted the part, but I was willing to bet none of them could do it*

The moment that Kurt will always remember, as he kicks Elvis's shins in It Happened At The World's Fair.

as well as I could. An actor has to think way. It hurts his ego to picture himself as one runner in a marathon race — so I si assumed that I'd got the part and ste learning how to be Elvis Presley.

"But don't start looking for an impers tion, though. I am an actor, not a singer, in every musical number in the movie, Ronnie McDowell's voice doing the sor Ronnie, by the way, is a perfect imitate the Presley singing style.

Kurt could feel that he was fated to the Elvis role. His first movie part, whe was 11 years of age, was in the film **It I pened At The World's Fair** and in it kicked the King of rock 'n' roll in the sh Says Kurt about that unforgettable mee with Presley: *"I only had a bit part in movie all those years back, but I worked Elvis for a couple of weeks and he was ter with me.*

"He took a genuine interest in me talked about baseball — at that time, I ca about baseball more than anything else, cluding acting — and he was gracious kind.

"I knew his music and I sort of liked it, b wasn't a fan. I rated him for the way he tree me, not for his records or for the girls yelled and jumped all over him all the ti Although I guess I thought all of that pretty neat, too."

Kurt is totally honest about how the

Turn to page 19 ⟫⟫

⟫⟫⟫ — the new one, that is — could affect his future.

"This film could give my career the biggest boost it's ever had, or by next summer I could find myself in early retirement, marked forever as the kid who messed with a legend and lost.

"We haven't made this project into a fairy-tale. We present an Elvis Presley who laughs and cries and throws things when he gets mad and I believe we offer some interesting new insights into the man.

"But most of all, the film is upbeat and optimistic. Presley gave a lot of people a good time and the least we owe him is to portray him sympathetically and show some respect for his generosity with his talent."

REAL-LIFE DRAMA

Behind the scenes on the set of **Elvis The Movie** there was some real-life drama taking place — a romantic drama between Kurt and Season Hubley, who plays Mrs. Priscilla Presley in the film. Now the two are married, and, as one film executive said about the blossoming love between the two on set: "I don't know whether it helped the scenes in **Elvis**, but it certainly didn't do them any harm!"

So who is Kurt Russell, the man destined to be on people's tongues in the coming months — maybe years? Well, he was born in Springfield, Massachusetts, on March 17th, 1951, and has been performing in TV and feature films regularly since 1961. Amongst his television work in the sixties were appearances in such famous series as **The Fugitive** and **The Man From U.N.-C.L.E.**

As we've mentioned, his first feature film was with Elvis in **It Happened At The World's Fair** in 1963, and from that debut,

Season Hubley as Priscilla and Kurt as Elvis in a scene from Elvis The Movie. (Below right) Priscilla Presley and daughter Lisa-Marie; recognise the unmistakable features of Elvis in his daughter?

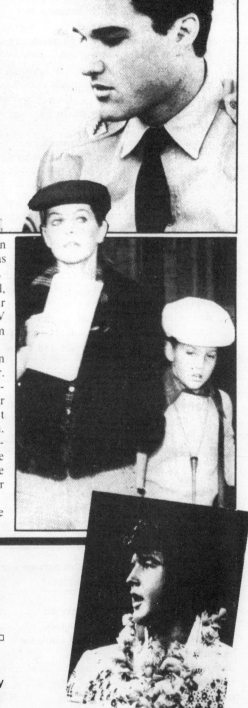

Walt Disney signed him up to appear in **Follow Me, Boys;** since then, Kurt has worked for Disney on numerous occasions.

Incidentally, Kurt's father is Bing Russell, a noted actor well-known for his 14-year stint as the sherriff in the hugely-popular TV series **Bonanza** — and about to gain acclaim for his role as Elvis's dad in the new film!

The two Russells are not only dad and son in real life and in **Elvis The Movie,** either. They also part-own a minor league professional baseball team, along with two other enthusiasts. Kurt is no mere figurehead at the club — he does a lot of work for the team, including publicity and promotion. He actually played three years of minor league baseball, starting in 1971, but had to quit the game at this level in '73 when a shoulder injury ended his career.

A loss to the game of baseball — but quite a gain for the world of films and TV!

The second article comes from *Look In*, another teenage magazine. It was published a week or so before the article by Jill Eckersley. It, too, is about Kurt Russell and the film of Elvis Presley's life.

■ 1 What similarities are there between the two articles?
2 What differences can you find in the way the articles are written and the way they approach their subject?
3 What use do you think the *Look In* journalist made of the film company's press release?
4 Imagine you had written the article in *Look In* and your editor decided that it was too long.

Rewrite the article, using half as many words as the original. You will have to decide whether to put the emphasis on the film or on Kurt Russell.
5 Using evidence from both articles, compile a press release on Kurt Russell. ▢

■ Some people criticise teenage magazines for being too commercial. They say that the magazines don't take enough account of what teenagers are really like or what they are really interested in. They say that the magazines exist mainly to take teenagers' money from them by selling them make-up, clothes, pop records and films like *Elvis*.

What are your reactions to criticisms like this?

Write an essay in which you explain your views about teenage magazines. ▢

Speech and Writing

A journalist's job involves writing things that people have said, and there are many differences between spoken and written language. Here is part of a conversation between five sixteen-year-old girls talking about their families. The conversation was tape-recorded and then written down. Supply your own names for the girls, if you like.

E I think what you mainly remember is when ... sort of ... to your knowledge ... your ... the first time you see your mother and father having a row ... Not a fight, but a row. (Yes) You always think ... you always look at them to be ... you know ... you think, That's my mother and father ... they're always so happy, you know, and I'm happy with them ... but when you see them angry with each other ... that just spoils everything. Sort of ... you can't say, you know ... then when you get older, you think, what if they got divorced ... or had to separate ... (Yes. Oh dear)

D It's on your memory all the while, isn't it?

E You think which one would you choose, and you can't ... well, I can't ... I couldn't choose between my mother and father.

A They seem to be one ... they are one. (Yeah. They are) Parents, you don't think of them as two separate people.

D You don't split them up into mother and father ...

A It's when they have rows that you realize they're two separate people ... what could go wrong. (Yes)

D I don't want to take sides ... I hate taking sides ... because my mum will explain ... she gets quite angry and she'll explain to me and tell me what happened ... and then my dad will explain. Both the stories may be different ... you know, the same sort of thing, but different ... but I can see one of them isn't quite right and I can't say which one of them it is. (No)

C Have you ever had them say ... whichever one it is ... say you're always on his side? (Yes)

E I could never take sides, you know ... if my father is ... you know ... shouting at my mother, I'd say, Don't shout at my mum like that! ... and then my mother will start shouting at my dad and I'd say, Don't shout at my dad like that! ... You know, I could never choose.

D I can't.

A I can remember the first row we ever had. It was ... I think ... my brother and I were in the kitchen and my mum and dad were rowing and it was so bad ... I'd never seen a row like this before, and my mum just started crying her eyes out and my dad felt terribly guilty, he was dead silent. Then I started crying, my brother started crying ... it was hell for about half an hour, you know. We all split up, there was nothing of the family left. And then we all crept back in, giggling and saying, Oh, I am sorry, you know.

D Yes, that's the best part ...

B Well, finally when my parents ... when they do have rows, you know, I ... er ... always saw both sides, because there was something in each ... one's explanation that ... that meant something. (Yes)

D You know, because each one's explanation was different, wasn't it?

B Yeah, and there was something right in each one ... So I just couldn't realize why on earth they did have the row in the first place, because you ... you both have perfectly good reasons but they just don't fit in.

D Sometimes they don't realize how upsetting it can be to the child. The child sometimes doesn't want to show they're upset in front of the parents, do they?

B Yeah.

C Sometimes it's something silly and the child could see it's silly and wondering why they're rowing over it 'cause they wouldn't think of anyone rowing over it ... it's just silly.

A Yes, it's funny isn't it, children don't row so much as adults.

D Really? [Laughter] My brother and I, we row.

C My sister and I are terrible ...

D I think that happens to all families, doesn't it, when they've got brothers and sisters ...

E Yes, but now I think you get most rows because they're *over* you, you know. (Yes ... Terrible) And you think you're the object of this row ... and you think, Ooh!

B You're always getting the blame for everything.

D ... and you're not really ... can't stick up for yourself.

B This is why sometimes ... sort of less contact with each other ... because you sort of come between them in a way ... you know.

■ 1 It is quite hard to read this passage at first. Try reading it aloud so that it makes sense.

Speech written down looks very different from ordinary written English. What differences do you notice? Look for examples of:
unfinished sentences;
repetitions;
pauses and hesitations;
words which fill in time while the speaker collects her thoughts (e.g. 'sort of').

When you speak, you can see from how your listeners react whether they have understood what you mean. Listeners can also encourage you to go on by agreeing with you or adding to what you say. Can you find any examples of that in this conversation?

2 When you write, you have time to stop and think and choose your words carefully. You can also go back and change what you have written. So we don't find pauses, hesitations and so on in writing; but you have to make your meaning very clear, because you may not be there to explain what you have written when someone reads it.

Take the first speech (the one that begins 'I think what you mainly remember ...') and make it into a piece of writing. Compare your version with what your partner has written. Discuss the different decisions you have each made. What did you have to leave out?
Did you add anything?
Did you need to change the order or the way the sentences were put together?

3 Using some of the ideas discussed by the girls in the conversation, write a short piece entitled 'Family Rows'. You will need to think about:

what points you want to mention;
what order you will put them in;
which examples you can use;
how to change what the girls say so that it can be written down. It should still mean roughly the same. Are there any words or phrases that can't be used in a piece of writing?

4 The conversation above has been transcribed from a tape-recording — this means that everything was written down just as it was said. If you can, try to make a tape-recording of an ordinary conversation. (If the speakers don't know they are being recorded, so much the better.)

Transcribe a part of it. Are the actual words enough to understand the conversation?

Can you find a way of writing down: pauses; emphasis; the expression in the speaker's voice; voices getting louder, faster, etc.? □

Here are two journalists writing about the art of interviewing.

When you write for a magazine or newspaper, you always have to think of your readers first. You need to know how old they are, what kind of people they are, and what they are interested in, before you can begin to write the kind of article that they will want to read!

Ideas for articles are all around you. Sometimes I get an idea from something I've read in the papers or seen on TV. Other ideas come from conversations with friends, or discussions with the Editor, or from information I have been sent by a film or record company. Even the most ordinary experiences can provide ideas to write about. Take getting up in the morning and going to work or school, for example. We all do that! You could write a funny article about the crazy things people do when they're still half-asleep; a serious article about what people in different parts of the country have for breakfast; or a campaigning article about the scruffy state of our buses and trains. See what I mean? Ideas are everywhere!

Many people think that journalists have to be experts on the subject they write about, but this isn't always so. Before I even begin to write an article, I have to do some research. This may involve going out and interviewing a real expert, or getting information about the subject from a library or from newspaper cuttings. Most companies, from BP and 20th-Century Fox to organisations like the Royal Society for the Prevention of Accidents, have a Press or Publicity Office whose job is to give journalists the right information to help them write their articles. In the same way, when a new film or record comes out, the artist's publicity agent will contact me to let me know that they are available for interview.

Some journalists use shorthand when they are interviewing. I prefer to use a cassette recorder as I think it makes for a much more natural, relaxed conversation. Some interviews are very easy and straight-forward; at other times I'm lucky to get a snatched ten minutes with a busy actor or pop star!

When I have all the information I need, I sit down to write my article. Quite often the first sentence is the most difficult part. In those first few words I want to grab the readers' attention, tell them what the article is going to be about, and make them want to go on reading.

I don't always use every bit of information I have got when I finally write the article. I pick out the most important things, and the things that are most likely to interest the readers. It's important to make your articles roughly the right length to fit the column or page. Usually, before I begin to write I have talked to the Editor about whether the article needs a page, two pages, or maybe just a few lines. It still sometimes happens that I find I've written too much, and then I have the job of 'cutting' my article, which means trying to say just the same things in fewer words! This is easier than trying to add lines to a finished article, if we find we have more space to fill than we thought.

Whether I am writing up an interview with a star, or an article on, for example, road safety, I re-read it carefully afterwards to check that I have got all the facts right and that people's names are spelt correctly. If I've quoted any figures — like the number of children killed on the roads every year, for example — I have to check that these are up-to-date. This will probably involve a couple more telephone calls.

Being a journalist doesn't just mean sitting down and writing. It means *knowing* your readers, *planning* what you're going to say to them, *checking* all the facts, and then *presenting* them in an interesting and entertaining way!

Jill Eckersley

The most important point is that the personality of the interviewee determines the kind of question that should be put, even perhaps the tone in which the interviewer puts them. . . . Some interviewees have got their answers pre-set into a well-worn groove. Trade union leaders sometimes fall into this category. They have become so used to the comforting sound of jargon, that they do not always appreciate how little they are conveying to viewers. It is in their own interests that the interviewer should confront them with short sharp questions. . . .

A good interviewer must listen carefully to the answers he gets, even if he is quite sure that he knows what the interviewee will say. Interviews that produce revelations do so, as a rule, because the interviewer has spotted something unusual and has kept probing the soft spot.

Brian Walden

■ 1 Research and plan your own interview.
(a) Compile a list of questions.
(b) Carry out the interview — with a tape recorder if possible.
(c) Make notes either during the interview, or later, when you listen to your tape.
(d) From your notes, write a short article which gives a good account of the interview and the person you interviewed.

Choose someone to interview. If you aren't sure who would make an interesting subject, here are some suggestions:
One of your parents or grandparents — you will be able to find out what life was like a generation ago.
One of your friends — this one should be easy to research, so concentrate most on the difficult job of capturing your friend's personality.
A teacher — this will require quite a lot of tact when it comes to questions!
A neighbour or friend of the family — choose someone who has something of interest about them: an unusual job or interesting hobby, perhaps.

Decide who you are writing for. When you are planning your interview, decide which kind of magazine you might be writing for. Then, when you write your article, aim to write in the appropriate style. Your article could be for:
a teenage magazine;
a newspaper;
a specialist magazine;
or you could aim — right from the beginning — to write an article for your own school magazine.
2 Journalists have to research into the background of their subject when they are going to write about an event or a general topic as well as when they are interviewing someone.

Choose a subject you are interested in or a local event and collect as much background information as you can. Then write an article about it, keeping in mind a particular audience. It could be for a popular daily or local newspaper, a children's comic, the school magazine, or a specialist magazine for people who are already interested in the subject.

Write the article imagining that you have been given a deadline by the editor of the paper or magazine. You have twenty minutes to produce an article of two hundred words, complete with headline.
3 You have now studied the way a professional journalist works, and tried your own interview. So, compile a list of 'Helpful Hints for a Good Interview'.

Present your advice either as a page from a book on *How to be a Journalist* or as a poster that you can pin up on your classroom wall to help younger pupils. □

Unit 2   Advertising

Making a Television Commercial

When a company has a new product it wants to sell, it often goes to an *advertising agency* to make a TV commercial to sell the product. In the same way, public information films are made, where advertising techniques are used to get across health or safety messages.

The Health Education Council want to encourage pregnant women to make full use of the National Health Service **ante-natal clinics**. They go to an advertising agency and commission them to make a TV advertisement to do this. The *advertising team* discuss the message they want to convey and decide what approach to take when making the advertisement. They decide to stress the fact that no one the expectant mother knows has as much experience of dealing with pregnancy as the doctors, nurses and midwives who work at the clinic. The team need to get across to the audience the experience and knowledge of the clinic staff.

They decide on a script which has an unusual approach to the problem. It's important to show just how experienced the midwives and specialists are, so the film starts with a close up of the senior midwife, while the commentary tells us

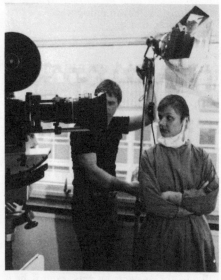

'This woman has had 3927 babies . . . . She's joined by her friend, who's 'only had 413.'

The script goes on to introduce the doctor, and to show a nervous young woman, in her first pregnancy, visiting the clinic. It's important to be informa-tive and reassuring about the clinic, so the film shows exactly what an expectant mother will find on her visits.

The film shows how the clinic is designed to help women through all stages of pregnancy.
Finally the film closes with the new mother and the sound of her baby's first cry. The experience of the clinic staff has proved invaluable yet again.

The film shows advertising methods at work and you can see the first script of this film at the end of this unit. Compare it with the script of a fruit juice advertise-ment shown opposite.

```
Client:    UNIGATE                    Title:        "Orange Trees"
Product:   St. Ivel Real Orange Juice  Job No:       FWM/30/2947
Date:      10.9.79                     Length:       30 secs
Producer:  Maggie Doyle               Colour-B/W:   Colour
```

<u>Vision:</u>   <u>Sound:</u>

Open on CU of animated orange tree
holding up right hand as he swears
his oath of St. Ivel purity. Pull
back to see that he is one of a group
of animated orange trees all with
their right hands up, all chanting
together. They are animated by stop-
frame and their branches and leaves   <u>Orange Trees</u>: We, the workers of
are like hair, and full of tons of   St. Ivel, do solemnly swear that
oranges. They have faces on their   St. Ivel Real Orange Juice isn't
trunks and talk to camera. One is   watered down, or sweetened up, or
featured in foreground.   mucked about with in any way....
                                           (fade)

Cut to pack of St. Ivel Real being   <u>SFX</u>: (pouring)
opened and poured.
                                           <u>MVO</u>: All you get in a carton of
                                           St. Ivel Real Orange Juice is the
                                           juice of about 15 oranges. Nothing
                                           more, nothing less.

Cut back to trees.   <u>Orange Trees</u>: ... (fade up) ...
                                           it will be as pure and delicious
                                           as the orange juice you'd squeeze
                                           yourself. So help us.

They all shake heads together and   <u>Lead Orange Tree</u>: Right boys, all
tons of oranges fall on to ground all   together.
round.   <u>SFX</u>: (leaves rustling)
                                           <u>SFX</u>: THUMPTHUMPTHUMPTHUMPTHUMP...

Cut to animated peel logo   <u>MVO</u>: St. Ivel Real Orange Juice.

                                           <u>Tree Chorus</u>: The Juice. The
                                           whole juice. And nothing but the
                                           juice.

■ 1 Make a study of one or two TV   (c) What particular atmosphere does the   aspects of the product should be emphas-
commercials that are on at the moment.   commercial create?   ised to sell it?
Answer the following questions about   (d) What features of the product are   (b) Devise a thirty-second TV commercial
them: emphasised?   to advertise your product, or write the
(a) How many times is the product   (e) Do you think the commercial is   script for a commercial advertising your
name repeated?   successful?   school. Set out your script like the one
(b) Is there a slogan used to sell the   2(a) Pick a fairly well-known product or   for St Ivel Real Orange Juice.
product?   invent one of your own. What special   (c) Film or act out your script. □
```
```

Advertisements in Newspapers and Magazines

Some advertisements give us a lot of information about the product — things you might need to know before deciding to buy. Others simply concentrate on creating a mood or an impression, making us feel enthusiastic about the product. Here are two examples:

Come home to a coal fire

Hitachi's latest music centre comes straight out of tomorrow's world. Pull out the control panel. And you find it works just as well when you're standing on the other side of the room.

And if that wasn't enough, it has a digital clock and timer you can use for recording programmes when you're not even there.

The four-band radio has a digital tuning system too. That makes it more precise than conventional dials. Then, once you're tuned in accurately, it has a quartz lock that eliminates drift.

There are no less than twenty different pre-set stations, over medium and long wave as well as FM.

And, when you're not using the pre-

sets, you can sweep across the wavebands and tune in automatically with a self-seeking device.

The automatic turntable uses the latest Unitorque direct drive technology.

And the cassette deck has two motors, Dolby* noise reduction and feather touch controls.

All these complete functions are fed into a powerful 50+50 Watt RMS amplifier, controlled by a micro-computer.

Drop into your nearest Hitachi dealer and try out all these amazing controls for yourself.

But don't forget to listen. The SDT 900 sounds superb.

This one has infra-red remote control and a built-in computer.

■ 1   Look at the hi-fi advertisement. What useful information does it give you? Is there anything you would want to know which is not included in the advertisement?

It uses several technical terms, such as *drift, Dolby, direct drive*. Does the advertisement give any help in understanding these words? Why do you think they are used?

2   Look at the advertisement for coal. What impression does the picture aim to create? What details in the picture add to that impression? What information would you need to know before deciding whether to choose solid fuel for heating?

3   Design an advertisement for a stereo system which gives the impression of relaxation and pleasure in music. Then

design a more informative one for a bike or a motor bike. First list all the facts and technical details you would need to know before buying the bike. Use the facts in your advertisement. Invent the information if you need to.

4   Choose a picture which could form the basis for an advertisement for a product — a chocolate bar, say, or an airline. You might find a suitable picture elsewhere in this book. Write the words to go with it — advertisers call this the *copy*. Your copy should match and emphasise the mood created by the picture.

5   Read the copy on the right and describe the sort of picture you would choose to illustrate it.   □

New Citrus Musk

Citrus Musk is the cool clean freshness of lemons blended with the warm excitement of musk. It's so perfectly balanced, so fresh and yet so mellow, that it has to be shared like good wine, music and love! In a man-sized lotion for him and perfume and sprays for her. Share it with a friend.

Making Words Work

As well as creating an atmosphere with the pictures they choose, advertisers create effects with words. Often it is the combination of words and pictures which is surprising, amusing or intriguing. The advertiser's aim is to write something which will attract our attention, keep it while we read the advertisement, and stick in our memory afterwards. To do this the advertiser uses words in special ways.

(a) Words can be chosen for the associations they have, the thoughts or feelings they bring into our minds. An advertisement for a low tar cigarette simply says:
MILD. BUT NOT MEEK.
How are the two main words different? What associations do they have?

(b) Advertisers often play with words by inventing new ones or using new spellings of existing words, for example:
IT'S A HEINZ SOUPERDAY
EVERY BUBBLE'S PASSED ITS
    FIZZICAL
FALMER JEANIUS

(c) You will frequently find language used with double meanings in advertisements. This is one way of getting the reader's attention, by making him or her stop, think and puzzle out what is meant. A car advertisement which emphasises the safety features of a well-constructed body has the caption:
YOU'RE IN THIS CELL FOR YOUR
    OWN PROTECTION

(d) *Puns* are another example of this — single words which have two meanings, both of which are important to the message of the advertisement. In this airline advertisement two good points about flying to Australia are emphasised with one word:
FLY TO THE SON

(e) Using the unexpected is a common way of catching the reader's interest. What do you think these two captions are advertising? What kind of pictures would you expect to go with them?
ALISON JONES JUST DID HER FIRST
    NUDE SCENE IN A MOVIE
WATCH LESS TV
The answers are at the bottom of the page.

(f) The sounds of words are very important in advertisements. *Rhyme* is one technique:
ROOSTER BOOSTER
Alliteration (words containing the same sound) is another:
MAKE MINE MACKESON

■ 1 Look through a newspaper or magazine, or listen to some television advertisements, and collect some more examples of these techniques.
2 You are a copy writer working for an advertising agency which is at present dealing with three products:
a fibre tip pen;
a digital watch;
a potato snack.
Choose one, and make some suggestions for an advertising campaign for the product. Design and write advertisements using some of the techniques discussed above in your slogans and in the copy of the advertisements. Remember your aim is to attract and keep the reader's attention. □

Here is an advertisement for a sports car, which uses many of the techniques discussed in this unit.

■ 1 Write down all the facts you learn about the Spitfire.
2 Write down any words or phrases the writer has used, not to give any information about the car, but to create a particular impression. Try to say what impression they create. Which is more important, the facts or the impression?
3 Pick out all the words and phrases the writer has used with more than one meaning. Explain how they have been used.
4 Read the copy aloud. Which words do you think are there for the effect of their sound?
5 What impression do you get from the name of the car, the Spitfire?
6 Why has the designer added the captions (0 mph; Oomph) to the pictures? What would be lost if they weren't there?
7 Advertisers frequently use commands which wouldn't be used in ordinary conversation because they would sound impolite. Find examples in this advertisement, and look for others in both filmed and printed advertisements.
8 Do you think this advertisement would attract your attention if you saw it in a magazine? How does it try to attract your attention, and how does it keep it? □

Even at the kerb, the Triumph Spitfire is a hard car to pass. Uncurbed, it bursts away with full thrust from its twin-carbed 1493cc engine.
Go and try a Triumph Spitfire at your showroom today and see what a great deal you'll get. It's the only sportscar that can do over 50mpg. And, at less than £3,400, it leaves all the others standing.

SPITFIRE TRIUMPH

The aim of an advertisement is to make whatever is being advertised appear as attractive as possible. So the information that is included in the advertisement is carefully selected. Favourable points are stressed, while unfavourable points are either made to appear unimportant or are not mentioned at all.

Study this advertisement for holidays at Lloret de Mar, in the Costa Brava, which is taken from a holiday brochure.

COSTA BRAVA—Lloret

1. A colourful floorshow at one of Lloret's leading nightclubs 2. Lloret's lovely beach 3. Lloret's tree and cafe-lined promenade 4. Everyone enjoys the local barbecue

Throughout the ages, countless races have visited and settled here, along what must claim to be one of Spain's most famous coastlines. Come yourself! Discover why so many people — in ancient and modern times — are attracted to the aptly-named 'Wild' Coast.

The savage beauty of the Costa Brava tumbles in a series of rocky inlets, forming hundreds of coves and wide bays, backed by magnificent pine forests and mountains. It's a marvellous resort area, blessed with a happy, carefree holiday atmosphere and long, golden stretches of beach warmed by the hot Mediterranean sun.

Small fishing villages dot the landscape in clusters of characteristic little cottages — perhaps you'll even be lucky enough to join in the merrymaking on one of the regional 'fiesta' days. But whatever else you do, be sure to sample the locally-caught fish — delicious shell-fish eaten at their best in a hundred-and-one Catalan specialities and washed down with the wine of the province.

With sport in abundance for the energetic; historical sights and monuments to satisfy the most ardent sightseer; shops and markets to excite the bargain hunter, and swinging nightlife for the liveliest extrovert — you can be sure of one thing: relaxed you may be, but bored never.

SIGHTSEEING

The grandeur and the beautiful scenery of the Costa Brava make every excursion a voyage of discovery and delight. Go to Barcelona, Spain's second city, to see the majestic gothic Cathedral, the picturesque 'Ramblas' lined with colourful flower stalls and the 'Spanish Village': go shopping amongst the wide variety of modern stores and well-stocked boutiques or see a bullfight. There's the 'mini' bullfight party too, harmless fun where you can try your skill against small bulls and possibly win a prize. Or what about taking a drive to admire the dramatic natural beauty of the region, with a visit to the famous monastery at Montserrat, set high amongst the lofty mountains. Take a trip along the rugged coast to the resorts of Tossa de Mar and San Feliu; enjoy a scenic tour, stopping first at Gerona market for bargain hunting, followed by a drive through beautiful countryside past Lake Banolas, finishing up at the charming little town of Blanes. Lively evenings too — at a leading night-club where you'll watch an excellent Spanish and international floorshow, or at the barbecue, an unforgettable experience incorporating wine, spit-roast meats, music and dancing.

You'll take home precious memories of many wonderful visits to new places.

LLORET
Costa Brava

Lively Lloret stands amidst beautiful countryside overlooking a broad, sheltered bay. The long sweep of beach is backed by a palm-fringed promenade and, beyond, there's the resort centre and the fascinating Old Town with its domed sixteenth century church.

With so many attractions and such a friendly atmosphere, you're all set for a happy, sunny, holiday. There's plenty to do by day — with pedalos and water-skiing at the beach; numerous shops for browsing in; scores of cafes, bars and restaurants and a colourful weekly market. You can go horse riding or hire a bicycle; play tennis; mini golf; skittles; enjoy folk dancing displays; watch a bull fight; or merely relax with friends in one of the open-air cafes. Yet, if you want to get away from it all, you can also find secluded coves and not-so-crowded beaches where you can swim and sunbathe in lovely surroundings.

By night, return to live it up still more . . . to the latest sounds at one of the lively discotheques; drinking sangria whilst listening to the haunting strains of guitar music in a typical Catalan bar or, by contrast, playing darts and drinking draught bitter in an English-style pub! Take your choice — and if you really want a night on the town, why not visit Lloret's new casino for a flutter at the gaming tables!

There's all this and more when you holiday in Lloret. No wonder that it's the most popular resort on the Costa Brava.

Hotel Flamingo ***

The Flamingo is a lively hotel with a friendly, informal atmosphere. We've been using it for 15 years now and particularly recommend it to holidaymakers who like to mix their leisure and pleasure evenly . . . with the emphasis on pleasure possibly? Certainly it seems that way from the enthusiastic letters we receive about the full-of-fun life here. For the hotel is just two minutes from a town which is brimming over with holiday pleasures — a shoppers' paradise by day and, by night, an exciting razzamataz of entertainments.

In the hotel itself, all public rooms are well furnished — there's a lounge and two dining rooms where you'll enjoy a choice of menu and, even more important good food and friendly service. Outside, a **swimming pool**, surrounded by an attractive terrace, offers temptation to sun worshippers and there's also another terrace up on the roof. Children aren't neglected either. They have their own section of the swimming pool and a playground too. In the evenings you'll enjoy lively entertainment, dancing in the hotel's own discotheque, or you can pop into the Frigola next door and join the weekly dances there.

There are lifts and all bedrooms have a private bathroom and a terrace.

The Flamingo offers very good value for money — certainly it's one of the most attractive and reasonably priced hotels in Lloret and, for his reason, we suggest that an early booking is desirable if you wish to avoid disappointment. *Full board.*

A The Costa Brava

1 What features of the Costa Brava area does the advertiser mention in the first three paragraphs to try to attract holiday-makers to go there?

2 Suggest some unfavourable features of the area that the advertiser might have deliberately left out.

3 What features of a holiday on the Costa Brava are suggested by the photographs? Discuss the captions for the photographs. Imagine you have been asked to expand these captions. Write new captions of approximately thirty words for each photograph.

4 What activities for the holiday-maker are mentioned in the section headed 'Sightseeing'? What impression of a holiday on the Costa Brava is the advertiser trying to give in this section? Pick out any particular words or phrases which he has used in order to create this impression.

5 Notice how the advertisement is written as if the writer were talking directly to you, the reader. For example, he invites you to 'Come yourself!' in the first paragraph. Find other examples of the writer directly addressing remarks to the reader.

B Lloret de Mar
Advertisements for holiday places are always full of adjectives. Lloret is described as being 'lively'. The surrounding countryside is 'beautiful'. Make a list of all the adjectives that are used in the description of Lloret. Talk about the words in the list. Why did the advertiser choose these particular words? What impression of Lloret does he mean these words to create?

C Hotel Flamingo
Make a list of all the facts about the Hotel Flamingo that the advertiser has included. Is there any other information about the hotel (apart from the details of prices, which were given elsewhere in the brochure) which you think the advertisement should have included?

Discuss the order in which the information is presented. How important is this order? Would the advertisement be more or less effective if the order of the information was rearranged?

Compare the adjectives used in the description of the hotel with those used in the descriptions of Lloret and of the Costa Brava. Look at the adjectives used in a number of advertisements in other holiday brochures. You could carry out a survey of a number of advertisements to see which words appear in several advertisements. Can you explain why certain words are used time and again in advertisements for holiday resorts and holiday hotels?

The Hotel Oasis Park
This description of another hotel in Lloret is taken from the same holiday brochure. The adjectives, which the advertiser included to try to make the hotel appear attractive, have all been left out. Copy out the passage, using your own adjectives. Then compare your version of the advertisement with those of the other members of the group. Decide whose advertisement is the most effective.

Hotel Oasis Park _____ and _____ , this hotel is, indeed, an oasis of holiday pleasures. It's well situated too, just a _____ five minutes' walk through pine trees from the _____ bay and _____ beach of Fanals. And Lloret, the _____ spot on the Costa Brava, is only 15 minutes' walk away — so you're all set for a _____ holiday from every point of view.

The Oasis Park offers you plenty of scope for enjoyment whether you're feeling energetic or not. A _____ swimming pool and _____ terraces provide ample opportunity to lap up the _____ Spanish sun, while the children amuse themselves in their own paddling pool and _____ playground. _____ parasols and _____ terrace furniture add colour to a scene that's all set for complete relaxation.

Design a brochure advertising your school or college. Aim to make it appear as attractive as possible. You could include a description of the school in general terms and then separate descriptions of particular subjects and courses.

How would you describe your town, estate or village, if you were advertising it in a holiday brochure to try to attract visitors? Make a list of all the favourable features you would want to include in your description. Think carefully about the order in which you would put the information, so as to make your advertisement most effective. Then write your description, addressing the reader personally as the writer of the description of the Costa Brava does.

Instead of writing a description designed to attract visitors to a place, write a description designed to put people off visiting a particular place. Make up your own name for it or call it Sludge-on-Sea. □

Brand Names

When companies decide on a name to give their products, they don't do it at random. The colour and shape of the package have an effect on what people think of it. The outside design of a car makes a difference to people's feelings about it. Just as important are the words chosen as brand names for products. Words make us think, not just about their meaning, but about the places where the words would be used. Brand names also make us think of particular things.

For example, SURF is a washing powder. The word 'surf' conjures up ideas of foamy waves, beating powerfully on the shore, just like suds in a bowl of washing being vigorously cleaned. Or the suds in a washing machine busy cleaning a load of dirty washing.

EMBASSY is the name of a brand of cigarette. An embassy is a building where diplomats from foreign countries work. The word makes us think of exciting, mysterious foreign places. It makes us think of rich, highly-paid officials who travel around in big, powerful cars.

Why did the manufacturers of DAZ and PICCADILLY choose these brand names?

■ 1   Look at the cars below and the names they have been given. List all the things that each name makes you think of. Then decide whether it is a good name for that particular model.

■ 2   Make a list of a dozen names of car models. Next to each name write all the things that name makes you think of. Then decide whether it is a good name for that particular model.

3   When you have finished your investigation into car names, think out answers to these questions.
(a)   Do motor companies give a similar name to all the models they make? Think about Rolls-Royce cars: Silver Cloud, Silver Wraith, Corniche, etc.
(b)   Here are some famous cars from the past. Is there anything special about the names they were given?
Ford Popular   Vauxhall Cresta
Sunbeam Rapier   Austin Ruby
Hillman Hunter   Triumph Herald
(c)   What is the effect of giving a car model a number rather than a name? Think about Renault cars: R4, R5, R6, R12, R14, R15, R16, R17, etc.   □

1   Austin Allegro   5   Jaguar XJ6
2   Talbot Alpine   6   Vauxhall Cavalier
3   Ford Fiesta   7   Morris Marina
4   Lotus Europa   8   Austin Princess

Brand names are particularly important to show the differences among products that are in other ways very much the same. That is why the names of washing powders are so important.

■ 1 Discuss with your friends and family what ideas come into their heads when they hear the brand names of well-known products.
Any dozen or so names will do, but a useful choice would be:
brand names of chocolate bars and sweets;
brand names of washing powders.
2 You could try the same kind of survey with:
names of pop groups;
names of teenage magazines.
3 Write a short report of your findings about people's reactions to brand names.
4 Make a list of names given to men's after-shave, deodorants, soaps, etc.

Compare your list with the names chosen for women's perfumes, anti-perspirants, beauty soaps and so on. What have the advertisers done to make men's cosmetics sound manly and the women's sound feminine? □

George Eastman, inventor of the simple box camera:

I chose that name because I knew a trade name must be short, vigorous, and incapable of being misspelled to an extent that will destroy its identity. The letter K had been a favourite with me — it seemed a strong, incisive sort of letter. Therefore, the word I wanted had to start with K. Then it became a question of trying out a great number of combinations of letters that made words starting and ending with K. The word 'Kodak' is the result.

This is part of an advertisement for Klorane shampoo.

This is part of a campaign by the Health Education Council to encourage parents to take their children to the dentist.

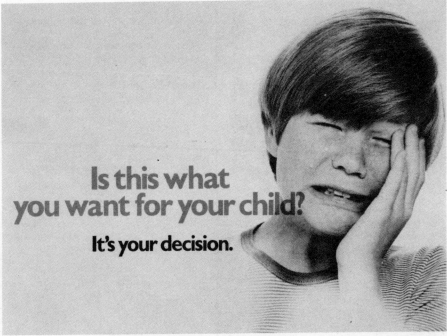

Is this what
you want for your child?
It's your decision.

Appealing to our Instincts

Just as brand names are chosen to conjure up particular ideas and feelings, some advertisements make a deliberate appeal to our instincts. Such advertisements arouse feelings that we cannot easily control. They have affected us before we can begin to think about their message.

■ 1 What instinct is aroused by the pictures above?
Do you think either advertisement is very successful?
2 What other instincts do advertisements appeal to?
Find some examples of such advertisements and explain how they work.
Make a list of a dozen different kinds of product. Say which instincts you would appeal to if you were devising an advertisement for each one. □

Public Information Advertisements

It is not only companies trying to sell things who use advertising techniques. Government organisations, charities, groups (for instance, political parties) who are campaigning for something, all use similar methods to inform or persuade us. We have already seen something of the making of a Health Education Council advertisement made for TV, to encourage pregnant women to go to ante-natal clinics. Here is the script that was used. Look also at the poster warning parents about dangers to children in the home.

How to injure your child without really trying.

Remember:
Children will try
anything once.
So protect them
from themselves.
Keep your home
safe from accidents.

The Health Education Council

Picture:

Open on pleasant woman aged about 40 entering ante-natal clinic (identified by sign). (Exterior shot: nursing school)

We see second woman, aged about 27, also entering. She greets man at door as if she is a regular there.

We see affable, middle-aged man in overcoat, also entering clinic.

We see nervous woman, slightly pregnant, entering clinic.

We enter clinic, where we see nervous pregnant woman being examined, reassured, advised, etc. by other three, whom we now identify as junior midwife, doctor and midwife. (3 fast cuts)

(She becomes more pregnant as these scenes progress)
Dissolve to woman, now a little more pregnant, being weighed by midwife. We see weight is 10 stone.

Dissolve to her being examined by doctor.

Dissolve to her being weighed again. We see weight is 11 stone.

Dissolve to midwife showing her diagram as she explains something. Cut to mother's face on pillow, lighting up with joy.

Cut to head and shoulders of junior midwife and midwife

Super: HEC logo

It will be clear by changes of costume etc. as well as by changes of size, that these are separate visits with several weeks between them. By the last two dissolves, woman should be wearing a maternity dress.

Sound:

MVO:
This woman has had 3,927 babies.

Her friend is a bit of a novice. She's only had 413.

(incredulously):
And this man has had hundreds of babies. And he's still as trim as ever.

This woman never had a baby in her life.

But she's glad the other three have.

As soon as you suspect you're pregnant...

See your doctor and he'll send you to the clinic.
They can make your pregnancy...

...a lot happier and healthier for both of you.
SFX:
Baby's first cry

Junior midwife to midwife:
Four hundred and fourteen.

■ 1   How do the Health Education film and the poster attract our attention?
What instincts and feelings do they appeal to?
Do you think they are effective?
Are they aiming mainly to inform or to persuade?
Rewrite the poster using words only. Which is the most effective way of putting the message across?
2   Think of a public information campaign that sticks in your mind. What was it about the campaign that made it effective?

3   Design a public information advertisement. It could be a poster or television script. Consider what facts you want to get over and how you can make the most impact. Your advertisement could be about:
safety in the laboratory;
cycling or motor cycling;
walking or camping in rough country.   □

Advertising and Children

The British Code of Advertising Practice is drawn up by the Advertising Standards Authority. Broadly, it requires that all advertisements should be legal, decent, honest and truthful. The code sets out a series of general rules: rules about misleading advertisements, price comparisons, worth and value claims, testimonials, the use of fear or superstition in advertisements, and many other matters. There is an appendix giving detailed guidelines about advertising to children.

The Code and children.

"Children should not be seen leaning dangerously over bridges." An extract from the revised British Code of Advertising Practice.

Appendix B Children.

General.

1.1 Direct appeals or exhortations to buy should not be made to children unless the product advertised is one likely to be of interest to them which they could reasonably be expected to afford for themselves.

1.2 Advertisements should not encourage children to make themselves a nuisance to their parents, or anyone else, with the aim of persuading them to buy an advertised product.

1.3 No advertisement should cause children to believe that they will be inferior to other children, or unpopular with them, if they do not buy a particular product, or have it bought for them.

1.4 No advertisement for a commercial product should suggest to children that, if they do not buy it or encourage others to do so, they will be failing in their duty or lacking in loyalty.

1.5 Advertisements addressed to children should make it easy for a child to judge the true size of a product (preferably by showing it in relation to some common object) and should take care to avoid any confusion between the characteristics of real-life articles and toy copies of them.

1.6 Where the results obtainable by the use of a product are shown, these should not exaggerate what is attainable by an ordinary child.

1.7 Advertisements addressed to children should wherever possible give the price of the advertised product.

Safety.

2.1 No advertisement, particularly for a collecting scheme, should encourage children to enter strange places or to converse with strangers in an effort to collect coupons, wrappers, labels or the like.

2.2 Children should not appear to be unattended in street scenes unless they are obviously old enough to be responsible for their own safety; should not be shown playing in the road, unless it is clearly shown to be a play-street or other safe area; should not be shown stepping carelessly off the pavement or crossing the road without due care; in busy street scenes should be seen to use the zebra crossings when crossing the road; and should be otherwise seen in general, as pedestrians or cyclists, to behave in accordance with the Highway Code.

2.3 Children should not be seen leaning dangerously out of windows or over bridges, or climbing dangerous cliffs.

2.4 Small children should not be shown climbing up to high shelves or reaching up to take things from a table above their heads.

2.5 Medicines, disinfectants, antiseptics and caustic substances should not be shown within reach of children without close parental supervision, nor should unsupervised children be shown using these products in any way.

2.6 Children should not be shown using matches or any gas, paraffin, petrol, mechanical or mains-powered appliance which could lead to their suffering burns, electrical shock or other injury.

2.7 Children should not be shown driving or riding on agricultural machines (including tractor-drawn carts or implements), so as to encourage contravention of the Agriculture (Safety, Health and Welfare Provisions) Act 1956.

2.8 An open fire in a domestic scene in an advertisement should always have a fireguard clearly visible if a child is included in the scene.

■ 1 Study the guidelines carefully, then design an advertisement for a new children's toy in which you deliberately ignore part of the code. Show your advertisement to your friends and see if they can spot how you have broken the code.

2 Imagine that you have found an advertisement which breaks one of the guidelines about advertisements to children. Write a formal letter of complaint to the Advertising Standards Authority giving full details of the advertisement. Remember to lay out your letter correctly. (The address of the Advertising Standards Authority is: Brook House, 2-16 Torrington Place, London WC1E 7HN.) □

Unit 3　Preparing a Television Programme

On weekdays immediately after the early evening news, BBC TV broadcasts its news magazine programme *Nationwide*. The programme goes out live and throughout the day the editor and his team of journalists are hard at work preparing the programme. The programme often contains one or two prerecorded items — perhaps a couple of short films, or a recorded studio item. But the bulk of the programme is put together on the day that it appears.

1　By 8.30 in the morning, the editor and his team of researchers are at their desks. First they scan the day's newspapers, looking for news stories that will make good television. At about 9.00 a.m. there is an editorial conference. The editor tells the researchers about prerecorded items that are available, then asks the researchers for ideas. *Nationwide* tries to balance lighthearted stories against more serious ones. The discussion becomes a free-for-all with everyone expressing their opinions.

2　The editor chooses which stories to go for and who will work on each. The items are written up on a board by the editor's desk. The researchers set about trying to find guests to appear on the programme. Some stories will be lost, so the editor constantly has to reshape the programme.

3　Neil has been asked to prepare an item on Keith Castle, who has just recovered from a heart transplant and is raising money for other heart patients. Neil telephones Mr Castle's agent and is told that Mr Castle cannot confirm yet whether he can come to the studio for a live interview in the evening.

4　Neil sets about finding the background to the Keith Castle story. He contacts News Information, a BBC department which keeps newspaper cuttings on everyone in the news, and is given a file of cuttings about Keith Castle which provide dates, facts and perhaps ideas. Here Neil is looking at clips from earlier news programmes on Keith Castle.

5　By 11 a.m. the whole *Nationwide* team has arrived: the floor managers, who find the props and run the studio; the designer, who looks after the set; the director; the film editor; and the technicians. And, of course, the presenters — the people who appear on the screen — who will spend the time until they go on the air in familiarising themselves with the items they will present.

6　At last, Neil gets hold of Keith Castle, who agrees to appear. In one phone call, Neil has to decide on what to cover in the interview. Now he must write the script. Every script is checked by the editor before it is passed to the presenter who is to introduce the item. Presenters look out for mistakes and may rewrite the odd word or phrase. The length of the item is timed with a stop-watch by the producer's assistant.

7 Other researchers have been preparing their items. One story about an actor is going to use still photographs and clips from some of his films. The researcher tells the director and the stills man about the order in which he will use them.

8 It is 3 p.m. In the main office the editor has decided on the running order. If an item is on the editor's board now you can be pretty sure it will appear in the programme. But if a big news story breaks, the chances are that the editor will include it — even if there is less than an hour before the programme starts.

9 Neil finds out who is to present the item about Keith Castle, and passes on the information he has. The presenter has to know his subject and ask the right questions. It's five to six and the programme starts. Keith Castle has arrived and in due course he is introduced and interviewed. The item on him is one of ten items in the fifty-minute programme. Next morning, the researchers will be back at their desks looking for news stories that will make interesting television.

Every weekday at five to six *Nationwide* is on the air, showing you the pictures behind the news stories of the day and interviewing the people in the news. The faces of the *Nationwide* team that you see are the familiar ones of reporters and presenters, but behind them are the 'backroom' boys and girls who make it possible for the programme to be broadcast.

As one of the researchers, I'm responsible for one of the several items which appear every day. It's my job to find the background to a news story and arrange for a suitable guest to be interviewed. I have to find the right pictures to illustrate the story on the television screen and write a script for the presenter to read which will explain the story to the viewers. It's a great deal of work to get through each day in the few hours before the programme is on the air!

When working under that sort of pressure I find it helps to arrange the things to be done in order of importance. That way, if I start running out of time, at least I know that I won't have forgotten something which is essential.

The first stage of a researcher's job is to find the right person to be interviewed. If that person is in the news, then it's a fair bet that many other newspapers, magazines, radio and television programmes will be after him as well, so the quicker you can speak to him the more chance there is that he will agree to appear on *Nationwide*.

Sometimes you are lucky. If he's at home or at an office, it's a simple matter of finding the telephone number and giving him a call. But many people in the news, like politicians, union leaders, and entertainers are constantly on the move, and you have to do a little detective work to track them down.

Once your guest has agreed to appear, it's time to speak to other members of the *Nationwide* team about the pictures you will need. The graphics department can make maps, charts, graphs or cartoons. The film librarian can help you to find pieces of film or video tape which will illustrate your story. The stills department have thousands of photographs for you to choose from, or they can arrange for a photographer to go out and shoot pictures specially for your story. A designer will build you a studio set, and a floor manager will help you to get hold of any props you may require — and props may mean anything

from a clothes peg to five million pounds' worth of precious jewels or an elephant! They've all been brought into the *Nationwide* studio at one time or another.

When you are confident that all the pictures are on the way, the story has to be researched in detail. Newspaper cuttings and library books will provide much of the background, but the up-to-the-minute information will come from speaking directly to the people involved. All big organisations have spokesmen who deal with Press enquiries, but there's no substitute for by-passing them and getting the information straight from the horse's mouth!

It's not possible to become an instant expert on a different subject every day, but at least you can expect to gain a clear understanding of the basic issues behind any story. Most important, you must check as many of the facts and figures as possible so that you can be confident that your script will be accurate.

The script has to be written quickly and kept as brief as possible so there's no time for anything fancy. It's essential to use only the most straightforward writing skills: arranging the facts in a sensible order and then keeping to the point, being concise and giving clear information.

Towards the end of the afternoon the pace hots up. The pictures are arriving and the director is checking how you want them to appear on the screen; you've given the presenter all the information he will need to conduct the interview; your script has been seen by the editor and has been read by the presenter to make sure that it will sound natural when spoken. Finally your guest arrives and you take him to the studio to prepare for the transmission.

At five minutes to six the signature tune begins the programme and there's little to do but cross your fingers and hope that nothing will go wrong!

Being a researcher on *Nationwide* is hard work. There's no doubt about that. But it's exciting and varied work. One day you can be speaking to a cabinet minister and the next to the owner of a skateboarding duck! There's certainly never a dull moment. And at the end of the day it's exhilarating to think that the results of your work will be seen by millions of people.

Brian Cook

On 11 November 1979, *Nationwide* included an interview with Keith Castle, who had been given a new heart in a transplant operation three months before.

Neil, the programme researcher who was assigned to this item, found lots of newspaper cuttings about Mr Castle in the BBC News Information Department. Here are some of them.

Heart Man Sits by Bed

BY DAVID FLETCHER
Health Services
Correspondent

MR KEITH CASTLE, 52, the retired Battersea builder who received a new heart in a five-hour transplant operation on Saturday, got out of bed and sat up in a chair yesterday.

He was said by the authorities at Papworth Hospital, near Cambridge, to be making a remarkable recovery.

Mr Terence English, the surgeon who led the transplant team, said that Mr Castle had recovered so quickly that he did not need to be kept on a ventilator breathing machine.

He said that this greatly reduced the chances of lung infection that "caused all the problems" with the last unsuccessful transplant operation last January.

Sixth patient

Mr Castle is Britain's sixth heart transplant patient. The patient to survive the longest died 107 days after his operation, but Mr English said: "I believe that we have a better than even chance of Mr Castle living longer than that."

He received the heart of a 21-year-old golf professional killed in a car crash whose kidneys and pancreas have also been used in a transplant operation.

Daily Telegraph 21 Aug 1979

Heart man's progress

HEART transplant patient Keith Castle today overcame another hurdle on his way to a new life.

The 52-year-old father-of-four from Latchmere Road, Battersea, has now out-lived four of the previous five people to undergo the operation in Britain.

It is now 48 days since the retired builder received his new heart — at least one day more than the fourth longest survivor.

And all the signs are that he will beat the 107-day record set by Mr Michael Hendrick in 1969.

"Mr Castle is satisfactory and he is up and dressed much of the day," said a spokesman at Papworth Hospital, Cambridge.

He disclosed that doctors have had to contend with some "rejection episodes" of the heart, donated by Duncan Prest, a 21-year-old golfer from St. Ives, Cambridgeshire, who died in Ely after a car crash.

Hopeful

Doctors are hopeful it will soon be possible to transfer Mr Castle from his germ-proof room into a normal hospital room. If all goes well, he may be allowed to return home next month.

The operation was carried out in August by a medical team led by 46-year-old Mr Terence English.

Evening Standard 5 Oct 1979

HEART MAN ENJOYS HIS FOOTBALL

HEART transplant patient Keith Castle, 52, was beaming with happiness yesterday when he was given VIP treatment at the Fulham versus West Ham football match at Craven Cottage.

A lifelong Fulham fan, Mr Castle met players and manager Bobby Campbell in the dressing room before the kick-off.

He was dined in the members' restaurant and greeted by Fulham chairman, Mr Ernie Clay.

"I feel marvellous," said Mr Castle as he tackled a meal of soup, scampi, and chocolate gateau for lunch, with a glass of wine.

Mr Castle sat in a chill wind without a coat to watch the match. And he tucked into ham sandwiches and a cup of tea at half-time.

Mr Castle, a retired builder from Latchmere Road, Battersea, London, had a heart transplant 85 days ago.

Sunday Express 11 Nov 1979

The newspaper cuttings helped Neil to write a short introduction to the interview. This is the script he wrote.

```
NATIONWIDE 15.11.79

KEITH CASTLE


                /BOB I/V: This week, Britain's most well known hospital patient
BOB I/V                  took a further step in his efforts to help sufferers
                         of heart disease. He is of course/Keith Castle, and
C/A CASTLE               yesterday he helped the boxer Eric Boone launch a fund
                         named after his own heart donor, Duncan Prest.
                /BOB I/V: Keith first hit the headlines back on August 20th/
BOB I/V                  the day after he became Britain's sixth heart-transplant
TJ 1 HOSPITAL            patient. So far he has outlived four of the five
TJ2 WITH WIFE            previous patients/and has astounded everyone with his
TK W'PAPER CASTLE        health and vitality. Ten weeks after the operation at
                         Papworth Hospital in Cambridge he was allowed to leave,
                         and has since stayed with his daughter and son-in-law at
                         their farm in Northampton. For a man who could only walk
                         thirty yards before the operation it's been a new life -
                         walking and cycling several miles a day.
```

■ 1 Discuss the following questions.
(a) Which part of the script could *not* be based on information from the newspaper cuttings?
(b) Is there any information in the script that must have come from a newspaper cutting that is not reprinted here?
(c) Do you think the researcher who wrote the script has followed the advice Brian Cook gives on the previous page?
(d) Would the script have been any different if it had not been written to be read aloud?
2 Do some research into TV news magazines.
(a) Find out what kinds of items are covered.
(b) Compare the news magazines on different channels and try to decide which is more successful and why. □

When the researcher has written his intro-duction, it is typed on to a special roll of paper which fits into a machine called the *autocue*. The autocue projects the script on to a screen near the camera lens. The roll of paper moves round at reading speed so that the presenter can read the script and look at the camera at the same time.

Here is part of the autocue roll that was made for the introduction to the inter-view with Keith Castle.

SEQ.6 KEITH CASTLE

BOB / This week, Britain's most well known hospital patient took a further step in his efforts to help sufferers of heart disease.
He is of course Keith Castle, and yesterday he helped the boxer Eric Boone launch a fund named after his own heart donor, Duncan Prest.
Keith first hit the head-lines back on August 20th the day after he became Britain's sixth heart-transplant patient.
So far he has outlived four of the five previous patients, and has astounded everyone with his vitality.
Ten weeks after the operation at Papworth Hospital in Cambridge he was allowed to leave, and has since stayed with his daughter and son-in-law at their farm in Northampton.
For a man who could only walk thirty yards before the operation it's been a new life — — walking and cycling several miles a day.
Whilst convalescing there, he managed to pop down to London last weekend to watch his favourite team — — Fulham — — play a local derby against West Ham.
Although he was under strict instructions not to get excited, Fulham lost 2—1 anyway.

■ 1 Imagine you are a presenter who has to read the introduction on the right. Can you read it aloud correctly without stopping or going back?
Why does the lack of punctuation marks make this piece so hard to read?
Where should the missing full stops and commas be inserted?
2 Give an introductory piece which you have written to someone else in your class. See if they can read it through without making any mistakes.
Did your punctuation help them or hinder them?
3 Discuss the following questions about punctuation.
(a) What is the main job of punctuation?
(b) Could we manage without punctua-tion marks?
(c) Which punctuation mistakes cause most confusion?
(d) Which do you think are the *three* most important conventions of punctua-tion? □

The autocue roll below was never used in a programme.

You may not be a pop fan but you must have been on holiday on the moon for the past year if you haven't heard of Elephants the group that has made its name by dressing up in felt carpet underlay and wearing umbrella stands on their feet the group has hit the headlines once more yet again they are in the news this time the lead singer Jumbo has decided to have himself and the rest of the group locked in a cage in London Zoo to publicise the dangers to the African elephant which is threatened with extinction the group have released a special single Ivory Trail which is the story of one man's fight against the big game hunter Tim Smith who went down to the zoo to find out more now reports. . .

Ideas for a News Item

Here are three poems and a short story describing unusual incidents. The poems tell a story but do not give all the details or background information we might want to know.

Choose one of them and use it as the basis for an item on a news magazine programme on television. You will need to work in groups to plan and prepare your item. There are various jobs to be done:

Presenter It is your job to announce the item and to get the viewers interested so they will go on watching. You also have to explain the background of the story briefly so that people can understand the item.

Reporter You will be 'on-the-spot' describing the scene, explaining what is going on, adding to what can be seen on the screen with your commentary.

Interviewer This may be the presenter, interviewing people involved in the story in the studio, or it may be the reporter talking to people at the scene of the event. Remember to think in advance about the important questions to ask, and about how to get your interviewee talking.

Interviewees People involved in one way or another. Try to build up a clear idea of the kind of person you are representing, and answer the questions in a way appropriate to the character.

Other things to consider
Autocue Write the presenter's script on to an autocue (see p. 23) so that he or she can read it easily and without mistakes.
Filming script Alongside your notes of the contents of the item (commentary, interviews, etc.) make a note of camera shots and stills that you would like to accompany the item.
Background material Write some of the material that could be used by researchers and reporters working on the preparation of the item. Suggestions are given with each poem or story. □

Welsh Incident

'But that was nothing to what things came out
From the sea-caves of Criccieth yonder.'
'What were they? Mermaids? dragons? ghosts?'
'Nothing at all of any things like that.'
'What were they then?'
      'All sorts of queer things,
Things never seen or heard or written about,
Very strange, un-Welsh, utterly peculiar
Things. Oh, solid enough they seemed to touch,
Had anyone dared it. Marvellous creation,
All various shapes and sizes and no sizes,
All new, each perfectly unlike his neighbour,
Though all came moving slowly out together.'
'Describe just one of them.'
      'I am unable.'
'What were their colours?'
      'Mostly nameless colours,
Colours you'd like to see; but one was puce
Or perhaps more like crimson, but not purplish.
Some had no colour.'
      'Tell me, had they legs?'
'Not a leg or foot among them that I saw.'
'But did these things come out in any order?
What o'clock was it? What was the day of the week?
Who else was present? How was the weather?'
'I was coming to that. It was half-past three
On Easter Tuesday last. The sun was shining.
The Harlech Silver Band played *Marchog Jesu*
On thirty-seven shimmering instruments,
Collecting for Carnarvon's (Fever) Hospital Fund.
The populations of Pwllheli, Criccieth,
Portmadoc, Borth, Tremadoc, Penrhyndeudraeth,
Were all assembled. Criccieth's mayor addressed them
First in good Welsh and then in fluent English,
Twisting his fingers in his chain of office,
Welcoming the things. They came out on the sand,
Not keeping time to the band, moving seaward
Silently at a snail's pace. But at last
The most odd, indescribable thing of all,
Which hardly one man there could see for wonder
Did something recognizably a something.'
'Well, what?'
      'It made a noise.'
      'A frightening noise?'
'No, no.'
      'A musical noise? A noise of scuffling?'
'No, but a very loud, respectable noise —
Like groaning to oneself on Sunday morning
In Chapel, close before the second psalm.'
'What did the mayor do?'
      'I was coming to that.'

Robert Graves

Interviewees could include:
1 *The mayor* Think how the conversation in the poem might continue. What would the mayor do next? What did he say to the creatures when he addressed them?
2 *A member of the silver band* What would his reactions be? Would they affect his playing?

3 *A scientist from the university* He or she might be able to provide a common-sense explanation for what happened.
4 *An eyewitness from the village.*

Background material Write a factual report on the incident by the scientist. This could be used by the presenter in his introduction to the item.

When you have finished your news item, ask yourselves:
How much did you have to add to what the poem tells you?
Does the poet want to give you information about the incident?
Why do you think he writes as he does, keeping you waiting?

The 'Alice Jean'

One moonlight night a ship drove in,
  A ghost ship from the west,
Drifting with bare mast and lone tiller;
  Like a mermaid drest
In long green weed and barnacles
  She beached and came to rest.

All the watchers of the coast
  Flocked to view the sight;
Men and women, streaming down
  Through the summer night,
Found her standing tall and ragged
  Beached in the moonlight.

Then one old woman stared aghast:
  'The *Alice Jean*? But no!
The ship that took my Ned from me
  Sixty years ago —
Drifted back from the utmost west
  With the ocean's flow?

'Caught and caged in the weedy pool
  Beyond the western brink,
Where crewless vessels lie and rot
  In waters black as ink,
Torn out at last by a sudden gale —
  Is it the *Jean*, you think?'

A hundred women gaped at her,
  The menfolk nudged and laughed,
But none could find a likelier story
  For the strange craft
With fear and death and desolation
  Rigged fore and aft.

The blind ship came forgotten home
  To all but one of these,
Of whom none dared to climb aboard her:
  And by and by the breeze
Veered hard about, and the *Alice Jean*
  Foundered in foaming seas.

Robert Graves

Interviewees could include:
1 *The coast-guard* who first saw the returning ship. What did he do? What information could he give about tides, winds, and so on?
2 *Ned's wife* What has her life been like since the ship disappeared?
3 *Ned's son* Remember he would have been only a baby when his father went missing, but would now be quite an old man.
4 *A local historian* from the museum. He might be able to provide records from the time of the original mystery.
5 *A village fisherman.*

Background material Write a newspaper report of the incident which appeared sixty years previously when the ship first vanished. This will be part of the records provided by the historian. ▢

Bradford June 1972

Dusty, bruised and grazed, and cut about a bit, but
cheerful, twenty men in white
are demolishing an old stone house
by karate.
They attack the worst part:
the thick cemented fireplace wall.
What a concert of chops is conducted
by him in the helmet, with KARATE INSTRUCTOR
across his back and Union Jacks and ideograms
along his sleeve: a deep-breathed plot
of timed and buttressed energies jabbing
one bare hand and two bare hands and
one bare foot and two bare feet and
one bare head at
stone: the pivot man,
swarming with badges, swings
on two friends' shoulders, clutches
their necks, leans back with knees
above his head and like a spring
uncoils two smart sharp whacks
from heels of steel,
and the wall keels.

Edwin Morgan

Interviewees could include:
1 *the karate instructor;*
2 *one of his team* of karate experts;
3 *the owner* of the house that is being demolished;
4 *a neighbour;*
5 *the council official* who decided to use the karate team to do the job (is the team being paid by the council, or are they doing it for practice? Is the council official himself a karate enthusiast?);
6 *a passer-by.*

Background material The researchers for the item will need some information about the martial arts. Write an article on the subject which they will find useful in preparing this news item.

You could prepare a news item in the same way, based on an incident in the books you are reading, or on an actual incident reported in a newspaper. ▢

Every Picture tells a Story

It is often said that every picture tells a story. That's quite true, but unless you know the circumstances in which the picture was taken, you might get quite the wrong idea about the story that the picture has to tell. For example, if you see a picture of a cricket match taking place in bright sunshine with only a few spectators watching, you might think that

it tells the story that not many people go to watch county cricket these days, But, if you were told that the picture was taken one day when there was not going to be more than about twenty minutes' play, because that was all that would be necessary for one side to win the match, then it is hardly surprising that there were very few spectators, and the picture tells quite a different story.

The story that a picture tells can depend on the caption that is printed beneath it, or the commentary that is spoken while it is being shown. This sequence of four pictures can be used to tell two quite different stories, as the two different commentaries show.

Commentary A

1   Cramped terraced houses like these had to be home for several generations of working people. Providing only basic accommodation and lacking modern facilities, in the course of time the houses deteriorated and streets such as this became the twilight zones of our cities.

Commentary B

1   Over the years, these compact terraced houses provided homes for several generations of working people. In streets like this one, there was a friendly neighbourhood spirit. Everyone knew everyone else, and you could rely on a helping hand, if ever you needed one.

2   Wherever possible, local councils have adopted policies of slum clearance, and such houses are being demolished to make way for the provision of more satisfactory accommodation.

2   Now, without taking into account the wishes of the residents, many local councils have decided to demolish such houses rather than to modernise them.

3   The rows of dingy terraced houses have been replaced by blocks of bright, modern flats.

3   Whole streets of houses have been knocked down, only to be replaced by dull, uniform blocks of flats.

4   Families who were once forced to live in overcrowded, sub-standard accommodation, now enjoy the facilities of a modern, centrally-heated flat.

4   Although the new flats offer many extra facilities, a lot of the residents state that they would prefer to be back in their old homes.

■ 1 Make a collection of pictures from newspapers and magazines, together with their captions. Write an alternative caption for each picture, so that you make it tell a different story.
2 Look at the pictures which are shown on this page, and write a commentary to accompany them that is either for or against fox-hunting, Then, see if you can write an alternative commentary to show how the sequence of pictures could be used to tell quite a different story. □

Unit 4 Words and Pictures

This unit looks at the ways people explain things to others using combinations of words and pictures.

Suzy Benghiat is a cookery writer, but her recipes look very different from those in an ordinary cookery book. She works with cartoonist Peter Maddocks to produce *Suzy Cookstrip* — a cartoon-strip recipe book. She cooks her dishes in her own kitchen and while she is cooking she talks about what she is doing into a tape-recorder. Then she and Peter discuss together the best way of showing the cooking process using a combination of Suzy's words and Peter's pictures. Here is an example of one of Suzy's recipes and alongside it a more conventional recipe for a similar dish.

■ 1 Compare the recipes below. Which one is easier to follow? Why? Which sort of cookery book would encourage you to try the recipes?
2 Look at the information they give. Make a note of any information contained in Suzy's recipe but not in the other one, and then vice versa. Is this information necessary? Is it helpful? Do they tell you everything you need to know? Could a beginner follow them?
3 Is the order of the instructions for the recipes different? Which one uses the best order?
4 Rewrite Suzy's version using words only. Does this make it easier to follow or harder? Where do the pictures help? What was the most difficult thing to explain in words?
5 Read what Suzy says below about writing the cookstrip.

Draw a cartoon strip to show someone how to do something you know how to do well, such as mending a puncture or taking or printing a photograph. Consider what needs explaining in words and what is best shown in pictures.

Swap your instruction strip with your partner. Try each other's out, if possible; if not, discuss them. What was hard to explain? Could you follow the instructions? Can you make them better? □

Cooking time: 1¼—1½ hr. Preparation time: 25 min. Main cooking utensils: saucepan, colander, sieve, frying pan/skillet, casserole. Oven temperature: very moderate, 350°F., 180°C., Gas Mark 3—4. Oven position: centre.

For 5—6 people you need:
1 lb. raw minced beef
3 oz. cooked rice
4 oz. mushrooms
2 medium-sized onions
3 medium-sized carrots
seasoning
1 egg
10—12 large, young cabbage
  leaves

For the sauce:
1 tablespoon lemon juice
2 oz. brown sugar
¼ pint water
1 lb. ripe tomatoes

To fry:
2 oz. chicken fat

1 Blend the minced meat, rice, chopped mushrooms, grated onions and carrots. Season well. Add egg.
2 Put the cabbage leaves into boiling salted water and cook for 3—4 minutes. Drain.
3 Put the stuffing on to each leaf and roll firmly. Secure with wooden cocktail sticks if wished.
4 Blend the lemon juice, sugar, water and sieved, skinned tomatoes.
5 Heat the fat in a pan and turn the cabbage rolls in this until slightly browned on the outside.
6 Transfer to a casserole, putting some of the sauce underneath and the rest on top.
7 Cover tightly and cook for 1¼—1½ hours.

To serve: With green salad or cooked beans.

To vary: Add raisins to the sauce.

When Peter and I first had the idea for doing the cookstrip, it struck me that the form would help me do what I wanted to do. I wanted to communicate in a very informal way what you cook and how you do it; to reproduce what you do when you talk to people. One of the interesting things about doing it this way is that it's not a written language, it's a spoken language. I'm a talker rather than a writer. You have to be a very skilful and talented writer to convey how you cook a dish just in descriptive writing, whereas in dialogue it works well.

Writing a recipe in this form helps me to explain in sequence what's happening. Very often, with written recipes, they don't go in the logical sequence. When I open an ordinary recipe book, I always read the recipe first, before the ingredients, because first of all I want to know if I feel like cooking whatever it is. I can only find out by reading the recipe. So if I wrote an ordinary

recipe, I would start with an explanation of how it's done, then I would put the ingredients at the end. Better still, I would have no list of ingredients, but they would also come in sequence as you describe the recipe, and I would have them printed in a different type, so you can see, just at a glance, the sequence in which you will need them.

When you think of the space you have on the page, you're limited in the number of words you can use. I came to realise very quickly that it wasn't words and then drawings; it had to be thought up as a whole. You had to be very economical. I try to plan the words and pictures together, because, very often, things that need explaining with three or four sentences, Peter will explain with a stroke of the pen. Sometimes, though, it's the other way round.

Suzy Benghiat

28

Making a Children's Toy

Here are some instructions for you to try out. Can they be improved in any way?

Lunar Surface Craft

You will need:
Four cotton reels
Small cardboard canister (about 10 cm long x 4 cm dia.)
Two strips of corrugated paper 20 cm x 2½ cm
Cap of plastic bottle
Two round sticks or ½ cm dowels 14 cm long
Four cardboard discs 2½ cm dia.
Four pins
Piece of 1½ cm drinking straw
Glue and Sellotape, scissors, coloured paints.

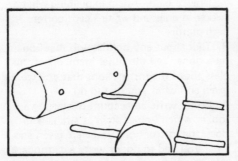

1. Make four holes in the cardboard canister and push sticks or dowels through.

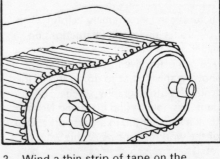

3. Wind a thin strip of tape on the sticks to keep the wheels on. Glue on corrugated paper for tracks.

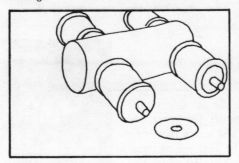

2. Put cotton reels on ends of sticks and put cardboard discs on outside.

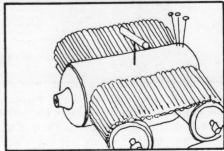

4. Stick pins at rear of craft. Push pin through straw for antenna. Glue bottle cap on nose.

■ 1 Make a collection of further examples of instructions — for example those for model kits, using a camera or a stereo system, wiring a plug, sewing and knitting patterns, woodworking, origami, car-repair manuals, using a petrol pump. Try some of them out if you can. Discuss the following questions and try to decide what makes instructions clear and easy to follow and what makes them confusing.

In what order is the information given?

Has the writer used any technical terms special to the subject?

If so, have they been explained?

Are the instructions precise or would you be unsure exactly what to do at any point?

Do you need the object there in order to understand the instructions?

What do you need to know already to be able to follow the instructions?

2 Write your own set of instructions for a simple action like opening a tin of sardines or a can of coke, or putting on a record. Use the best combination of words and pictures in each case. Try out one another's instructions and see if you can improve them.

3 Invent a machine or gadget, such as a dog-exercising machine or an orange peeler, or design a toy or game. Draw labelled diagrams to show how your design works, and write a set of operating instructions to go with it. □

Working in the Glassworks

■ 1   Read the extract through twice and work out exactly what Archie had to do as a 'tekker-in'. Join up with a partner and take it in turns to explain in your own words exactly what Archie's job was.
2   Draw a picture-strip explaining what a tekker-in does and write a caption for each picture.
3   Talk about any holiday job that you have done. Tell the other members of the class about the instructions that you were given and what you had to do.
4   Either write an account of starting a job, in which you explain as Archie Hill does, the instructions you were given and what you had to do; *or* write a cautionary tale about a teenager who is given a set of instructions, but who fails to carry them out because he or she misinterprets them (does not understand them properly).

5   The terms 'Lear', 'Chair' and 'Tekker-in' are examples of what is known as *technical language* or *jargon*. They are part of the specialised vocabulary used by workmen in a glassworks. Many other occupations and activities have a technical language of their own.
   Collect examples of technical language, e.g. from motor-cycling and other 'special interest' magazines. Choose a passage from one of them and try to rewrite it, substituting your own words for any technical terms that are used. Afterwards, discuss the problems that you had to face in trying to avoid using any technical terms. Discuss what you learned from this exercise about the nature and function of technical language.   □

Pictures can be extremely helpful when you are trying to give instructions on paper, but if you are talking to someone you can often give instructions by showing them what to do. In this extract from his autobiography, Archie Hill describes how he and his friend Noggie took a summer job in a glassworks. One of the workmen shows Archie what his job is.

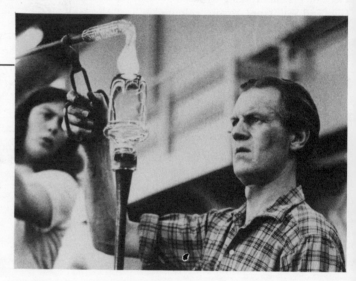

The gaffer took me and Noggie across to the far side of the shop, paused at a man sitting in his work-bench. The bench had two long arms sticking out in front of it, and across these two arms the man had a long iron rod which he kept rolling backwards and forwards, while he shaped the molten glass which was stuck like treacle to one end. 'Which one o' these two dos't want as tekker-in 'til yo're chap comes back from holiday, Walt?' the gaffer asked him. The man grunted at his work, never taking his eyes from the job he was doing.

'Either one 'ull do me, gaffer,' he said, 'just as long as he'll werk and don't play the idle-sod.'

'Yo' stop with him,' the gaffer said to me, and took Noggie off to the next man and left him there. I stood watching my bloke finish off the water-jug he was making. By the time he'd finished it the red-hotness had left it, and it glowed only amber-warm, almost as if there was no heat left in it. It looked cool enough to pick up, but I knew if you did try to pick it up it would burn your hands down to the bone. Walt stood up from his chair, walked over to a trough lined with asbestos, laid the end of the iron containing the jug over it. He rapped the iron-pole a sharp rap with the steel scissors he carried, and the jug parted company with the iron and lay in the trough. Walt motioned me over to him. He gave me a pair of wooden tongs and a wooden pole which had a 'Y' at one end, like a catapult.

'These'm yo're tools,' he told me, 'yo're tekking-in tools. Do it like this. For jugs, put one end of yo're pole inside the jug. Careful not to knock it about – the jug, not the pole – although it amounts to the same thing in the end. Bad tools means bad work. Now use the tongs to mek sure the jug is secure on the pole. When yo' lift it, lift it like this – upwards, so's it won't fall off and smash on the floor. Dos't see?'

I nodded.

'Right then. When yo've picked it up like ah've shown thee, yo' has to carry it to that place over there. The Lear, it's called. It's an annealing oven. Come on and I's'll show thee.'

I followed him. When we got to the lear I saw that it had got a moving bottom, a sort of belt ever moving away from you as you stood there, moving easy and slow. Walt placed the jug on to the start of the moving belt, pushed it upright with the tongs, and I watched the object creep away from me. It passed between asbestos curtains which lifted for it to enter the long annealing oven, and then it was gone from view.

'That's easy enough then, bisn't it?' Walt asked me, and I nodded again.

'Ah'm on jugs all day,' he said, 'so there's little more to learn than what ah've shown thee. Every different shape has to be carried in a different way, and I's'll show you how to carry as I makes 'em. Now come on back to my chair and ah'll explain. Can't spend too much time explaining, though, 'cos ah bist on piece-work. We'll go through it quick.'

He sat down at his wooden bench, reached down besides it and fetched up a bottle of cold tea. He drank from it, wiped the neck with his hand then passed it across to me for me to take a swig. I just sipped from it for politeness's sake, then gave it back to him.

'This bit of wood ah'm sitting on,' he said, 'it's took me twenty years to get to sit here. Nobody sits in this chair but me. It's not a ornament, it's not a piece of furniture to put yo're arse on. It's a work-tool and it's *mine* and anybody other than me 'ud get away with it better by putting his arse on the King's throne than on this. *It's* called the Chair and the blokes like me are called the Chairmen, meaning we'm top-craftsmen. Mostly we gets called the Workmen. Ah'm *yo're* Workman whilst yo' bist here. The team ah've got werking for me is known as 'a chair o' workmen', and they'm called a Chair for short. Is all this sinking into yo're head?'

'Yes,' I said, because it was.

from Summer's End by Archie Hill

Training a Kestrel

In this extract from *Kes*, Billy Casper explains to his teacher, Mr Farthing, and to the rest of his class, how he trained his kestrel.

'Kes wa' as fat as a pig though at first. All young hawks are when you start to train 'em, and you can't do much wi' 'em 'till you've got their weight down. You've to be ever so careful though, you don't just starve 'em, you weigh 'em before every meal and gradually cut their food down, 'til you go in one time an' she's keen, an' that's when you start getting somewhere. I could tell wi' Kes, she jumped straight on my glove as I held it towards her. So while she wa' feeding I got hold of her jesses an' . . .'

'Her what?'

'Jesses.'

'Jesses. How do you spell that?'

Mr Farthing stood up and stepped back to the board.

'Er, J-E-S-S-E-S.'

As Billy enunciated each letter, Mr Farthing linked them together on the blackboard.

'Jesses. And what are jesses, Billy?'

'They're little leather straps that you fasten round its legs as soon as you get it. She wears them all t'time and you get hold of 'em when she sits on your glove. You push your swivel through . . .'

'Whoa! Whoa!'

Mr Farthing held up his hands as though Billy was galloping towards him.

'You'd better come out here and give us a demonstration. We're not all experts you know.'

Billy stood up and walked out, taking up position at the side of Mr Farthing's desk. Mr Farthing reared his chair on to its back legs, swivelled it sideways on one leg, then lowered it on to all fours facing Billy.

'Right, off you go.'

'Well when she stands on your fist, you pull her jesses down between your fingers.'

Billy held his left fist out and drew the jesses down between his first and second fingers.

'Then you get your swivel, like a swivel on a dog lead, press both jesses together, and thread 'em through t'top ring of it. T'jesses have little slits in 'em near t'bottom, like buttonholes in braces, and when you've got t'jesses through t'top ring o' t'swivel, you open these slits with your finger, and push t'bottom ring through, just like fastening a button.'

With the swivel now attached to the jesses, Billy turned to Mr Farthing.

'Do you see?'

'Yes, I see. Carry on.'

'Well when you've done that, you thread your leash, that's a leather thong, through t'bottom ring o' t'swivel . . .'

Billy carefully threaded the leash, grabbed the loose end as it penetrated the ring, and pulled it through.

'. . . until it binds on t'knot at t'other end. Have you got that?'

'Yes, I think so. Just let me get it right. The jesses round the hawk's legs are attached to a swivel, which is then attached to a lead . . .'

'A leash!'

'Leash, sorry. Then what?'

'You wrap your leash round your fingers and tie it on to your little finger.'

'So that the hawk is now attached to your hand?'

'That's right. Well when you've reached this stage and it's stepping on to your glove regular, and feeding all right and not bating too much . . .'

'Bating? What's that?'

'Trying to fly off; in a panic like.'

'How do you spell it?'

'B-A-T-I-N-G.'

'Carry on.'

'Well when you've reached this stage inside, you can try feeding her outside and getting her used to other things. You call this manning. That means taming, and you've got to have her well manned before you can start training her right.'

While Billy was talking Mr Farthing reached out and slowly printed on the board BATING; watching Billy all the time as though he was a hawk, and that any sudden movement, or rasp of chalk would make him bate from the side of the desk.

'You take her out at night first and don't go near anybody. I used to walk her round t'fields at t'back of our house at first, then as she got less nervous I started to bring her out in t'day and then take her near other folks, and dogs and cats and cars and things. You've to be ever so careful when you're outside though, 'cos hawks are right nervous and they've got fantastic eyesight, and things are ten times worse for them than they are for us. So you've to be right patient, an' all t'time you're walking her you've to talk to her, all soft like, like you do to a baby.'

He paused for breath. Mr Farthing nodded him on before he had time to become self-conscious.

'Well when you've manned her, you can start training her right then. You can tell when she's ready 'cos she looks forward to you comin' an' there's no trouble gettin' her on to your glove. Not like at first when she's bating all t'time.

from *Kes* by Barry Hines

■ 1 Prepare a talk about how to train an animal or how to look after a pet. Bring in any diagrams or equipment which will help you to demonstrate what to do.

2 Give a talk to the class describing any hobby or activity in which you are particularly interested. Remember that you will need to explain any technical language you use, just as Billy had to stop to explain terms such as 'jesses' and 'bating'. □

Words and pictures can also be used to present factual information. Often, a visual presentation of facts can have more impact than an explanation in words. In particular, numbers and statistics mean a lot more to us when they are presented in the form of charts and graphs.

Compare the illustration on the right with the paragraph below it.

National morning newspaper circulation, 1973

In 1973, by far the most popular national morning newspaper was the *Daily Mirror*. With a circulation of 4 261 683, it beat its nearest rival, the *Daily Express* (3 296 988) by nearly a million copies. The *Sun*, selling 2 931 466 copies each day, came a close third. Of the remaining daily papers, only the *Daily Mail* (1 703 215) and the *Daily Telegraph* (1 423 031) had a circulation of more than a million copies. *The Times* (345 044) and the *Guardian* (344 356) sold just under twice as many copies as *The Financial Times* (194 651).

■ 1 Which way of presenting the circulation figures has more impact? Why?
2 Does the visual presentation tell us anything more than just the size of the paper's circulation?
3 How easy would it be to adapt the written paragraph or the illustration to include the following information:
the price of the paper, relative to its circulation;
whether the circulation is going up or down;
how good the sports reports are in each paper? □

There are other ways in which quite complicated information can be presented in a simple visual form. The visual presentation usually makes a single point in a straightforward and immediate way.

Here is a way of showing how a total number is broken down into various parts. It shows at a glance the relative size of each part. A circle represents the whole figure and is divided into segments. The size of the segments, like the newspapers above, reflects the size of the part they represent. This way of showing figures in visual form is called a *pie chart*, because it looks like a pie divided into pieces of varying size.

For every £1.00 spent on records, this is where the money goes.

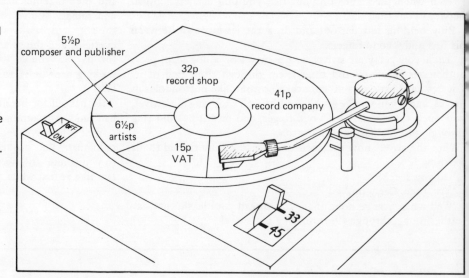

■ 1 Write a short paragraph in which you explain in words all the information contained in the pie chart. Then compare your paragraph with the chart. Which is easier to understand?
2 Work out how your school day is divided. What proportion of the day is spent on each of the following activities:

lessons;
sports and clubs;
form periods;
eating;
breaks;
other activities?
Present your answers in the form of a pie chart.

The pop music chart has been drawn in the form of a record on a turntable. Try to think of a way to design your school day chart to make it interesting. □

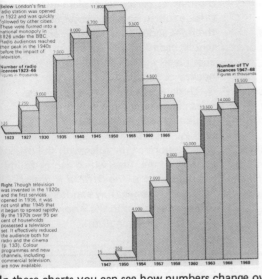

In these charts you can see how numbers change over a period of time. The size of each block in these block graphs shows the number of radio and TV licences bought in the years since the BBC began broadcasting.

■ 1 What do the two charts tell us about the effect of the coming of television on the number of people who listen to the radio?
2 Why isn't there a block for every year between 1923 and 1968?
3 Do you think the pattern of TV and radio use has changed since 1968? □

Another way of showing numbers in a visual form is to use symbols. In this chart, each little figure sitting in his cinema seat represents the equivalent of 50 000 000 visits to the cinema.

■ Is there any link between this chart and the one which showed the number of TV licences issued during the same period?

Imagine the photograph inset in the chart is to be printed in a book about changes in society since the war. Use the information in the chart to write a caption which explains the significance of the photograph. □

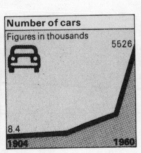
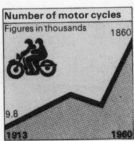
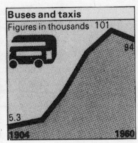

Of course, it is possible to show how numbers change over a period of time by drawing a simple graph. These graphs show how road transport has changed this century.

■ Compare the graphs and use them to discuss the following questions:
1 Why does one of the graphs show a decline in numbers?
2 Why hasn't the total road mileage increased at the same rate as the number of vehicles? □

Your Own Charts

Road deaths in Britain

1934	7300
1941	9200
1948	4500
1956	5400
1963	6900
1972	7800

No. of motor vehicles per mile

1947	18
1950	24
1957	39
1960	49
1967	70

■ 1 What do these figures tell us about the level of safety on the roads in this country?
2 Study the figures and discuss the various ways in which you could present them in a visual way.
3 Design and draw a chart that presents the figures in an interesting and clear way. □

■ 1 Look up your favourite football team in the league table. Design a chart that shows how they have performed so far this season.
2 Conduct your own survey among the people in your year in school. Then present your results as vividly as you can. Your survey might aim to find out:

which record stars are most popular in your year;
how people in your year spend their leisure time;
what people in your year think about how to improve the school.

When you have chosen a subject, you will need to take care making up the questions. Think up questions that invite answers that can easily be turned into numbers.

When your survey has been completed, be as imaginative as you can in the way you present your results. □

Rules and Regulations

When we want to convey information, such as rules and regulations, the most effective way is often a combination of words and pictures.

Sports

■ 1 Cover up the diagram of the throwing area with either a piece of paper or a book. How easy is it to follow the rules giving the specifications of the throwing area without referring to the diagram?

2 Choose a sport you know well. Write out the rules giving the details of the pitch or court on which it is played, without drawing a diagram.

3 Using someone else's instructions, draw a diagram of the pitch or court on which the sport they have chosen is played.

4 Having drawn the diagram, discuss it with the person who wrote the rules. Suggest ways in which the wording of the rules might be improved.

5 Bearing in mind the points that have been made about your set of instructions, rewrite your rules, giving details of the pitch or court, and using a diagram to help to explain them.

6 Using words and pictures (either diagrams or cartoons) explain either the offside rule in hockey, soccer or rugby, the rules about how a point is scored in tennis, badminton or squash, or the rules about legal and illegal tackling in soccer, hockey or rugby.

7 Using words only, write out some rules concerning fouls in a game which you know well, such as soccer, netball, hockey, basketball or rugby. Compare your versions of the rules with the official versions of the rules, which can be found in books such as *The Official Rules of Sports and Games* (Kaye and Ward) and in individual titles in the *Know the Game* series (EP Publishing Ltd).

Javelin

Throwing Area   The runway shall be between 30 m and 36.5 m long and marked by two parallels, 5 cms wide and 4 m apart.

The scratch line shall be the arc of a circle of 8 m radius drawn across the end of the runway nearer the landing area, and should be **7 cms** wide.

Where it intersects the parallels of the runway, the scratch line should be extended at right angles to them for a distance of 1.5 m.

Where constructed in wood or metal the scratch line should be sunk flush with the ground.

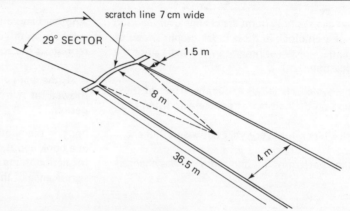

The landing area is enclosed by radii of the circle of which the scratch line is an arc, extended through the points at which it intersects the runway parallels. This will enclose a landing area of approximately 29°.

from *Know the Game — Athletics*

Board Games

1 Choose a well-known game such as ludo, draughts or snakes and ladders. Each write an account of how you would play it.

2 In groups, compare your accounts and draw up a set of rules, explaining how to play the game.

3 Try playing the game, using the rules drawn up by another group, and then your own rules. Suggest any changes that are necessary because:

(a) some things have been taken for granted and are not explained in the rules;

(b) the wording of a rule is not clear enough.

4 Look at the instructions for how to play a number of board games, which belong either to you or to younger members of your family. Discuss which are easy to follow and which are difficult to follow. Can you suggest any ways in which the rules which are difficult to follow could be expressed more clearly?

5 In groups, invent a simple board game and write a set of rules for it. □

Playground Games

■ 1 Discuss the games such as hopscotch, prisoners' base and conkers, that you used to play in the area round your home or in the playground. Can you remember any times when there was an argument over the rules?

2 Prepare and deliver a talk to the group, explaining the rules of one of the games you used to play. If it would be helpful, draw diagrams to illustrate your talk.

Rules of the Road

1 Look at a copy of the *Highway Code*. Read it carefully and then either draw a series of cartoons showing a cartoon character called Careless Charlie breaking the rules, or write a story about Careless Charlie, in which you show him breaking many of these rules.

2 In the *Highway Code* and in RAC or AA handbooks there are pictures of road signs. Discuss how the orders and warnings are conveyed by using symbols rather than words. Are all the signs easy to understand? □

Notices

1 Study these notices. All of them convey information of some kind. Some of them are warnings. Others issue advice. The tone of a notice depends on the language that has been used. In some cases, e.g. 'Please do not walk on the grass', the notice is presented as a request. In others, e.g. 'Any unauthorised person found on these premises will be prosecuted', the notice is presented as a threat. In many instances, notices take the form of a command, e.g. 'Stick No Bills', 'Shut the Gate'.

Collect examples of different notices which are presented as (a) requests, (b) threats, (c) commands.

2 Today many notices, e.g. road signs, use signs or symbols rather than words to convey their messages. Collect examples of notices, other than road signs, in which the message is conveyed by symbols rather than by words. Discuss:
(a) What words would the notices have contained if symbols had not been used?
(b) Are any of the symbols misleading or difficult to understand?
(c) What are the advantages and disadvantages of using signs and symbols instead of words?

3 Redesign some notices which use words only, so that they are conveyed by symbols. Does the use of symbols mean that you have altered the message in any way? How far can symbols be used to convey (a) requests, (b) threats, (c) advice?

4 Design a notice for one of the following purposes:

to warn visitors to a beach that it is dangerous to climb the cliffs;

to advise people eating in a cafe that it is unwise to leave valuables with their coats in the cloakroom;

to tell people that the current in a river is swift and that no one should swim in it;

to inform people that public fishing is not allowed on a particular stretch of river and to give details of where permits can be purchased;

to tell people that a wooden footbridge is unsafe and that no one should attempt to cross it. □

Many pamphlets giving us advice use pictures as well as words to convey their messages.

1 The advice on the right is from a Health Education Council pamphlet *Home Safe Home*, which gives hints on preventing accidents in the home. Design similar pages giving advice on safety In the kitchen, In the living room, In the bedroom, In the garage or In the garden.

2 Design a pamphlet called *School Safe School* giving hints on avoiding accidents in your school. Some of the sections you should include are: In the laboratory, In the workshop, On the games field, In the playground.

3 Draw cartoons or a comic-strip or write a story about Careless Charlie, either at home or at school, designed to show the mistakes that Careless Charlie makes and to give the reader information about what causes accidents. □

Unit 5   Inside Radio

Noel Edmonds is one of Britain's most popular disc jockeys.
In the following interview, he discusses the ways he tackles
his job.

Q: What sort of people make good disc-jockeys?
N: There are many different sorts of disc-jockey, like there are many different sorts of athlete or footballer. I think a successful radio station ought to be run like a successful football team. A number of personalities and individuals are tied together in a team. You have someone who does the hard work; you have the slightly flamboyant sort; you have the sheer personality and you have the big name who, in a football team, only touches the ball a couple of times but when he does he's worth his money.

    If you are part of a team, then you have to decide what you are going to be. You must decide whether to be a personality disc-jockey or a good technician, or a musical expert, like John Peel.

Q: What kind of disc-jockey do you think you are?
N: The music I play tends to be the kind of music I like myself. I think the music is important, but I go out to try and make the listeners notice what happens between the records. I try to get my audience to entertain themselves by taking part in the programme. That way I can also tell how successful I am being.

    I have asked people to contribute to a *Posh Person's Dictionary*; we asked women to send in adverts for their boyfriend or husband; we asked for slogans that could be printed on the front of tee-shirts. Another idea was something I called *The Grovel Path* where people were asked to write exaggerated praise of me and the show. One fellow wrote in to say that he worshipped the water I walked on. I thought that was a lovely line.

Q: How many letters do you receive each week?
N: Between two and three thousand. They are mostly in response to the ideas I mention on the show, but there are always a lot which might give me an idea that I can try to use later.

    I never take the mail for granted. It's a terribly cruel thing not to use a letter when somebody's bothered to type a card or letter and to get a stamp, put it on the envelope and send it to me. I always consider every single one that goes in the bin, but you can't put them all on the air or you'd never play a bit of music.

Q: How much planning goes into each programme?
N: When I go into the studio on Sunday morning, the records are all listed and I know the mail, because I've spent three or four hours the previous evening sorting it. So, I've worked most of it out and then the rest is just bolted together as we go along.

Q: Are you nervous when you start a live programme?
N: I can't honestly say that I was nervous the first time I ever did anything. Tense, yes, but not nervous. I've always drawn a very clear line between nervousness and tension. I think you've got to be tense in order to perform properly. If you are nervous, though, it can be very dangerous because people make mistakes when they're nervous.

    The beginning of the programme is very important to me. It's quite strange, because considering the amount of preparation that goes into the programme, we always seem to end up at ten o'clock in a bit of a flurry. Then I make a point of playing a few records without saying too much, because I think that sets the mood of the show. The first twenty minutes sets the mood and then we tend to gradually get into a number of the set spots.

    I am virtually my own transmission producer, because there is no one who tells me to speed up or slow down. My producer helps me, but really it is down to me. Maybe I won't pick up that fourth letter because I realise the link has gone a bit too far. I have listened to shows — particularly on Sunday mornings — where items have gone on just a bit too long. So your own timing as a disc-jockey is very important.

    Sometimes I don't know what I'm going to say until I switch on the microphone. Usually, though, when I am talking about a letter or a set thing in the programme, I've got a rough idea of what I want to say. I've had ten years of experience and I can cope with all the technical problems without that affecting what I say. I've never worked on Radio 1 with a script that actually tells me what to say, apart from occasions when I am obviously reading — a traffic flash or a piece of programme information, for example. As a disc-jockey you have to be able to talk off the top of your head.

Q: Do you think about the audience when you are presenting a show?
N: I've always thought that it's important to know what the listener might be doing, what the listener might be thinking. Doing the *Breakfast Show* was great from that point of view because I knew that ninety per cent of the people listening to me were getting up and facing a new day. Sunday morning is also very nice from that point of view. It is one of the few other times when you've got a rough idea of what people are doing.

■ 1   What does Noel Edmonds have to say about:
disc jockeys' different styles;
involving the audience in the programme;
how he uses the many letters that he receives;
his knowledge of the audience?

2   If you can, listen to part of Noel Edmonds' show. Find examples of the way his ideas were put into practice in the show.

3   Make up an entry for one of Noel Edmonds' 'write-in' spots. You could write:
a slogan for the front (or back!) of a Radio 1 tee-shirt;
an entry for *The Posh Person's Dictionary*;
praise of Noel Edmonds for *The Grovel Path*.
Or think up your own 'write-in' spot and make up some entries for that.

4   Select two or three different disc-

jockeys and compare their styles. It will help if you can make a tape recording of a few minutes from each of their programmes. Then you will be able to make a detailed analysis of their radio styles. □

Here are some letters typical of those sent to Noel Edmonds. With them is part of the list of records used in a programme.

These are the raw elements that go into a Radio 1 show. Noel Edmonds combines the letters he receives and the records he plays into an interesting and amusing entertainment.

12 Conistone Street,
walmington,
sussex.
21st November 1979.

Dear Noel,
My friends at school bet me you wouldn't answer my letter. So don't let me down, please!!! We have had a competition to guess what colour your underpants are! Tell us the answer and say primrose yellow that's what I guessed.
My favourite groups are Abba, The Manhatten Transfer and Police.
lots of love
Mildred Kay
x x x x

Elmbank
Streatley Avenue
MALBORROW
29th November 1979

Hello Noel,
I could say that your programmes on television and radio are the best thing since Des O'connor stopped singing and how I love your smooth voice and perfect hair ...... but I won't. What are you? a retarded 'Weeny bopper' or a member of the 'Kid Jensen' fan club? Why do you play the commersialised clap trap which ind- octrinates the younger people of our society. Since when have the Bee Gees, John Travolta and similar groups been termed as musicians. Am I right to assume that your Sunday morning programme is a musical programme? Well if so why don't you play some Neil Young or Bob Dylan and similar types of music. So don't keep up the good work.
Here's hoping
Phil Johnson.

I hope Posh Paws becomes extinct like the others of his race.

MUSIC REPORTING						
MUSIC CODES	TITLE COMPOSER = PUBLISHER = ARRANGER RECORD LABEL = PREFIX = SUFFIX		LP TITLE PERFORMER COMMISSIONED	SIDE/BAND ARRANGEMENT NO.	DURATION mins	secs
C	DON'T IT MAKE YOU WONDER Mason/Nicholas=April Music=NA CBS=S=82625		LP: Mariposa De Oro S.1 B.1. Dave Mason		02	50
C	KISS YOU ALL OVER Chapman/Chinn=Chinnichap Music/ RAK Music=NA SPRING=2095=091		Millie Jackson		03	10
C	WALKING ON THE MOON Sting=Virgin Music=The Police A&M=AMLH=64792		LP: Reggatta De Blanc S.2. B.1. The Police		04	50
C	LONDON BRIDGE Gates=Screen Gems/Columbia Music= NA ELEKTRA=K=42029		LP: Bread S.1 B.2 Bread		02	10
C	SHOOTING STAR Courtney=Interworld Music/Brighton Rock=NA CARRERE=CAL=111		LP: Shooting Stars S.1. B.2 Dollar		03	25
C	FAUVETTE Browne=Logo Songs=NA LOGO=GO=361		Duncan Browne		03	50

PRODUCTION NUMBER
QIA252P510

1 Compile your own list of singles and LP tracks that would fill a twenty-minute section of a Radio 1 music programme.

You should aim for variety, but keep roughly to a particular kind of music. Your listeners have to know more or less what kind of music to expect from you.

Note on your list all the details which the disc jockey might need.

Noel Edmonds's list has:
the name of the piece of music;
the composers and the publisher;
the record company and the record number;
the name of the performer or group;
(in the case of LP tracks) the name of the LP;
the length of the piece.

For some songs, it would be useful to know the length of the introduction as well, so that the disc jockey knows how long he can talk before the singer comes in.

2 Write some letters to your favourite disc jockey.

Work out who would be able to listen to the show and write some letters from a variety of imaginary people. Remember that teenagers aren't the only ones who listen to pop music programmes.

Disc jockeys receive letters about all kinds of things:
there are personal questions about the disc jockey's likes and dislikes (particularly in music);
there might be reactions to a remark he made on the air;
disc jockeys hear about listeners' experiences — especially where a particular record is involved;
people send in stories and questions about pets.

3 Now combine all the separate elements of a Radio 1 music programme to present your own twenty-minute show. Make a tape of the show or present it live to the rest of the class.

Before you start, you will need:
a list of the records you will be playing — and the records themselves;
the letters you have decided to use — and a rough idea of that you will say about them (use letters written by other members of your class);
at least one regular feature that you have asked listeners to contribute to;
one or two scripted items — a piece of traffic information, a programme announcement or an advertisement.

You will also have to decide:
what kind of audience you hope to reach;
what kind of style you are aiming for.

You could include a phone-in feature in your programme.
Don't forget Most of what you say will be made up as you go along. Don't write it all down or your show won't sound authentic at all. □

Working for a Local Radio Station

For a while after leaving school, Michelle Morris was unemployed. Then she got a job working for BBC Radio Leicester. She describes how she came to get the job.

I left school at 16 with three O levels. I'd taken five, and I was hoping to go on to further education and do a normal electrician's course, but I wasn't accepted, because I didn't have enough O levels. I went along to the careers office and told them I wanted to do sound work. They couldn't really help me and I went on the dole.

Then, one day, I went back to school to see one of the teachers. It was lucky, really, because he had been a DJ when he was younger, and he sympathised with me. He told me that he'd heard there was a course going at Radio Leicester, a government-run scheme, and he said it could be just clerical work but at least I'd be working with the people who I want to know.

So I contacted Radio Leicester and they invited me along for an interview. I had an interview with the station manager and he told me that the job would last for nine months, because it was part of a government job opportunities scheme, and that only unemployed people could apply. At first, I wasn't sure. Then I went to see one of the producers and he told me all about the different things I would be doing. It sounded something worth trying. So I said that I'd take the job, if they offered it to me, and a couple of days later they got in touch with me and said come along and start.

One of the programmes that Michelle Morris worked on was called *Hot Air.*

Hot Air is a two-hour music-based programme for young people, especially unemployed people, between the ages of 15 and 22. That's the main target range. The reason we have plenty of music in it is to keep the kids interested. You're at the sort of age when you don't want just to listen to interviews and boring talk. So we space out the interviews and the information by putting music in between. What we do is have a bit of music, go into an interview, have a bit more music, go into a bit of information.

I think any programme for young people must have a young person, or two or three young people, behind the scenes. They must come up with the ideas, even if it's a case of kids writing in. I also think you should have a young person presenting it.

Of course, some of the ideas for the programme come from older people. They could be ideas that the producer had thought of, but they're always presented from a young person's point of view. For example, one week the producer was doing something about the law. So we said, let's have a young person who's been in trouble with the law, and a young police officer. We don't want a 40-year-old bloke, otherwise people will be thinking, well, he's 40, we're 16.

Preparing for an Interview When I go along to do an interview, I've researched into it. I've picked out certain points I want to ask about and I've drawn up a list of questions I might ask.

Before I start the interview, I've got to check that there are no technical problems. First of all, I make sure that the tape recorder is working, that the batteries aren't flat and that there is enough power to make a good recording. It's always worth checking that it is recording properly, by recording yourself and then playing it back. Another thing you've got to check is the level — the level of volume that someone is going to talk at. People often check the level by getting the person they're going to interview to talk about what they had for breakfast.

You've also got to think about the place where you're doing the interview. What are the acoustics like? Will the interview sound okay, or will it sound echoey? You might be able to do something about it — like pull the curtains. Also, you've got to think about background noise, such as traffic or people moving about. You've often got to ask other people if they can try to avoid moving about while you're recording, and provided you ask them politely they usually oblige.

Speaking with an Accent At first, my accent wasn't accepted. In fact, I didn't know I had an accent until it was pointed out to me by the people on the station, because being broadcasters they didn't have accents. But then I heard round and about: 'Well, she's got a Leicester accent.' And they pointed out things I'd say, like 'eh' on the end of a word. I'd say 'Traceh' and 'trolleh', whereas they'd say 'Tracy' and 'trolley', and there's the 'uh' sound in words like 'buhs' and 'duhck'. Then there's certain words I'd use that they wouldn't, such as 'mardeh' which means 'soft', and 'laireh' which means 'boisterous'.

I was nervous at first, so I tried to change the accent. Then, one of the producers told me to stop worrying about it. He said there's nothing wrong with having an accent. Besides, he said, it's the young people of Leicester our programme's for. If there's someone talking without an accent to Leicester kids, they probably won't relate to him as much as they will to a young person like you with a Leicester accent.

Michelle Morris

■ 1 What do you learn from Michelle Morris about how the programme *Hot Air* tries to appeal to young people?

What topics do you think a programme like *Hot Air* should feature?

Which programmes produced by your local radio station are most popular with teenagers? Why are they the most popular?

If you were the producer of a radio programme for young people, what would you do to try to make it appeal to them?

Discuss what Michelle Morris says about her accent. What is the difference between accent and dialect? Is there such a thing as a 'proper accent'?

Should you try to change your accent when you talk on the radio? Why?

A Local Radio Programme Work in groups and plan a local radio programme. First, decide what type of programme you are going to make, how long it will be, and what audience you are going to aim the programme at. Then, discuss what the content of the programme is going to be. You will need to draw up a programme outline.

Research and record any interviews, music or live events. Listen to the recordings, decide on an order in which to present them, and write a script for a presenter to use to link the various items together.

When you have finished, listen to each other's programmes. Decide whose was the most successful and why. □

As part of one of the *Hot Air* programmes, it was decided to do an item on *Groundation*, a local reggae band. Michelle Morris went along to interview them.

When I went to interview Groundation I'd decided I wanted to ask them about the religion and how it gets into the music. I wanted to get them talking about the beliefs of the religion, and if that comes out on the records as well. I also wanted to ask them about the band — where they do their gigging round Leicester, so that people will know where they can go and see them; why they decided to take up music and how the group was formed; whether they've got any records released and what their future plans are; and about their kind of music and who their music is aimed at.

MICHELLE: Right, Henry, how is the Rastafarian religion connected to reggae music?

HENRY: Well, reggae music is teaching the people something if the people then want to listen. You know, Rastafarian religion is, um, a kind of direction. You know, show them a way to go if they - again if they want to listen. If they want to listen they will hear what we're singing about, you know. What we're telling the people and everything, you know? Right.

MICHELLE: Why do you wear your hair like you do in dread-locks?

HENRY: Identity. It's a form of identity.

MICHELLE: What - just to show off?

HENRY: No, no - not just to show off. Identity. Identity - so that people can identify Rastafarian people from the other people. You know, if I have my hair like, well, they can know who is Rasta and who is not Rasta, you see.

MICHELLE: So it's just to identify with the religion.

HENRY: Yeah. Sure.

MICHELLE: Why do you think that a lot of local black kids have suddenly gone into Rastafarianism? There seem to be more and more, going around with their hair like that.

HENRY: Well, some people do it for fashion, the guy who don't understand it. Then again, you find some people going Rastafarian religion because they believe in it, you see.

MICHELLE: Right. Right, Dave can you tell me who do you play your music for? The black people or the white people?

DAVE: We, um try to put our music for, um, Indian, white, black, you know, for a majority of, you know, everybody. We, you know, everybody who would like to listen to our music. You know, we try to put forward, you know every-thing that we have during the music. And, um, also our music is, you know, consisting of, you know, things that go on throughout the, um, world. Like, um, you know, maybe we'll put fighting wars, you know, um, politics, and just things like that - politics and um, like um, oh boy, could you cut - cut it, sorry, oh dear, I'd like to do it again because I...

MICHELLE: Right - who do you play your music for - the black people or the white people?

DAVE: Our music, we'd like to put forward to everybody cos we feel that everybody should know what's really going on, you know, during the music that we put forward. So we try to make our music consist of things that go on in life, you know, as it is now. You know, it's like there's fighting, there's war, and you get people whose, um you know, there's so many things like, you know, being on the dole and various things that go on like that, you know. So we try to put all these things forward to the people in our music.

MICHELLE: Right. Last of all, Ellis, you write your own music. Now where do you get your ideas from?

ELLIS: Well, the ideas come from the members of the group. When the group first started we decided to ourselves that we weren't going to be another Steel Pulse or another Bob Marley and the Wailers, so we're trying to make an original Groundation sound. At the moment, the sound, it's not really defined but the main thing is the ideas. That each man is able to express himself in the way he wants, and through that we kind of bring all the musical ideas together and kind of work from a framework towards a song. The basic element usually comes from one man who brings an idea towards the group, and he'll forward it to the group and the group will say whether they like it or not; and often the original idea has to be kind of shaped to suit the different kind of, you know, abilities in the group and various styles. So usually in the end - usually they're tested out on the public, you know, often we have a song, we try it out, it doesn't quite work - the message that we're trying to put forward doesn't work, so we have to change it. You know, the ideas do come from the group.

MICHELLE: Okay, then. Thank you very much.

Editing an Interview After the interview, Michelle Morris discussed with her producer which parts of the interview they could use in the programme. One of the pieces they decided to use was Henry's answers to Michelle's question about dreadlocks.

After listening carefully to the tape they decided that Henry repeated his point about identity and that it would be best to edit the tape to cut out the repetition. They did this by cutting out Michelle's second question — 'What — just to show off?' and squeezing together Henry's answers. Here is the edited version of that part of the tape, as they used it in the programme:

Michelle. Why do you wear your hair like you do in dreadlocks?
Henry. Identity. So that people can identify Rastafarian people from the other people. They can know who is Rasta, and who is not Rasta.

■ 1 Compare the edited version of this part of the interview with the unedited version.
2 Go through the interview and edit it, so that any part of it could be used in a radio programme. Before you begin, discuss together how you will decide what to keep in and what to cut out. Talk about the importance of keeping the objective of the interview firmly in mind, the need to cut irrelevances and repetitions, and to cut out hesitations and pauses, such as 'ums' and 'ers'.
3 Compare your edited version of the interview with those of others in your group. Whose version is best? Why?
4 Prepare and conduct a number of *vox pop* interviews — interviews in which you ask members of your group, or members of the general public, to express their views on topical subjects. Play the un-edited tapes and discuss how you would edit the tape. Remember that timing is important when preparing a radio pro-gramme. Which parts of your recording would you use, if you were told that there was only room in the programme for an item lasting 90 seconds? □

The Broadcaster as Presenter

David Self works for the morning radio programme *Round About East Anglia*. Every fortnight he contributes a feature called 'Parish Pump'. On this occasion he visited the Suffolk village of Mildenhall where the villagers were running a festival to raise money to restore the church. The festival included a medieval street market, medieval plays, music and dancing, and a display of the Mildenhall treasure.

The parish council wrote to David two months in advance of the event suggesting he might like to feature it in the programme. He receives many letters like this and he has to decide which ones to follow up. He decided that the Mildenhall festival would make a lively feature and planned to visit the village.

He found out in advance who would be the most useful people to interview, and worked out what he wanted to find out. Beyond that his aim was to capture the atmosphere of the village and to convey some of the sound and colour of it all. He recorded several interviews and excerpts from various events: he spoke to festival organisers, actors in the mummers' play, the vicar, the producer, and ordinary people in the street (he calls these 'vox pop' interviews). His job then was to select from all the material he had collected those bits that he wanted to use, to put them into order, and lastly to add his own commentary.

Here is the first part of the completed feature:

```
        P A R I S H   P U M P


RECORDED: 5.10.79     XMISSION: 8.10.79      No. 106

1.  DAVID            Thank you John.  Good morning and
                     today in "Parish Pump" we go to to medieval Mildenhall.

2.  TAPE B (Band 1)  FX: MARKET PLACE NOISES
                     MIXED WITH:

3.  TAPE C (Band 1)  (MUSIC)
                     DIP AND HOLD MUSIC BEHIND:

4.  DAVID            For the last two Saturdays, there's
                     been a medieval market in the middle of Mildenhall.
                     One of those involved in the organisation of it all,
                     Sue Hurrell, took me on a tour.

5.  TAPE A
```

```
        Sue Hurrell (Festival Organiser): We've had all sorts
        of local people producing various plays and displays,
        tumbling, maypole dancing, Saint George and the Dragon.

        David: And as we go down the main part of the market
        place down here, what have we got at the different
        stalls?

        Sue: We have stalls from local traders.  On our right
        at the moment is a basket work stall, hot dogs, baked
        potatoes, plant stalls.

        David: Who are they all organised by?

        Sue: Some by the Round Table, some by the Lion's Club,
        there's a church Stall and also local traders.

        David: A lot of the stall holders and a lot of other
        people too have dressed up.

        Sue: Yes indeed.

        David: For instance the children behind us, what are
        they?

        Sue: Well, they're dressed as knights, medieval knights,
        complete with horses and helmets.

        David: They really are rather splendid horses.

        Sue: Yes very colourful.
```

```
                     BACKED BY:

TAPE C (Band 3)      (MUSIC)

                     TAPES OUT TOGETHER:

1.  DAVID            And just as colourful were those
                     Mummers that Sue Hurrell was talking about earlier,
                     acting out the medieval story of Saint George and
                     the Dragon.

2.  TAPE B (Band 3)  MUMMERS

                     ESTABLISH, THEN LOSE BEHIND:

                     MUMMER: We're members of Mildenhall Mummers...
```

■ 1 How does David Self try to get the listeners' attention and persuade them to listen to his item?

2 Why do you think he begins with Sue Hurrell, rather than with, say, the vicar, who explained what the festival was for?

3 Why does he ask her to describe what is going on when he can see it for himself? □

The order of items is very important. David Self writes down all the various components at random on the page, and then decides which one should come first. He draws an arrow from it to the one he thinks should come next, and so on until all the parts are connected in a sensible order. This helps him give the feature a clear sequence.

■ 1 Plan a short talk to give to your class on any subject that interests you. Jot down any ideas which occur to you in the way David Self has done. Then link them up so that you can present your ideas in order.
2 Write an article or essay on any controversial topic using the same technique. □

David Self talked about his work as a radio presenter and explained how he goes about putting a feature together. Here are some extracts from what he said.

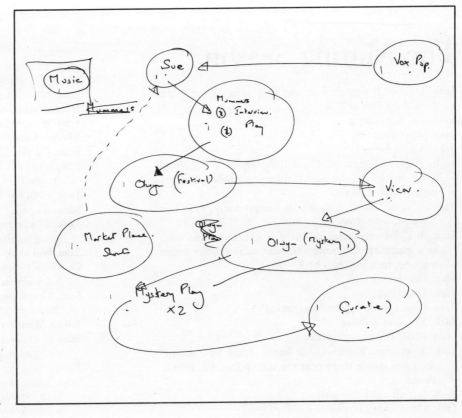

I suppose I think of myself as a writer, because a lot of my work is quite literally biro on paper. Writing for radio is also a matter of collecting sounds — a lot of people talking, a lot of interviews, sound effects, music, and fitting them together, as a kind of building, in a way, putting together a package, which is a radio programme. I think writing, whether you do it in school or for your job, is very like the kind of work that's done for example by a carpenter, by a craftsman, it's actually making something, there's an end product. . . .

In an interview, the key thing is not so much worrying about what I'm going to ask next, but listening. I think the greatest danger is that you're so worked up about what you ask next, that you don't listen to what you're being told. You do it by trial and error. You learn that some people are not good interviewees, so you try and avoid them.

There are two kinds of radio interview, really. There are the factual ones where you want to get hold of definite points, and then you have to plan in advance. You've got to decide what are the key questions, and plan those in advance. There's the other kind of interview, where you really want to get the colour, the interest, you want to find out from that person what they are doing, and why it matters to them. Don't worry about what's going to be the next question. Then it's simply a matter of listening hard to that person and appreciating what they say, and then asking, not some cold

questions you've had up your sleeve for hours, but simply what do I want to know next, what is there that I don't understand in what they were saying; what is it that I want to know more about them, what will the listener be thinking, what will the listener want to know?

What I have to do now is listen to all the material I've collected, perhaps twice. Then I chop out and throw away the rubbish. Now it can be rubbish for two reasons. One, the person I was interviewing was just deadly dull, or it can be for technical reasons (for example, there's a lot of the wrong sort of background noise, which has drowned an interview). Then I begin to get some sort of idea of the shape of the programme. What have I got available to build it out of? What will I need to write to fill in the background? How will I order the programme, what's a good thing to choose to start it off, which of all the various sounds I've got will really grab my audience by the ears and make them want to listen? So really I've got to find a headline, an attention-catcher, then I've got to explain what the event is, and that's going to be a part which I shall probably write.

I'm not trying to make an angled report saying this was a good thing, or a bad thing. I'm trying to present a picture of what it was like to be at the Mildenhall festival, and as a bonus, perhaps get the listener to say, 'Oh, I wish I'd been at that!'

David Self

■ 1 Using the points David Self makes, write a short article giving advice to radio presenters.

You could use his method to plan your article. First make a note of the main points you want to use, arranged on a page in a random way. Link them in a suitable order, and then write your article using the plan you have decided on.
2 Choose an event which is happening locally or in your school, or decide on a topical issue which people disagree about. Work with a small group to prepare a short radio feature about it. Using David Self's advice, plan whom you will interview, and what factual questions you must ask.

Prepare other questions that might be useful.

Conduct the interviews and tape them, trying to obtain as clear a recording as you can and remember to listen carefully to your interviewee.

As a group, decide:
(a) what kind of audience you are aiming at;
(b) which bits of the interviews you want to use;
(c) what order you are going to use them in;
(d) what you need to add as an introduction or to link the various parts together. If you can, edit your material and add your contributions. This is a very time-consuming job and needs two tape-recorders! If this is not possible, use the material you have collected to write a newspaper or magazine feature. □

The Mating Season

Jack. OK, we'll just go over the drill again. What's the first thing you do?

Stan. Get her talking.

Jack. What about?

Stan. About herself.

Jack. Right. Women all like talking about themselves. Find out where she works, then you know where to ring up. What else?

Stan [*a little wearily*]. Don't let her get away. Take her for a cup of coffee.

Jack. It's not very original, but it works. Now watch it, he's going to announce the next dance. Shirt collar undone, tie dangling, check?

Stan. Check.

Jack. Good lad.

Stan. Have I to do my hollow cheeks?

Jack. Yes, you do that.

Stan. Blast! It's a lady's desire . . .

Jack. That doesn't matter. Ask her to desire you, go on, she's just down there near the next pillar, don't mess about . . .

Stan. Is it all right though?

Jack. Get on with it, you're wasting time . . .

(Pause.)

Stan. Excuse me, I wonder if you'd like to desire me . . .

Eileen. Oh, my feet are ever so tired . . .

Stan. Are they? Er . . .

Jack. Improvise, improvise . . .

Stan. I only dance very slowly.

Eileen. All right then.

(They dance to a waltz time.)

Stan. It's . . . er . . . crowded then.

Eileen. Yes.

Stan. Suppose it's with it being Saturday . . . and that.

Eileen. I expect so.

Stan. Long time since I've been here, don't really like it very much.

Eileen. Don't you?

Stan. Gets a bit crowded.

Eileen. Suppose it's with it being Saturday.

Stan. Yes, Yes, I suppose that's it.

(Pause.)

Jack. You're breaking every rule in the book, Stan.

Stan. Oh, button it, can't you?

Jack. Well stop messing about.

(Pause.)

Stan. What's your name then?

Eileen. Eileen.

Stan. Oh aye. Er . . . nice name. Do you work? I mean where do you work?

Eileen. Cracker works.

Stan. You what?

Eileen. Cracker works.

Stan. Don't think I've heard of that.

Eileen. It's a big place.

Stan. Yes, yes, I expect it is.

Eileen [*suddenly forthcoming, suggesting she's been weighing Stan up*]. They make cream crackers and cheese biscuits and them nylon buns for slimming with.

Stan. Yes, my mam likes them. What do you do then?

Eileen. Me?

Stan. Yes, what do you do? Butter them?

Eileen [*laughing*]. No, I'm a private secretary.

Stan. What, like a typist, you mean?

Eileen. No, a secretary.

Stan. What's the difference, then? I've often wondered.

Eileen. I don't know. It just says so on my card.

Stan. Do you like it then?

Eileen. It's not bad. Money's all right.

(Pause.)

Jack. Hold hard, Stan.

Stan. Why?

Jack. That's enough about her for the moment. If she's going to bite, she'll ask about you.

Stan. Will she?

Jack. Nice touch about buttering the biscuits. Always helps if you can get a laugh. Breaks the tension.

Stan. Thank you. I'll wait then.

(Pause.)

Eileen. What's your name then?

Stan [*without thinking*]. Funny you should say that. He said you might . . .

Eileen. What you taking about?

Stan. Sorry. I was thinking about something else. Er . . . Stan, Stanley for short, no, the other way about. [*He is a little nervous.*]

Eileen. What's the matter?

Stan. Nothing. Just call me Stan.

Eileen. I suppose I ought to ask you where you work, if we're being polite and that. [*She knows the rules.*]

Stan. I'm just a clerk. Sort of low-class civil servant.

Eileen. Where? Up at the Town Hall?

Stan. Down the Labour Exchange.

Eileen. Do you like it?

Stan. It's lousy.

Eileen. Oh.

(Pause)

Jack. You big nit! Saying a thing like that.

Stan. It is lousy.

Jack. You don't have to tell the flaming truth. She doesn't know what to say now.

Stan. Sorry, Jack.

Jack. You're getting cocky with it, that's the trouble. You'd better try to sort it out.

(Pause.)

Stan. Mind you, we have some good fun in the office, it's just the paperwork gets a bit much sometimes. . . .er, would you like a cup of coffee?

Eileen. I don't know.

Stan. What do you mean, you don't know?

Eileen. It's a bit difficult.

Stan. It's all right, I'll pay.

Eileen. Do you mind waiting five minutes?

Stan. Five minutes? No, I don't think . . .

Eileen. Well wait at the bottom of the stairs, you know where I mean, and if I don't come in five minutes I'm not coming, OK?

Stan. All right. That is, it's all right as long as you come.

Eileen [*coy*]. Well, that's up to you, isn't it? [*She moves away.*]

adapted from *The Mating Season* by Alan Plater

The Broadcaster as Script Writer

The Mating Season was written several years ago (how can you tell?) and is set in a dance hall. Stan has an 'inner voice' — his friend Jack, who gives him advice and encouragement about chatting up Eileen. The audience can hear Jack too, but the other characters in the play can't.

■ In groups, rehearse and record a performance of this extract from the play. You will need three actors, and a producer to give advice to the actors and explain to them what impression is to be created. It is also useful to have a fifth person to manage the tape recorder and any sound effects.

Acting
An actor in a radio play has to create a character using voice only. You cannot use any of the other things which normally tell us something about a character: facial expression, clothes, way of moving, and so on. We can't even tell a person's age unless the sound of the voice gives us a clue. What can you do with your voice to create different effects? You can:
make your voice louder or quieter;
change the speed at which you speak;
make your voice go up and down in pitch;
give your voice different characteristics, e.g. speak hoarsely, whisper, whine, etc.;
change your accent to create a character from a different place or background from your own.

Think about the characters in this play. What sort of voice do you think would give the right impression of each of them? How are you going to make a difference between Stan and Jack in the way they speak?
Will you be able to tell from Stan's voice when he is talking to Jack and when he is talking to Eileen?
When Stan first starts talking to Eileen, he can't think of anything interesting to say. How will you show this in his voice? The author suggests that Eileen has been 'weighing up' Stan. Could that be heard in her earlier speeches?

Remember that *pauses* can be very useful in suggesting to the listener what the characters are doing or thinking. Should there be any, apart from where the author has put them?

Sound effects
Other sounds besides voices can be used to create atmosphere and to tell the audience what is happening. Music will be important in this play; what music will you choose? When will it stop? Make sure it is not so loud as to drown the actors' voices.

Other sound effects can be used too — to convey the fact that Stan and Eileen are dancing, for example, or to provide the background noises of a dance hall.

You could experiment to find a way of showing that Jack isn't actually there. For example, try out the effects of speaking close to and far from the microphone, muffling your voice, or having a particular noise heard in the background each time Jack speaks.

When you have made your recording, compare your interpretation with those of other groups in the class. Try to explain why you chose to do it the way you did. Discuss the differences between the versions. Which is the best and why? Does everyone agree about the characters? □

Writing a Radio Play

When you write a radio play the main thing you have to work with, your raw material, is the dialogue: what the characters say. There is no scenery or costume to help you set the scene and create your characters. So the first thing the dialogue must do is to show the audience what sort of people are involved in the play: the whole character must be built up through the words he or she speaks.

The second job of the dialogue, and equally important, is to explain what is happening, to allow the audience to follow the story without actually telling them directly. All the events of the plot must be clear from the words spoken by the characters.

As well as doing these two jobs, the speeches must sound natural, and must convince your audience that the characters are real people talking.

There are advantages in writing a play for radio. You can have frequent scene-changes without worrying about scenery or props. You can include unrealistic events and make them convincing, which would be very difficult if the audience could see what is happening. Supernatural events, fantastic creatures, unexplained noises, dreams and imaginings can all be used in radio plays.

Look again at the extract from *The Mating Season*.
■ 1 Do the characters come over clearly from what they say?
2 How does the author let us know what is happening?
3 Does the dialogue sound natural?
4 How has Alan Plater used the fact that he is writing for radio? □

Write Your Own Play
■ 1 Rewrite this scene but add another character: Eileen's 'inner voice', which gives her advice and comments just as Jack does for Stan. At the same time you could try modernising this extract: it will

mean changing the remarks about fashions, music, and so on.
2 Take a script or excerpt of a stage or TV play and adapt it for radio.
3 Write an original radio play bearing in mind the points above. Some ideas:
— a morning scene: the family at the breakfast table. Concentrate on making the characters distinct, e.g. one bright and breezy, one still half asleep, one worried about the day's events, and so on;
— a play with a supernatural theme: perhaps a ghost story with an everyday setting;
— a play in which animals or objects talk;
— a new boy or girl joins your class. As the other members of the class tease, talk to or ignore the new pupil, we can hear their inner voice telling us their true feelings;
— the invisible man;
— a short scene in which you are told off for something you have done wrong at home or at school. Again, we hear a voice giving your true thoughts, things you dare not say out loud.

Produce Your Own Play
Now you have tried acting a radio play, and writing your own. The next step is to prepare a performance of one of your own plays. A group working together can make a recording of a play one of you has written. You will need a producer, actors and a sound recordist who may also be responsible for sound effects.
Producer Cast the play. Choose the best people in the group for each of the parts. Decide on what sort of effect you want to create. Advise the actors in how to develop their characters and speak their lines to fit in with your ideas.
Actors Concentrate on using your voice in different ways to create your character and show how he or she feels about what is going on.
Recordist Make sure the microphone is kept still and that no one touches it. Place it the right distance from the actors — not too close or too far away. Try to choose a place for recording which is as quiet as possible.
Sound effects Experiment with different methods and effects. Some sound effects can be made and recorded at the same time as the actors speak their lines.

Some effects may need to be recorded separately, perhaps out of doors using a battery-operated cassette recorder — birdsong, traffic noise and so on. You then play the tape while the actors record their parts on to another tape recorder.

You may also be able to use records of special sound effects such as those produced by the BBC. □

Unit 6   Hiroshima

Hiroshima — a city in the south of Japan. One August morning in 1945 a noiseless flash — many times brighter than the sun — brought total destruction to the city and killed 100 000 people in a single second.

Ten days earlier President Truman and Prime Minister Churchill, seeking a quick end to the war with Japan, issued a warning: surrender unconditionally or face the complete devastation of the Japanese homeland. Japan ignored this warning.

Unknown to the Japanese, the Americans had developed, in total secrecy, a weapon which could bring about such destruction — the Atom Bomb. Now President Truman ordered it to be used.

At 1 a.m. on 6 August, 1945, the *Enola Gay,* an American Air Force bomber, took off from an island in the Pacific Ocean. Its destination was Hiroshima.

At 8.15 the *Enola Gay* was over its target. A second bomb was dropped on Nagasaki on 9 August. Six days later Japan surrendered unconditionally. The war was over.

Reports of the bombing of Hiroshima were like most reports of bombing raids during the Second World War. They dealt with the destruction of military and industrial targets. Little was reported about the fate of the people of the city.

In May 1946 an American journalist, John Hersey, was asked by the *New Yorker* magazine to go to China and Japan and write a series of articles. Hiroshima was to be one of his subjects. Nearly a year after the bombing, he found the city devastated, the people still dazed and suffering.

The story he brought back so moved the editors of the *New Yorker* magazine that although they had intended it to be a serial, they devoted an entire issue to it, adding only an introduction. They wanted to show clearly the human consequences of using such a terrible weapon. As a book it was translated into many languages. Newspapers all over the world serialised it; radio stations broadcast it. Hersey told for the first time the story of the people of Hiroshima.

The survivors on that day were people who had lived through the unimaginable. The following extract will give you some idea of the horror and confusion that were left in the wake of the explosion. John Hersey concentrated on a few of the survivors, and told of their experiences. They included: a young girl, Miss Sasaki, aged 20, an office worker; Doctor Fujii, who owned a small private hospital; a German priest, Father Kleinsorge; Rev. Tanimoto, a Methodist Minister, with a wife and baby.

Their stories provided a detailed record of that time.

In what had been the personnel office of the East Asia Tin Works, Miss Sasaki lay doubled over, unconscious, under the tremendous pile of books and plaster and wood and corrugated iron. She was wholly unconscious (she later estimated) for about three hours. Her first sensation was of dreadful pain in her left leg. It was so black under the books and debris that the border-line between awareness and unconsciousness was fine; she apparently crossed it several times, for the pain seemed to come and go. At the moments when it was sharpest, she felt that her leg had been cut off somewhere below the knee. Later, she heard someone walking on top of the wreckage above her, and anguished voices spoke up, evidently from within the mess around her; 'Please help! Get us out!'

Father Kleinsorge stemmed Father Schiffer's spurting cut as well as he could with some bandage that Dr. Fujii had given the priests a few days before. When he finished, he ran into the mission house again and found the jacket of his military uniform and an old pair of gray trousers. He put them on and went outside. A woman from next door ran up to him and shouted that her husband was buried under her house and the house was on fire; Father Kleinsorge must come and save him.

Father Kleinsorge, already growing apathetic and dazed in the presence of the cumulative distress, said, 'We haven't much time.' Houses all around were burning, and the wind was now blowing hard. 'Do you know exactly which part of the house he is under?' he asked.

'Yes, yes,' she said, 'Come quickly.'

They went around to the house, the remains of which blazed violently, but when they got there, it turned out that the woman had no idea where her husband was. Father Kleinsorge shouted several times, 'Is anyone there?' There was no answer. Father Kleinsorge said to the woman, 'We must get away or we will all die.' He went back to the Catholic compound and told the Father Superior that the fire was coming closer on the wind, which had swung around and was now from the north; it was time for everybody to go.

Just then, the kindergarten teacher pointed out to the priests

Mr. Fukai, the secretary of the diocese, who was standing in his window on the second floor of the mission house, facing in the direction of the explosion, weeping. Father Cieslik, because he thought the stairs unusable, ran around to the back of the mission house to look for a ladder. There he heard people crying for help under a nearby fallen roof. He called to passers-by running away in the street to help him lift it, but nobody paid any attention, and he had to leave the buried ones to die. Father Kleinsorge ran inside the mission house and scrambled up the stairs, which were awry and piled with plaster and lathing, and called to Mr. Fukai from the doorway of his room.

Mr. Fukai, a very short man of about fifty, turned around slowly, with a queer look, and said, 'Leave me here.'

Father Kleinsorge went into the room and took Mr. Fukai by the collar of his coat and said, 'Come with me or you'll die.'

Mr. Fukai said, 'Leave me here to die.'

Father Kleinsorge began to shove and haul Mr. Fukai out of the room. Then the theological student came up and grabbed Mr. Fukai's feet, and Father Kleinsorge took his shoulders, and together they carried him downstairs and outdoors. 'I can't walk!' Mr. Fukai cried. 'Leave me here!' Father Kleinsorge got his paper suitcase with the money in it and took Mr. Fukai up

pickaback, and the party started for the East Parade Ground, their district's 'safe area.' As they went out of the gate, Mr. Fukai, quite childlike now, beat on Father Kleinsorge's shoulders and said, 'I won't leave. I won't leave.' Irrelevantly, Father Kleinsorge turned to Father LaSalle and said, 'We have lost all our possessions but not our sense of humor.'

The street was cluttered with parts of houses that had slid into it, and with fallen telephone poles and wires. From every second or third house came the voices of people buried and abandoned, who invariably screamed, with formal politeness *Tasu-kete kure!* Help, if you please!' The priests recognized several ruins from which these cries came as the homes of friends, but because of the fire it was too late to help. All the way, Mr. Fukai whimpered, 'Let me stay.' The party turned right when they came to a block of fallen houses that was one flame. At Sakai Bridge, which would take them across to the East Parade Ground, they saw that the whole community on the opposite side of the river was a sheet of fire; they dared not cross and decided to take refuge in Asano Park, off to their left. Father Kleinsorge, who had been weakened for a couple of days by his bad case of diarrhea, began to stagger under his protesting burden, and as he tried to climb up over the wreckage of several

houses that blocked their way to the park, he stumbled, dropped Mr. Fukai, and plunged down, head over heels, to the edge of the river. When he picked himself up, he saw Mr. Fukai running away. Father Kleinsorge shouted to a dozen soldiers, who were standing by the bridge, to stop him. As Father Kleinsorge started back to get Mr. Fukai, Father LaSalle called out, 'Hurry! Don't waste time!' So Father Kleinsorge just requested the soldiers to take care of Mr. Fukai. They said they would, but the little, broken man got away from them, and the last the priests could see of him, he was running back toward the fire.

Mr. Tanimoto, fearful for his family and church, at first ran toward them by the shortest route, along Koi Highway. He was the only person making his way into the city; he met hundreds and hundreds who were fleeing, and every one of them seemed to be hurt in some way. The eyebrows of some were burned off and skin hung from their faces and hands. Others, because of pain, held their arms up as if carrying something in both hands. Some were vomiting as they walked. Many were naked or in shreds of clothing. On some undressed bodies, the burns had made patterns—of undershirt straps and suspenders and, on the skin of some women (since white repelled the heat from the bomb and dark clothes absorbed it and conducted it to the skin), the shapes of flowers they had had on their kimonos. Many, although injured themselves, supported relatives who were worse off. Almost all had their heads bowed, looked straight ahead, were silent, and showed no expression whatever.

After crossing Koi Bridge and Kannon Bridge, having run the whole way, Mr. Tanimoto saw, as he approached the center, that all the houses had been crushed and many were afire. Here the trees were bare and their trunks were charred. He tried at several points to penetrate the ruins, but the flames always stopped him. Under many houses, people screamed for help, but no one helped; in general, survivors that day assisted only their relatives or immediate neighbors, for they could not comprehend or tolerate a wider circle of misery. The wounded limped past the screams, and Mr. Tanimoto ran past them. As a Christian he was filled with compassion for those who were trapped, and as a Japanese he was overwhelmed by the shame of being unhurt, and he prayed as he ran, 'God help them and take them out of the fire.'

He thought he would skirt the fire, to the left. He ran back to Kannon Bridge and followed for a distance one of the rivers. He tried several cross streets, but all were blocked, so he turned far left and ran out to Yokogawa, a station on a railroad line that detoured the city in a wide semicircle, and he followed the rails until he came to a burning train. So impressed was he by this time by the extent of the damage that he ran north two miles to Gion, a suburb in the foothills. All the way, he overtook dreadfully burned and lacerated people, and in his guilt he turned to right and left as he hurried and said to some of them, 'Excuse me for having no burden like yours.' Near Gion, he began to meet country people going toward the city to help, and when they saw him, several exclaimed, 'Look! There is one who is not wounded.' At Gion, he bore toward the right bank of the main river, the Ota, and ran down it until he reached fire again. There was no fire on the other side of the river, so he threw off his shirt and shoes and plunged into it. In midstream, where the current was fairly strong, exhaustion and fear finally caught up with him—he had run nearly seven miles—and he

became limp and drifted in the water. He prayed, 'Please, God, help me to cross. It would be nonsense for me to be drowned when I am the only uninjured one.' He managed a few more strokes and fetched up on a spit downstream.

Mr. Tanimoto climbed up the bank and ran along it until, near a large Shinto shrine, he came to more fire, and as he turned left to get around it, he met, by incredible luck, his wife. She was carrying their infant son. Mr. Tanimoto was now so emotionally worn out that nothing could surprise him. He did not embrace his wife; he simply said, 'Oh, you are safe.' She told him that she had got home from her night in Ushida just in time for the explosion; she had been buried under the parsonage with the baby in her arms. She told how the wreckage had pressed down on her, how the baby had cried. She saw a chink of light, and by reaching up with a hand, she worked the hole bigger, bit by bit. After about half an hour, she heard the crackling noise of wood burning. At last the opening was big enough for her to push the baby out, and afterward she crawled out herself. She said she was now going out to Ushida again. Mr. Tanimoto said he wanted to see his church and take care of the people of his Neighborhood Association. They parted as casually—as bewildered—as they had met.

Mr. Tanimoto's way around the fire took him across the East Parade Ground, which, being an evacuation area, was now the scene of a gruesome review: rank on rank of the burned and bleeding. Those who were burned moaned, 'Mizu, mizu! Water, water!' Mr. Tanimoto found a basin in a nearby street and located a water tap that still worked in the crushed shell of a house, and he began carrying water to the suffering strangers. When he had given drink to about thirty of them, he realized he was taking too much time. 'Excuse me,' he said loudly to those nearby who were reaching out their hands to him and crying their thirst. 'I have many people to take care of.' Then he ran away. He went to the river again, the basin in his hand, and jumped down onto a sandspit. There he saw hundreds of people so badly wounded that they could not get up to go farther from the burning city. When they saw a man erect and unhurt, the chant began again: 'Mizu, mizu, mizu.' Mr. Tanimoto could not resist them; he carried them water from the river—a mistake, since it was tidal and brackish. Two or three small boats were ferrying hurt people across the river from Asano Park, and when one touched the spit, Mr. Tanimoto again made his loud, apologetic speech and jumped into the boat. It took him across to the park. There, in the underbrush, he found some of his charges of the Neighborhood Association, who had come there by his previous instructions, and saw many acquaintances, among them Father Kleinsorge and the other Catholics. But he missed Fukai, who had been a close friend. 'Where is Fukai-san?' he asked.

'He didn't want to come with us,' Father Kleinsorge said, 'He ran back.'

When Miss Sasaki heard the voices of the people caught along with her in the dilapidation at the tin factory, she began speaking to them. Her nearest neighbor, she discovered, was a high-school girl who had been drafted for factory work, and who said her back was broken. Miss Sasaki replied, 'I am lying here and I can't move. My left leg is cut off.'

Some time later, she again heard somebody walk overhead and then move off to one side, and whoever it was began burrowing. The digger released several people, and when he had uncovered the high-school girl, she found that her back was not broken, after all, and she crawled out. Miss Sasaki spoke to the rescuer, and he worked towards her. He pulled away a great number of books, until he had made a tunnel to her. She could see his perspiring face as he said, 'Come out, Miss.' She tried. 'I can't move,' she said. The man excavated some more and told her to try with all her strength to get out. But books were heavy on her hips, and the man finally saw that a bookcase was leaning on the books and that a heavy beam pressed down on the bookcase. 'Wait,' he said. 'I'll get a crowbar.'

The man was gone a long time, and when he came back, he was ill-tempered, as if her plight were all her fault. 'We have no men to help you!' he shouted in through the tunnel. 'You'll have to get out by yourself.'

'That's impossible,' she said. 'My left leg . . .' The man went away.

Much later, several men came and dragged Miss Sasaki out.

Her left leg was not severed, but it was badly broken and cut and it hung askew below the knee. They took her out into a courtyard. It was raining. She sat on the ground in the rain. When the downpour increased, someone directed all the wounded people to take cover in the factory's air-raid shelters. 'Come along,' a torn-up woman said to her. 'You can hop.' But Miss Sasaki could not move, and she just waited in the rain. Then a man propped up a large sheet of corrugated iron as a kind of lean-to, and took her in his arms and carried her to it. She was grateful until he brought two horribly wounded people—a woman with a whole breast sheared off and a man whose face was all raw from a burn—to share the simple shed with her. No one came back. The rain cleared and the cloudy afternoon was hot; before nightfall the three grotesques under the slanting piece of twisted iron began to smell quite bad.

from *Hiroshima* by John Hersey

Reading about the events at Hiroshima and John Hersey's account of them will have set you thinking about war and the threat of nuclear war. While the impact is still fresh, discuss possible answers to the following questions:

■ 1 Were the Allies justified in dropping atom bombs on Japan?

2 In what circumstances would the use of nuclear weapons be justified today?

3 Are nuclear weapons too destructive to make their use worthwhile?

4 Why do countries go to war with one another when so much suffering is bound to follow?

5 Can war ever be justified?

6 How much responsibility do individual people have for actions taken by their governments?

7 Are there ways of preventing war from happening in the future? ▫

Documentary Journalism

John Hersey's book about Hiroshima gets most of its effect from the way he wrote about real, identifiable people. He showed how a world-shattering event affected a few individuals.

■ Compile your own piece of documentary journalism in which you reconstruct an event through the experiences of people involved in it.

There might have been a happening which affected your town or village:

A local flood or snowstorm: include accounts from several people who were stranded or marooned. These could then be cut together to give an overall picture of the event.

The 1977 Queen's Jubilee Celebrations: cover the preparations for the big day and various viewpoints on the day itself.

The temporary evacuation of an area: people may have been moved out of their houses because of a leaking gas main or the discovery of an unexploded bomb. You could use the same technique on a much smaller scale, aiming to build up a complete picture of what happened by showing the different points of view of the people involved.

Here are some suggestions:
a day in the life of your family;
the day you were born;
a family reunion;
your form's first day at secondary school;
Speech Day. ▫

There Will Come Soft Rains

Clock Voice: Tick-tock, Eight o'clock, Time to get up, Time to get up, Eight o'clock.

Narrator: The morning house lies empty. The clock ticks on, repeating its sound into the emptiness.

Clock Voice: Tick-tock, Eight — nine, Breakfast time, Eight — nine.

(Musical theme — the kitchen)

Narrator: In the kitchen, the breakfast stove has switched itself on.

(Musical effect)

Narrator: It has ejected eight pieces of perfectly browned toast . . .

(Musical effect)

a jug of coffee . . . and two cool glasses of milk.

(Music out)

Woman's Voice: Today is August 4th in the year 2026. Today is August 4th in the year 2026.

Today is Mrs. Featherstone's birthday. Today is the anniversary of Tilita's marriage. Insurance is payable, as are the water, gas and light bills.

Clock Voice: Tick-tock, Nine-one o'clock, Tick-tock, Nine-one o'clock, Off to school, Off to work, Run, run, Nine-one.

Narrator: But no doors slam. No carpets take the soft tread of rubber heels.

Barometer Voice: *(singing).* Rain, rain, Go away, Rubber and raincoats for today, Rain, rain, Go away, Rubber and raincoats for today.

(Rain music has come in under voice and continues. There is a chime.)

Narrator: The garage chimes and the door rolls up. It reveals a car waiting inside. . . . After a long wait the door rolls down again.

(Music out. Pause.)

Nine-thirty. The eggs are shrivelled and the toast is like stone. An aluminium wedge scrapes them into the sink, then hot water whirls them down a metal throat, which digests them and flushes them away to the distant sea. The dirty dishes are dropped into a hot washer and emerge twinkling dry.

Clock Voice: *(singing).* Ten-fifteen, Time to clean, Ten-fifteen, Time to clean.

(Musical theme. Cleaning mice.)

Narrator: Out of warrens in the wall, tiny robot mice have darted, all rubber and metal. . . . They thud against chairs, they whirl their moustached runners, knead the pile of the carpet, suck gently at hidden dust.

(Music ends rather abruptly.)

They have popped back into their burrows. Their pink electric eyes have faded. The house is clean.

Clock Voice: Tick-tock, Eleven o'clock, Tick-tock, Eleven o'clock.

Narrator: The sun has come out now from behind the rain. The house stands alone in a city of rubble and ashes. This is the one house left standing. At night the ruined city gives off a radioactive glow which can be seen for miles.

(Garden music)

The garden sprinklers fill the soft morning air with scatterings of brightness. . . . The water pelts against the window panes, it runs down the west side of the house.

(Music out)

The entire west face of the house is black, save for five places. Here the silhouette in white of a man mowing a lawn. Here, as in a photograph, a woman bent to pick flowers. Still farther over, their images stamped in the house in one titanic instant, a small boy, hands flung in the air; higher up, the image of a thrown ball, and opposite him a girl, hands raised to catch a ball which never came down. The five spots of white — the man, the woman, the children, the ball — remain. The rest is a thin layer of black.

(Garden music continues)

The gentle sprinkling rain fills the garden with falling light. . . . Until this day, how well the house has kept its peace! How carefully it has enquired. Who goes there? What's the password? And getting no answer from lonely dogs and whining cats, it has shut its windows and drawn its curtains in an old-maidenly preoccupation with self-protection. The house quivers at every sound. If a sparrow brushes a window, the sun-blinds snap up. The bird is startled and flies away. Not even a bird must touch the house.

(Music out)

The house is an altar with ten thousand attendants, big, small, servicing, attending. But the gods have gone away and the ritual of the religion continues senselessly, uselessly.

Clock Voice: Tick-tock, Twelve o'clock, Tick-tock, Twelve o'clock.

Narrator: A dog whines, shivering, on the front porch. The front door recognises the dog's voice and opens. The dog, once huge and fleshy, has now gone to bone and is covered with sores. It moves in and drags itself through the house, leaving a trail of mud.

(Cleaning mice music)

The angry mice come whirring along behind it, angry at having to pick up mud, angry at inconvenience. For not a leaf fragment can blow under the door without the wall-panels flipping open and the copper scrap mice flashing swiftly out. The offending dust, hair or paper is seized in miniature steel jaws, and raced back to the burrows. From there, it goes down tubes into the cellar where it is dropped into the sighing vent of an incinerator which sits like evil Baal in a dark corner.

(Music out)

The dog runs upstairs. It yelps hysterically at each door. At last it realises, as the house has realised, that only emptiness is here. . . .

(Kitchen music)

In the kitchen, the stove is making pancakes now and filling the house with a rich smell of baking. . . . The dog scratches desperately at the door. The door remains shut. . . . The dog froths at the mouth and its eyes turn to fire. . . . It runs wildly in circles, biting at its tail. . . . And at last it dies.

(Music out)

It lies in the parlour for an hour.

Clock Voice: Tick-Tock, Two o'clock, Tick-tock, Two o'clock.

(Cleaning mice music)

Narrator: The cleaning mice have come out. They have caught the scent of decay. They go humming along as softly as blown grey leaves in an electrical wind.

(Music continues for a little and then stops)

The dog is gone now. In the cellar, the incinerator gives out a sudden glow and a whirl of sparks goes leaping up the chimney.

(Change to rather formal party music)

And now it is afternoon. Bridge tables are sprouting from the walls. Playing cards are fluttering down in a shower of pips. A tray of tea has appeared on a side table. There are tiny sandwiches and a large iced cake.

[Eventually, with no one living there to prevent it, there is an accidental fire. The house's automatic devices try to save it but cannot.]

from the story *There Will Come Soft Rains* by Ray Bradbury. Adapted by Nesta Pain.

The dark porch air in the late afternoon was full of needle flashes, like a movement of gathered silver insects in the light. The three women's mouths twitched over their work. Their bodies lay back and then imperceptibly forward, so that the rocking chairs tilted and murmured. Each woman looked to her own hands, as if quite suddenly she had found her heart beating there.

'What time is it?'

'Ten minutes to five.'

'Got to get up in a minute and shell those peas for dinner.'

'But — ' said one of them.

'Oh yes, I forgot. How foolish of me. . .'

'Go hull them if it'll make you feel good,' said the second woman.

'No,' said the first. 'I won't. I just won't.'

The third woman sighed. She embroidered a rose, a leaf, a daisy on a green field. The embroidery needle rose and vanished.

The second woman was working on the finest, most delicate piece of embroidery of them all, deftly poking, finding, and returning the quick needle upon innumerable journeys. Her quick black glance was on each motion. A flower, a man, a road, a sun, a house; the scene grew under hand, a miniature beauty, perfect in every threaded detail.

'It seems at times like this that it's always your hands you turn to,' she said, and the others nodded enough to make the rockers rock again.

'I believe,' said the first lady, 'that our souls are in our hands. For we do *everything* to the world with our hands. Sometimes I think we don't use our hands half enough; it's certain we don't use our heads.'

They all peered more intently at what their hands were doing.

'Yes,' said the third lady, 'when you look back on a whole lifetime, it seems you don't remember faces so much as hands and what they did.'. . .

And suddenly they were crying. The tears rolled softly down their faces and fell into the material upon which their fingers twitched.

'This won't help things,' said the first lady at last, putting the back of her thumb to each under-eyelid. She looked at her thumb and it was wet.

'Now look what I've done!' cried the second lady, exasperated. The others stopped and peered over. The second lady held out her embroidery. There was the scene, perfect except that while the embroidered yellow sun shone down upon the embroidered green field, and the embroidered brown road curved toward an embroidered pink house, the man standing on the road had something wrong with his face.

'I'll just have to rip out the whole pattern, practically, to fix it right,' said the second lady.

'What a shame.' They all stared intently at the beautiful scene with the flaw in it.

The second lady began to pick away at the thread with her little deft scissors flashing. The pattern came out thread by thread. She pulled and yanked, almost viciously. The man's face was gone. She continued to seize at the threads.

'What are you *doing*?' asked the other woman.

They leaned and saw what she had done.

The man was gone from the road. She had taken him out entirely.

They said nothing but returned to their own tasks.

'What time is it?' said someone.

'Five minutes to five.'

'Is it supposed to happen at five o'clock? . . . And they're not sure what it'll do to anything, really, when it happens?'

'No, not sure.'

'Why didn't we stop them before it got this far and this big?'

'It's twice as big as ever before. No, ten times, maybe a thousand.'. . .

'We won't hear anything, will we?'

'They say not.'

'Perhaps we're foolish. Perhaps we'll go right on, after five o'clock, shelling peas, opening doors, stirring soups, washing dishes, making lunches, peeling oranges. . . .'

'My, how we'll laugh to think we were frightened by an old experiment!' They smiled a moment at each other.

'It's five o'clock.'

At these words, hushed, they all busied themselves. Their fingers darted. Their faces were turned down to the motions they made. They made frantic patterns. They made lilacs and grass and trees and houses and rivers in the embroidered cloth. They said nothing, but you could hear their breath in the silent porch air.

Thirty seconds passed.

The second woman sighed faintly and began to relax.

'I think I just *will* go shell those peas for supper,' she said. 'I — '

But she hadn't time even to lift her head. Somewhere, at the side of her vision, she saw the world brighten and catch fire. She kept her head down, for she knew what it was. She didn't look up, nor did the others, and in the last instant their fingers were flying; they didn't glance about to see what was happening to the country, the town, this house, or even this porch. They were only staring down at the design in their flickering hands.

The second woman watched an embroidered flower go. She tried to embroider it back in, but it went, and then the road vanished, and the blades of grass. She watched a fire, in slow motion almost, catch upon the embroidered house and unshingle it, and pull each threaded leaf from the small green tree in the hoop, and she saw the sun itself pulled apart in the design. Then the fire caught upon the moving point of the needle while still it flashed; she watched the fire come along her fingers and arms and body, untwisting the yarn of her being so painstakingly that she could see it in all its devilish beauty, yanking out the pattern from the material at hand. What it was doing to the other women or the furniture or the elm tree in the yard, she never knew. For now, yes, now! it was plucking at the white embroidery of her flesh, the pink thread of her cheeks, and at last it found her heart, a soft red rose sewn with fire, and it burned the fresh, embroidered petals away, one by delicate one. . . .

from the story *Embroidery* by Ray Bradbury

■ Both stories are by the same writer. Compare them, in particular discussing:
what the stories say about a world without people;
what makes people different from machines;
whether you think Ray Bradbury wrote the stories as warnings. □

Here are some ideas for longer pieces of written work:
■ 1 Write a play set in the Automatic House when the family were alive.

You will be able to show what kind of people they were, and what it was like having everything done for you by machines. Was it a paradise or was it dull?

2 Write the life story of one of the old ladies in *Embroidery*. She was born in the nineteen-seventies and has lived through many changes.

Or you could write her memories as if you had interviewed her.

3 Write a story or play about the threat of nuclear war. □

Making a Statement about War through Poetry

One way of saying something about war is through poetry — but there are many ways of writing on this subject. Here is a collection of very different poems on the same theme; also included is a short extract from a novel which treats the subject in an imaginative way. As you discuss them, consider which you prefer, which makes the most impact on you, and which you think is most effective in making its point.

Paul Dehn and Adrian Henri both use parody — copying the style of nursery rhymes, hymns and advertisements to point out the stupidity of war.

Do you think nuclear war is a suitable subject for this sort of humorous treatment?

Do you prefer these or the poems with a more serious approach?

Both James Kirkup and Kurihara Sadako had actually been in Hiroshima — Kurihara at the time of the bomb and Kirkup later as a visitor.

Do you think this experience makes their poems better than those of people who write without themselves knowing what the city is like?

Do you prefer the poem by the victim (Kurihara's *Giving Birth to Life*) or the one by the outside observer (Kirkup's *No More Hiroshimas*)? Why?

These two poems are realistic: they try to tell us, as far as they can, what things are actually like. In contrast, the extract from Kurt Vonnegut's novel *Slaughterhouse Five* uses fantasy — the idea of time going backwards.

Which approach has the greatest effect on you?

Do you think Vonnegut is simply trying out an interesting idea, or is he making a point about war?

Adrian Mitchell uses horror in his poem about germ warfare, *Open Day at Porton*, to shock us into reacting.

What effect does it have on you?

Try writing two or three poems on a subject you feel strongly about, using some of the approaches used by these writers. □

Bomb Commercials
(for two voices)

1 A. Get PAD nuclear meat for humans.
   B. Don't give your family ordinary meat, give them PAD.
   A. P.A.D. — Prolongs Active Death.
   B. Enriched with nourishing marrowbone strontium.

2 A. All over the world, more and more people are changing to

   BOMB

   B. Bomb — The international passport to smoking ruins

3 B. . . . so then I said 'well let's all go for a picnic and we went and it was all right except for a bit of sand in the butties and then of course the wasps and Michael fell in the river but what I say is you can't have everything perfect can you so just then there was a big bang and the whole place caught fire and something happened to Michael's arms and I don't know what happened to my Hubby and its perhaps as well as there were only four pieces of Kit-Kat so we had one each and then we had to walk home 'cos there weren't any buses . . .'
   A. Have a break — have a Kit-Kat

4 A. Everyday in cities all over England people are breathing in Fall-out
   B. Get the taste of the Bomb out of your mouth with Oval Fruits.

5 A. General Howard J. Sherman has just pressed the button that killed 200 million people. A big job with big responsibilities. The General has to decide between peace and the extinction of the human race . . .
   B. But he can't tell Stork from Butter.

Adrian Henri

Rock of ages cleft for me,
Let me hide myself in thee.
While the bombers thunder past,
Shelter me from burn and blast;
And though I know all men are brothers
Let the fallout fall on others.

Ring-a-ring o' neutrons.
A pocket full of positrons,
A fission! A fission!
We all fall down.

Rain before seven,
Dead before eleven.

Onward, Christian soldiers,
  Each to war resigned,
With the Cross of Jesus
  Vaguely kept in mind.

Paul Dehn

50

From *No More Hiroshimas*

In the dying afternoon, I wander dying round the Park of
  Peace.
It is right, this squat, dead place, with its left-over air
Of an abandoned International Trade and Tourist Fair.
The stunted trees are wrapped in straw against the cold.
The gardeners are old, old women in blue bloomers, white
  aprons.
Survivors weeding the dead brown lawns around the Children's
  Monument.

A hideous pile, the Atomic Bomb Explosion Centre, freezing
  cold,
'Includes the Peace Tower, a museum containing
Atomic-melted slates and bricks, photos showing
What the Atomic Desert looked like, and other
Relics of the catastrophe.'

The other relics:
The ones that made me weep;
The bits of burnt clothing,
The stopped watches, the torn shirts.
The twisted buttons,
The stained and tattered vests and drawers,
The ripped kimonos and charred boots,
The white blouse polka-dotted with atomic rain, indelible,
The cotton summer pants the blasted boys crawled home in,
  to bleed
And slowly die.

Remember only these.
They are the memorials we need.

James Kirkup

Open Day at Porton

These bottles are being filled with madness,
A kind of liquid madness concentrate
Which can be drooled across the land
Leaving behind a shuddering human highway . . .

  A welder trying to eat his arm.

  Children pushing stale food into their eyes
  To try to stop the chemical spectaculars
  Pulsating inside their hardening skulls.

  A health visitor throwing herself downstairs,
  Climbing the stairs, throwing herself down again
  Shouting: Take the nails out of my head.

There is no damage to property.

Now, nobody likes manufacturing madness,
But if we didn't make madness in bottles
We wouldn't know how to deal with bottled madness.

We don't know how to deal with bottled madness.

We all really hate manufacturing madness
But if we didn't make madness in bottles
We wouldn't know how to be sane.

Responsible madness experts assure us
Britain would never be the first
To uncork such a global brainquake.

But suppose some foreign nut sprayed Kent
With his insanity aerosol . . .
Well, there's only one answer to madness.

Adrian Mitchell

Giving Birth to Life

At night, in the basement of a building destroyed,
a dark room without even a candle for light
crowded with wounded from the atom bomb.

The smell is the smell of blood, the smell of death,
the smell of sweat and suffocation, and moaning.
A strange voice is heard
'a baby is about to be born.'

In this basement, at the bottom of hell,
this young woman comes into labour.
What can be done
in the darkness without even a match?

But the people care, forgetting their pains.
'I am a midwife, I will help her'
comes this voice out of the sounds of moans.
So, in the depths of this hell of darkness,
a child is born.

With strength that cannot last till dawn,
the midwife dies in blood,
helping give birth to life,
giving birth to life
giving her own life.

Kurihara Sadako, Hiroshima

From *Slaughterhouse Five*

Billy looked at the clock on the gas stove. He had an hour to
kill before the saucer came. He went into the living room,
swinging the bottle like a dinner bell, turned on the television.
He came slightly unstuck in time, saw the late movie backwards, then forwards again. It was a movie about American
bombers in the Second World War and the gallant men who
flew them. Seen backwards by Billy, the story went like this:
    American planes, full of holes and wounded men and corpses
took off backwards from an airfield in England. Over France,
a few German fighter planes flew at them backwards, sucked
bullets and shell fragments from some of the planes and crewmen. They did the same for wrecked American planes on the
ground, and those planes flew up backwards to join the
formation.
    The formation flew backwards over a German city that was
in flames. The bombers opened their bomb bay doors, exerted
a miraculous magnetism which shrunk the fires, gathered them
into cylindrical steel containers, and lifted the containers into
the bellies of the planes. The containers were stored neatly in
racks. The Germans below had miraculous devices of their
own, which were long steel tubes. They used them to suck
more fragments from the crewmen and the planes. But there
were still a few wounded Americans, though, and some of the
bombers were in bad repair. Over France, though, German
fighters came up again, made everything and everybody as
good as new.
    When the bombers got back to their base, the steel cylinders
were taken from the racks and shipped back to the United
States of America, where factories were operating night and
day, dismantling the cylinders, separating the dangerous
contents into minerals. Touchingly, it was mainly women who
did this work. The minerals were then shipped to specialists
in remote areas. It was their business to put them into the
ground, to hide them cleverly, so they would never hurt anybody ever again.

Kurt Vonnegut

CND

The Campaign for Nuclear Disarmament (CND) is an organisation which campaigns for a world free of nuclear weapons and of all other weapons of mass destruction. CND's immediate policy is for Britain unilaterally to abandon nuclear weapons, and policies based on nuclear weapons, as a first step to the creation of a British foreign policy based on the principles of peace and cooperation. Such a policy would seek, as a priority, to rid the world of nuclear weapons.

CND is not only opposed to British nuclear weapons, but also to all other nuclear weapons, and it campaigns against any international development which threatens the survival of the world. During the 1960s the CND organisation received a great deal of publicity for the protest marches that were organised each year to the nuclear weapon research centre at Aldermaston in Berkshire.

■ CND produces its own bi-monthly newspaper, called *Sanity,* in addition to numerous posters, pamphlets and leaflets. The members of the organisation, who write and design these materials, try to influence public opinion in a number of different ways. In the pamphlet *How Many More? The spread of nuclear weapons* the authors, David Griffiths and Dan Smith, begin by presenting their readers with information about nuclear weapons in a clear and concise way. The extracts from the pamphlet printed below show that it is essentially a piece of factual writing, designed to influence the reader by allowing the facts to speak for themselves. Only occasionally do the writers use emotive words and phrases which reveal their own feelings about nuclear warfare. Study the passage and find examples of where this occurs. ▫

The first nuclear weapon used in war was dropped on the Japanese city of Hiroshima at 8.14 a.m. on Monday August 6, 1945. The bomb's explosive power was 14 kilotons (i.e. equivalent to 14,000 tons of TNT). Hiroshima was devastated.

Three days later, the only other nuclear weapon yet used in war was dropped on Nagasaki, missing the city by two miles. Slightly more powerful, it destroyed half of Nagasaki.

To this day it has been impossible to state definitively how many people died as a result of those two weapons. At least 80,000 died almost instantly in Hiroshima, a further 120,000 in the following three months. At Nagasaki, as many as 50,000 died instantly, and as many again in the next three months. In each year since 1945 there have been about 1,000 deaths in Hiroshima from delayed radiation effects; over the same period, 50,000 have died in Nagasaki. The hospitals of each city have over 1,000 in-patients suffering from after-effects of the bombs, and many thousands more are treated as out-patients – 49,000 in Hiroshima in 1971 alone.

Many of those now suffering, and many who have died, were not born when the bombs were dropped – perhaps it is that which makes nuclear weapons so especially horrifying.

Yet the weapons used against Hiroshima and Nagasaki were relatively crude. By today's standards their explosive power was small, and the method of getting them to their target unreliable. The power of nuclear weapons can now be measured in megatons (1 megaton is the equivalent power of 1,000,000 tons of TNT), and they can be delivered more accurately.

A single 10 megaton bomb would smash everything within a radius of 3½ miles; it would destroy brick buildings up to 6 or 7 miles away, and cause serious damage up to 30 miles away. Immediate deaths would be caused by the intense heat of the 'fireball', by collapsing buildings and flying debris, by blast, and by firestorms started by the fireball or by damage to electric circuits. Radioactive fallout would cover an area 40 miles wide and 100 miles downwind of the explosion with great intensity, and would spread over much larger areas. A dozen such bombs dropped on Britain would cover most of the country with radiation many times more intense than the lethal level. All basic services would break down and the fabric of society be destroyed. The country would be nothing but a graveyard....

The Extra Dangers With very few exceptions, nuclear proliferation–the spread of ownership of nuclear weapons to more states than now possess them–has universally been regarded as a terrible prospect.

In one sense the extra dangers are a matter of odds. The mere existence of nuclear weapons means that they can be used. Already at least five countries have them, and the more countries that have them, the more likely they are to be used. But it is not just a matter of odds, for two reasons.

Firstly, the countries most likely to 'go nuclear' are all involved in some kind of conflict with other states; in some cases these conflicts have boiled over into war. When the pressure of war is on, if things are going badly, if decisions have to be made under stress, even when war seems the possible outcome of a crisis–use of nuclear weapons might seem like a handy 'solution'.

Secondly, new nuclear powers' forces will be inherently even more dangerous than those of the established nuclear powers. The bombs themselves are the cheapest and simplest elements of the American and Soviet nuclear arsenals; the major effort is in developing the delivery systems–bombers and missiles. And missiles, buried in specially protected underground siloes, or carried in submarines, are very hard to destroy; together with the awesome power of the two arsenals this has been something of a deterrent to their use.

Because of the expense and complexity of long range missiles (the technology of which is easier to keep secret than that of the bomb itself), a new nuclear power will probably deploy its nuclear weapons on delivery systems it already has–bombers and, possibly, short range missiles. Stored on the surface, these will be vulnerable to attack in a war, raising the incentive to use them early on.

We are not saying that the Soviet/American relationship is safe. Quite the opposite: it is very dangerous, always open to the danger of war by accident, miscalculation or misunderstanding (apart from deliberate intent). It is made worse by the presence in Europe of thousands of very vulnerable tactical nuclear weapons. But all these problems would be multiplied for new nuclear powers, with their entire arsenals vulnerable to attack. ...

However, we can see that in a later passage from *How Many More?* the writers allow their opinions to appear much more openly than in the passages you have just read. In this passage they aim to present their point of view in such a way that readers will find their arguments convincing. They use facts in order to support particular points in their argument.

■ 1 What points do the authors make in this passage?
2 How do they support the points that they make?
3 Do you find their arguments convincing? Why? □

Our Responsibility It is an easy thing to define what is needed to prevent nuclear proliferation, less easy to ensure that it happens.

We have only one factor to throw into the equation—the force of public opinion. The problem of nuclear weapons may seem vast and intractable. But in the end no government can resist the strength of a great movement of the people, working together for a common objective.

In this respect, we in Britain have a special responsibility. Our government claims to put non-proliferation among its highest priorities; it has been a vigorous supporter of the NPT,[1] and has taken an active part in the diplomacy of nuclear trade controls. Yet its sincerity is constantly called into question by the fact that it clings tenaciously to its own nuclear arsenal. Its condemnation of the Indian nuclear test in 1974, for example, was followed in a few weeks by a nuclear test of its own.

A non-nuclear British government, in contrast, would be in a unique position to challenge the drift towards a nuclear-armed world.

It used to be argued that Britain's moral example alone could lead the world to nuclear disarmament. That is perhaps too grand a view. But the example of at least one country which had developed nuclear weapons and then decided to renounce them could only strengthen the hands of those in other countries arguing against nuclear weapon development. It would also give Britain the opportunity to challenge NATO[2] nuclear strategies, to press upon the USA and the USSR the urgency of nuclear disarmament, and to develop a foreign policy which, freed of the confrontation of East and West, could take peace as its priority.

Such a policy would involve no sacrifice for Britain. British nuclear weapons are a feeble joke at best, a gun at our own heads at worst. To use them would be to invite retaliation and the total destruction of our densely populated country. Any threat to use them is a threat to commit suicide.

Britain would be safer without nuclear weapons, even if British nuclear disarmament were ignored by the rest of the world. Any impact it had upon the rest of the world would in that sense be a bonus. There is much to be won, and nothing to be lost.

[1]*NPT* Non-Proliferation Treaty
[2]*NATO* North Atlantic Treaty Organisation

from How Many More? The spread of nuclear weapons
by David Griffiths and Dan Smith

In these posters, the writers and designers use emotive language to express their point of view and to try to influence people. The use of words such as 'national suicide' and 'the prostitute of war' leaves the reader in no doubt as to the writers' attitude towards nuclear weapons.
■ 1 Find other examples of the emotive use of language in these posters.
2 Discuss the slogan 'The Arms Race is Killing'. How effective is it? Suggest other slogans that CND might use.
3 Why did the designer choose Philip Noel-Baker's statement for his poster? How effectively does it make the point which the designer wants it to make?
4 Would the 'Polaris-No' poster influence you to march against the missiles?
5 Can you suggest ways that it might be redesigned or rewritten to make it more effective?

Organise a debate on a topic about which members of the group have strong feelings, e.g. nuclear warfare, vivisection, euthanasia. In addition to preparing speeches, produce posters and leaflets designed to influence others to come round to your point of view. □

Unit 7　　Notes on Trial

SCENE 1 INT . LONDON CROWN COURT

THE SCENE IS A SMALL LONDON CROWN COURT. THE PRISONER - HAINES - A YOUNG
WIRY COCKNEY, LOOKING COMPOSED BUT QUIETLY BELLIGERENT - IS SEATED IN THE
DOCK, A COURT OFFICIAL SITTING BEHIND HIM. ALSO PRESENT AND SEATED ARE THE
JUDGE, THE COUNSELS - FOULKES, PROSECUTING, YOUNG, KEEN, BESPECTACLED, AND
WALSH, DEFENDING, OLDER, RELAXED, CYNICAL - THEIR JUNIORS, THE CLERK AND THE
JURY. THE JURY HAVE OBVIOUSLY JUST RECENTLY TAKEN THEIR PLACES, AND ARE
COVERTLY STEALING GLANCES AROUND THE ROOM NERVOUSLY, A LITTLE EXCITEDLY -
THAT IS, WITH TWO EXCEPTIONS. THESE ARE A HEAVILY BUILT STOLID INDIVIDUAL
SEATED IN THE CORNER SEAT NEAREST THE JUDGE - THE FOREMAN OF THE JURY, AND
ALREADY ASSUMING AIRS HE CONSIDERS APPROPRIATE TO THE POSITION - AND A GIRL
OF ABOUT EIGHTEEN, COMPOSED, INTERESTED, BUT RELAXED, WHO IS SEATED TWO
PLACES FROM THE FOREMAN. THESE TWO ARE GIVING THEIR FULL ATTENTION TO THE
JUDGE. BETWEEN THEM SITS A BOY WHO - OBVIOUSLY TAKING HIS CUE FROM THEM -
IS CONCENTRATING ON THE JUDGE, OPEN-MOUTHED. THE JUDGE IS IN THE MIDDLE OF
HIS ADDRESS TO THE JURY - THOUGH WE HAVE ENTERED THE COURT WHILE HE IS
APPARENTLY PAUSING RELAXEDLY TO CONSIDER HIS FINAL POINTS, FINGERING SOME
NOTES AND PAPERS BEFORE HIM.

1

JUDGE: And finally, ladies and gentlemen of the jury, let me stress that
I am here to guide you only in matters of the law. It is for you - and you
alone to decide on matters of fact: whether the accused is guilty or not
guilty. Therefore you will understand it is of the utmost importance that
you pay close attention throughout this trial. I would strongly advise you
to take notes of the evidence to help guide your deliberations when you come
to give your verdict.

(JURY STIR, NERVOUSLY REACHING FOR THE PAPER, SOME SEARCH HURRIDLY FOR PENS.
THE BOY ESPECIALLY, LOOKS AGITATED. HE REALISES HE HAS NO PEN. JUDGE WAITS,
TOLERANTLY - HE'S SEEN ALL THIS BEFORE.)

BOY: Oh...(WHISPERING TO FOREMAN) I...you...you couldn't lend me a pen?

JUDGE (OVER THE BUZZ): It is especially important of course, that your
foreman takes adequate notes, I'm sure that's understood.

(FOREMAN, PREENING HIMSELF AT THIS, NODS EAGERLY TO THE JUDGE.)

BOY (STILL MORE TIMIDLY, AGITATED): I...I haven't -

FOREMAN (PEN AND PAPER CONFIDENTLY AT THE READY, WHISPERS): Don't you bother.
You can leave it to me.

(BOY, RELAXED, SINKS BACK GRATEFULLY. GIRL MEANWHILE HAS PRODUCED A SPARE
PENCIL, OFFERS IT. HE SHAKES HIS HEAD, MOTIONS, SMILING, 'doesn't matter'.
FOREMAN IS WRITING GRANDLY AT THE TOP OF HIS FIRST SHEET OF PAPER: 'FOREMAN'S
NOTES'. GIRL MERELY BUSIES HERSELF NEATLY NUMBERING HER PAGES.)

CLERK (HAVING GOT THE NOD FROM THE JUDGE, RISES): Bring up George Robert
Haines.

(HAINES COMES FORWARD, GRIMACING WEARILY)

CLERK: George Robert Haines, you are charged that on the 16th of June this
year you did attempt to steal a sum of one hundred and two pounds and a
wallet from Charles Edward Mariner. How do you wish to plead? Guilty or
not guilty?

HAINES (DELIBERATELY, EXPLOSIVELY): Not guilty. Definitely.

(JUDGE LOOKS UP, URBANE, BUT SLIGHTLY STARTLED. THEN SCRIBBLES BRIEFLY.
FOREMAN IS SCRIBBLING FURIOUSLY, EAGER, APPARENTLY, TO TAKE DOWN EVERY
WORD. GIRL WRITES NEATLY, SMOOTHLY: 'CHARGE - ATTEMPT STEAL £102 & WALLET.
NOT GUILTY PLEA?' BOY WATCHES FOREMAN'S EFFORT, IMPRESSED.)

CUT/FADE TO WITNESS BOX, WHERE NOW STANDS NEATLY DRESSED MIDDLE-AGED MAN.

PROSECUTING COUNSEL: Please give the court your name and address.

MARINER: I am Charles Edward Mariner of 11 Billington Street, S.W.5

PROS. C.: Can you tell the court what transpired on the morning of the 16th
June last?

(FOREMAN SCRIBBLES AWAY, GIRL, PEN POISED, LISTENS.)

2

MARINER: Yes. Certainly. Well, it was a Saturday and my wife and I were
shopping in the West End. We ended up in Marks and Spencers, in Oxford
Street.

PROS. C.: And about what time of the morning would this be?

MARINER: Oh, it was about lunchtime by then. Almost half past twelve.

(WE SEE FOREMAN'S PAGE AS HE WRITES, WORDS HURTLED DOWN IN WILD DISARRAY.
GIRL IS NEATLY WRITING: 'MARINER & WIFE - SHOPPING MARKS & SPENCERS,
OXFD. ST., APPROX 12.30'.)

PROS. C.: (AGREEING): Ah, indeed. And what happened then?

MARINER: Well, while I was looking in the mirror, all the time I could see
my coat hung up on the rail behind me and then I saw this man hovering -

PROS. C.: Just a moment, Mr. Mariner. You observed this man 'hovering', as
you say. Did you have the opportunity to observe him closely?

MARINER: Oh yes, 'cos he was kind of standing still 'hovering'. Oh, yes.

PROS. C.: And do you see this man in the court at this moment?

MARINER: Yes, I certainly do. (POINTING TO HAINES, FIRMLY) It was him!

HAINES (MUTTERING HALF INAUDIBLY): Leave it out! Stroll on.....

JUDGE (WITH MILD SEVERITY): Please ask your client to keep quiet, Mr. Walsh.

(HAINES'S MUMBLINGS DIE AWAY)

PROS. C.: And so, Mr. Mariner, you took note of this man...

MARINER: Yes, and I thought to myself, he looks suspicious -

PROS.C.: Why did you think that?

MARINER: Well, because of - well, because the way he was hovering - as if
making up his mind to do something or other.

PROS. C.: And did he? Do something?

MARINER: Yes. He suddenly put his hand in the pocket of my coat and pulled
out my wallet with £100 in it.

PROS. C.: And what was your reaction?

MARINER: Why, I shouted, of course. I said 'Hey!', and he immediately
started to run.

PROS. C.: Still holding your wallet.

MARINER: Yes. So I started off after him. He ran through the store out
towards the main entrance, into Oxford Street.

3

PROS. C.: And you followed.

MARINER (SLOWING, EMBARRASSED): Well, I tried to. But just as I was running through the doors, I was jumped on.

PROS. C.: Jumped on? By whom?

MARINER (SUBDUED): The store detective.

(JUDGE'S EYEBROWS RISE, PUZZLED)

He, well, I was still wearing one of their sports jackets...

(HAINES LAUGHS, SOFTLY. JUDGE GIVES HIM A QUICK GLARE)

JUDGE (TO MARINER): An unfortunate misunderstanding.

MARINER (GLARING AT HAINES, DEFIANTLY): Yes. Luckily my wife was there to do the necessary.

JUDGE (PUZZLED TO PROS. C.): His wife?

PROS. C.: Mrs. Mariner is my next witness, your honour. No further questions.

(HE SITS. DEFENCE COUNCIL RISES.)

DEF. C. (SMUGLY): I have no questions for this witness. (SITS)

(HAINES GRINS, SMUGLY. PROS. C. LOOKS MILDLY SURPRISED. IN THE JURY BOX, GIRL HAS LEISURELY TO OBSERVE THIS. FOREMAN, HEAD DOWN, IS STILL SCRIBBLING FURIOUSLY.)

CUT/FADE. Mrs. MARINER, A LARGE POWERFUL-LOOKING WOMAN, IS IN THE WITNESS BOX.

PROS. C.: Mrs. Mariner, could you tell the court what happened after your husband was detained by the store detective?

MRS. M.: Well, I was following up, close behind. It was total confusion. The stupid fool.

PROS. C.: Er, who, precisely?

MRS. M.: Why, the store detective. You see, I was screaming 'Stop, thief', and that fool thought I was shouting at my husband - cos he could see he was wearing the coat with all the tags hanging off it -

PROS. C.: Yes, yes, we realise that, but -

Mrs. M.: Well, when he jumped him, I went smack into the both of them and we all flopped down in a heap!

4

PROS. C.: I see. Very unfortunate. What happened then?

MRS. M.: I left them two to fight it out. I jumped and went running out onto the pavement. I couldn't see any sign of him. (INDICATING HAINES) Course, the street was crowded with shoppers. Being a Saturday. But then I saw something in the gutter.

PROS. C.: What?

MRS. M.: It was the wallet. So I ran to it and picked it up. Empty! All the money was gone. So I looked around again. And what do you think?

PROS. C. (SMILING SLIGHTLY): Well, please tell us.

MRS. M. (DRAMATICALLY): There was one of those barrows that sell hot chestnuts and some fruit - you know - just a few yards away, and I could see some legs sticking out underneath.

JUDGE (PUZZLED): Legs? Underneath?

PROS. C. (SWIFTLY): I think the inference is, my lord, that there was a body attached to the legs.

MRS. M. (INDIGNANT): Well, of course there was a body. His body! (POINTING TO HAINES) He was hiding behind the barrow.

HAINES (EQUALLY INDIGNANT): Hiding? I object, your honour!

JUDGE (ANGRILY): Kindly instruct your client to be silent. This is your last warning. (NODS TO PROS. C. TO CONTINUE) Mr. Foulkes.

PROS. C.: So having seen him, what did you do?

MRS. M.: I run and grabbed him, of course.

PROS. C.: Did he struggle?

MRS. M.: I'll say. But I got him in a half-Nelson.

(HAINES GLOWERS)

JUDGE (PUZZLED AGAIN): Why is she talking about Nelson?

PROS. C.: I believe it to be a well-known wrestling hold, your honour.

MRS. M. (MILDLY AMAZED): It's very simple. Would you like me to show you, your honour? (MAKES SLIGHT MOVEMENT TOWARDS HIM, HELPFULLY)

JUDGE (SHRINKING BACK AN INCH, SMILING): No thank you. That will not be necessary....Mr. Foulkes.

(SLIGHT LAUGHTER IN COURT)

5

PROS. C. (RESUMING TO MRS. M.): So, having secured the defendant in this wrestling hold...

MRS. M.: I frogmarched him back into the store.

PROS. C.: And was he there searched by the store detective and your husband?

MRS. M.: Yes, he was. And we found the money, stashed in his trouser pocket. Intact!

PROS. C.: Finally, Mrs. Mariner, are you positive this was the same man you both saw taking that money from your husband's jacket?

MRS. M.: I certainly am. (SHE GLARES AT HAINES WHO GLARES BACK)

PROS. C. (SITTING): And that, your honour, concludes the case for the prosecution.

(HE GLANCES ACROSS AT DEFENDING COUNSEL, WITH A QUIET SMIRK. DEFENDING COUNSEL LOOKS IMPERTURBABLE.)

FOREMAN (WHISPERING ACROSS TO BOY AND GIRL): Gah! It's an open and shut case.

GIRL (MILDLY, TIMIDLY): But we haven't heard the defence yet.

FOREMAN: Defence? What defence can there be? No, open and shut - (AS HE IS LEANING OVER, HIS EYE LIGHTS ON THE GIRL'S NOTES). Those all the notes you've managed?

GIRL: Yes.

FOREMAN (EXULTANT): Gah! Look how much I've got. Practically every word here. (SHOWING HIS SPRAWLING MASS OF NOTES)

GIRL (HESITANT): Yes, but...

FOREMAN (PROUDLY, TO GIRL): A complete record!

BOY (IMPRESSED, BUT NOTICING MOVEMENT ELSEWHERE, THE WITNESS BOX, INDICATING) Yes...ssh.

FOREMAN (NODDING, ALERTED, REACHING FOR HIS PEN AGAIN): Oh, yes, yes.

(THEY CONCENTRATE ON THE COURTROOM. HAINES IS IN THE BOX. USHER'S VOICE COMES INTO FOCUS.)

USHER (CONCLUDING): ...the truth and nothing but the truth.

HAINES (FIRMLY): ...the truth and nothing but the truth.

6

DEFENDING C.: Now, Mr. Haines, could you give us your version of what happened on this morning of the 16th June last?

HAINES: Yes, I can. I don't know nothing about it.

DEF. C.: How do you mean?

HAINES: I was never in Marks & Sparks that morning.

DEF. C.: No? Then where were you?

HAINES: At work, wasn't I?

DEF. C.: (FEEDING HAINES WITH A WELL SIMULATED WIDE-EYED PUZZLEMENT): At work? Where's that?

HAINES: Serving on the hot chestnut barrow!

(SENSATION IN COURT)

JUDGE: Do I understand you correctly? You claim to work on this hot -

HAINES: Too right, m'lud.

(PROSECUTING COUNSEL IS ON HIS FEET)

(PROS. C. SITS, GLOWERING, BEWILDERED THEN BEGINS HURRIEDLY WHISPERING WITH HIS JUNIOR. JUDGE, FROWNING NODS.)

JUDGE: Continue, Mr. Walsh...continue.

DEF. C.: And so, Mr. Haines, you could not possibly have been this man who, it is alleged, attempted to steal Mr. Mariner's wallet?

HAINES: Dead right. The only time I set foot in the store that morning was when that incredible hulk dragged me in!

JUDGE: Mr. Haines. Please moderate your tone. I will not have that language in this court.

HAINES (SPIRITEDLY): Well, it's all very well, your honour, but how would you feel?

JUDGE (OUTRAGED): Will you control your client, Mr. Walsh!

DEF. C. (HURRIEDLY): Yes, your honour. Mr. Haines, I'm sure the court sympathises with you in your distress, but please, please, keep to the point. I have only one more question. How do you explain the hundred pounds found in your possession?

7

HAINES: Why, that was the takings, wasn't it. The morning's takings. Nothing to do with <u>their</u> money.

DEF. C. (NODS SATISFIED): I have no further questions.

(SITS WITH A MILD FLOURISH, AND A MALICIOUS GRIN TO THE PROS. C.)

PROS. C. (RISING IN SOME CONFUSION): Mr. Haines - Mr. Haines, why, when you were arrested, why did you not tell the police, why did you not tell them this story about working on the barrow?

HAINES (WARILY): Why? Well...because I wasn't with it was I? After being knocked half unconcious by her over there.

PROS. C.: Oh, come now, Mr. Haines. You were with it enough, apparently, to give your occupation as that of 'barrow boy'. Wasn't that rather peculiar? Why should you do that? Were you lying when you said you were a bricklayer?

HAINES: No.

PROS. C.: (SEEING LIGHT, POUNCING): Oh! Now we're getting to the truth of it. So you are a bricklayer and not a barrow boy after all!

HAINES: Oh, yes, I am...I'm both.

PROS. C.: Both?

HAINES: I work on the buildings during the week, and help out on the barrow on Saturdays.

PROS. C. (SWALLOWING THIS, RALLYING): Oh, how very convenient for you. I see. So you were serving on that barrow for the whole of that morning? Were you? Is that what you're trying to tell us?

HAINES: Yes. How many more times?

PROS. C.: Working...on the...barrow. (FURIOUS, DRAMATIC) Do you expect this court to believe you?

HAINES (AFTER CONSIDERATION): No, I expect it to believe Mr. Peacock.

PROS. C. (SET BACK AGAIN): Who's Mr. Peacock?

DEF. C. (RISING BLANDLY): Perhaps I may be permitted to answer that. Mr. Peacock is my next witness.

(PROS. C. HESITATES, THEN SITS, BEWILDERED)

PROS. C. (ANGRILY): No further questions.

8

(HAINES PERMITS HIMSELF A COVERT SMILE)

CUT/FADE TO PEACOCK IN THE WITNESS BOX. PEACOCK IS PLUMP, THIRTYISH, VERY SELF-POSSESSED.

DEF. C.: Mr. Peacock, are you the proprietor of the hot chestnut and fruit barrow that commonly stands near the junction of Maryville Lane and Oxford Street?

PEACOCK: I am.

DEF. C.: Adjacent to the main entrance of Marks and Spencers, in fact.

PEACOCK: You betcher, chief.

DEF. C. (SMILING): Er..yes. Thank you. Now, my learned friend has cast doubt on the defendant's testimony that he is customarily employed to assist you each Saturday in your retailing operations.

PEACOCK: Come again?

DEF. C. (SLOWING): Mr. Haines assists you on the barrow.

PEACOCK: Oh, I get you. Yes chief. He's my assistant.

JUDGE: What is this 'chief' business?

PEACOCK (IMPERTURBABLE): Sorry, your worship. Just my way of speaking.

JUDGE (TESTILY): Well please amend your way of speaking. Answer the questions without giving Counsel these elaborate titles.

DEF. C. (SUPRESSING A SMILE): Now Mr. Peacock, how was trade on this particular Saturday? Can you remember?

PEACOCK: I can. Real brisk it was.

DEF. C.: And so Mr. Haines would have had no opportunity of, shall we say, slipping off into Marks and Spencers during the course of that morning.

PEACOCK: I should say not. If he'd popped off, I would have noticed, wouldn't I.

DEF. C.: Precisely. And trade being brisk, as you say, it would not be at all surprising that Mr. Haines would have had in his possession one hundred pounds. One hundred pounds of <u>takings</u>, in other words?

PEACOCK: No. Definitely.

9

DEF. C. (SITTING SMUGLY): Thank you, Mr. Peacock. No further questions.

(PROS. C. RISES, GAME BUT RUFFLED)

PROS. C.: Mr. Peacock, this is an extraordinary story, isn't it? Come on, be honest. An extraordinary story.

PEACOCK: What is?

PROS. C.: This story you are telling the court. Your assistant is assaulted before your very eyes, he is dragged into Marks and Spencers with one hundred pounds of your money in his possession and you apparently stand there and do nothing!

PEACOCK: Do nothing?

PROS. C.: Well, isn't that so? You made no protest.

PEACOCK: No, well, the fact is I didn't notice it, to be honest.

PROS. C.: Didn't notice it?

PEACOCK (IMPERTURBABLE): No. I was serving customers at the other end of the barrow. First I knew of it, I looked round and there he was - gone.

PROS. C. (SARCASTIC): Oh. Suddenly. Just wasn't there. So what did you think had happened to him? (LAUGHS) That he'd vanished in a puff of smoke? Gone off on holiday? What?

PEACOCK: No, I thought he'd gone for a slash.

PROS. C. (INTERRUPTING HURRIEDLY): But he did not come back, did he?

PEACOCK (PONDERING): No, well, I did think that a bit queer...I must admit.

PROS. C.: Oh, you admit that?

PEACOCK: Yes.

PROS. C.: Well, weren't you worried?

PEACOCK: Why?

PROS. C.: That he'd run off with your hundred pounds.

PEACOCK: What? Georgie? (OUTRAGE SLOWLY GROWING) Georgie Haines? Oh, you're joking. I've known him since he was a kid. Honest as they come - No. I never thought that. (WAXING VERY INDIGNANT) Why, you could trust him with the crown jewels, that boy. The whole idea of him trying to half-inch anything - what that bloke said - pinching his wallet, ridiculous I call it.

10

PROS. C.: Mr. Peacock.

PEACOCK (SUBSIDING, AMIABLY): Well, you did ask my opinion.

PROS. C. (SWALLOWS HARD, THEN): Mr. Peacock. Let me put it to you plainly. Mr. Haines has never been your assistant. I am suggesting to you that this is all a tissue of lies, cooked up between you and the defendant.

PEACOCK: I...I'm speechless. Can he say things like that to me, my lord?

JUDGE (WEARILY): Just answer the questions, Mr. Peacock.

PROS. C.: Mr. Peacock, you run a small barrow. A small two-wheeled barrow. You have no need for an assistant. You don't employ an assistant on any other day of the week, do you?

PEACOCK (APPARENTLY SLIGHTLY DISCONCERTED): Er, no, I grant you that.

PROS. C.: So why, on this particular Saturday should it happen, providentially, that the defendant, a bricklayer, apprehended skulking behind your barrow, suddenly turns out to be your assistant? Why should you need an assistant only on a Saturday?

PEACOCK: Trade's very brisk on a Saturday.

PROS. C. (SENSING VICTORY): Oh, but, surely, trade is also brisk on - a Friday, say? Or any other day of the week?

PEACOCK: Well, yes...on and off.

PROS. C.: So then why? Why? I want an answer, Mr. Peacock.

PEACOCK (GRINNING SLOWLY, AT LAST): Weekdays I work half-day.

PROS. C.: What difference does that make?

PEACOCK: Oh, I'll tell you. Saturdays. Full day. (SHRUGS) Lunch breaks.

PROS. C.: Lunch...

PEACOCK: Yes. We have one hour for lunch. We take turn and turn about. (SWEETLY) I have to have an assistant. (AS PROS. C., DEFEATED NOW, KNOWING IT, STARES AT HIM) Oh yes, people don't realise, you see. You can't expect to keep going full stretch all day without a break. Georgie goes off first. Then I have my break. At one, Religiously. On the dot. And that's not the end of it. There's tea breaks. Four o'clock. Oh, I could never manage without Georgie. Never. (ENJOYING HIMSELF, TURNING TO THE JUDGE), Cos you see, your honour, we don't pack up till gone six - later sometimes -

JUDGE: Yes, all right Mr. Peacock. I think we get the picture. Any further questions, Mr. Foulkes?

PROS. C.: No, your honour. No further questions.

JUDGE: You may step down.

PEACOCK: Thank you, chief.

(PEACOCK CEASES, WITH A SLY GRIN. SLY GRIN ON DEF.C'S FACE. AND A SLY GRIN FROM HAINES. BOY SUITABLY IMPRESSED, DUMBFOUNDED. GIRL LOOKS THOUGHTFUL, PEN IN HAND.

INCIDENTALLY, FOREMAN BY THIS TIME HAS GIVEN UP NOTE TAKING. NOTES IN DISARRAY IN FRONT OF HIM.)

CUT/FADE TO JURY TROOPING INTO JURY ROOM. FOREMAN LEADING THE WAY, BOY AND GIRL IN IMMEDIATE REAR.

FOREMAN (GLOOMILY AS THEY STRUGGLE INTO THEIR SEATS): Well, open and shut case.

GIRL: You think so?

FOREMAN: Ah, don't be stupid. Prosecuting Counsel threw in the towel, didn't he. You heard his final speech.

GIRL: Yes, but according to my notes...

FOREMAN (SCORNFULLY): Notes. (LAUGHS) We can forget them. Look, I've got notes - thousands of 'em. You don't need notes when the truth is staring you in the face.

BOY (SIGHING AGREEMENT): I did think he'd done it in the beginning.

FOREMAN: Yes, but then we hadn't heard the other side of the picture. No, myself, I could feel there was something fishy about it. Right from the start. After all, they never even got a proper sight of the thief in Marks and Spencers, did they.

GIRL: Didn't they? Mariner said they did.

FOREMAN: What? Where? (STRUGGLING WITH HIS NOTES) Half a mo, I'll check.

GIRL (READING COOLLY): 'Did you get a close look at the man?' 'Yes,' he said.

FOREMAN (PLAINTIVELY, SEARCHING): All my bloody papers are mixed up.

GIRL (MILDLY): Why didn't you number them?

FOREMAN (IRRITABLY PUSHING HIS NOTES ASIDE): Oh, anyway, doesn't matter. Mistaken identity, that's all it was. This sort of thing's always happening. Mistaken identity.

GIRL: I'm not so sure...

FOREMAN (SCORNFUL): Be your age. The barrow boy clinched it. You can't argue with the evidence. Come on, let's have a vote and get it over with. Not guilty! (STICKING UP A HAND)

GIRL (AS THE OTHERS HESITANTLY BEGIN TO RAISE THEIR HANDS): But...listen...

FOREMAN: Oh, Gawd. (LAUGHING TO THE OTHERS) There's always one awkward one, isn't there.

GIRL (EMBARRASSED, BUT INSISTENT): According to my notes...

FOREMAN: Her notes!

GIRL: These lunch times -

FOREMAN: I know one thing - if we don't settle this verdict quick, none of us are going to get any lunch. Ah, come on! (RAISES HAND AGAIN IMPATIENTLY TO INITIATE ANOTHER VOTE)

GIRL: Peacock said they had 'an hour each for lunch'.

FOREMAN: So what? Good luck to them. (RAISING HAND HIGHER) Not guilty!

GIRL (PERSISTING, AMID THE GENERAL MOVEMENT): The crime took place at twelve-thirty.

FOREMAN (AGGRESSIVELY): Who said?

GIRL: Mariner. (TAPPING NOTES) 'Half past twelve.'

BOY: Yes. I remember. He did say that.

FOREMAN: Well, what's it matter if he did?

GIRL: Precisely this. If Peacock and Haines had their hour off for lunch - only one of them would have been on the barrow at that time.

FOREMAN (STIRRING SUDDENLY, BLUSTERING): Wait a minute, let me check this out. We'll settle this. (PLOUGHING THROUGH HIS NOTES) Where is it - here - no. (AGONISED) Can't quite read it - (RALLYING) But it's all here. They each go to lunch - that doesn't prove anything. People go to lunch at any old hour.

GIRL: Not Peacock. 'I have my break at one'.

BOY (EXCITEDLY): Yes, that's right.

FOREMAN: Ah, but Haines might have gone after him.

GIRL: No, Haines went first. (BANGING HER NOTES) 'Georgie goes first'.

FOREMAN (RELUCTANT): So that means...

GIRL: Either those two did cook up this story, as the counsel said. Or Haines could have been in the store at that time.

BOY: Either way they're lying.

FOREMAN: Blow me. He's guilty.

BOY (GAZING WITH ADMIRATION AT THE GIRL): That was brilliant...

GIRL (MODESTLY): No.. Just good note-taking.

(SMILES AT BOY, HE SMILES BACK AVIDLY)

from a play by Leonard Kingston

Notes on Trial

■ 1 What do you think happened? Do you think the jury found Haines guilty? Do *you* think he was guilty? Give your reasons.

2 Talk about each of the characters: (a) Mr and Mrs Mariner; (b) Haines and Peacock; (c) the members of the jury; (d) the judge; (e) the lawyers and (f) the policeman.

What is a stereotype? How many of the characters are stereotypes?

3 Choose two of the characters. Imagine that you are each of them in turn, and write two separate paragraphs in which you describe their thoughts and feelings as they leave the court after the trial.

Note-taking

When you are making notes, remember these points:

(a) the use of headings and sub-headings;

(b) the importance of numbering pages/sections;

(c) the need to be selective;

(d) how to use abbreviations;

(e) how to group points and make cross-references;

(f) the use of asterisks, arrows and underlinings;

(g) the value of neatness and a clear layout;

(h) the value of writing up notes that are to be filed for future reference.

1 Why did the girl take better notes than the foreman?

2 Act out scenes in which either a store detective or a policeman interviews (a) Mariner, (b) Mrs Mariner and (c) Haines. Take it in turns to be the policeman or store detective. During the interview take notes on the answers to your questions. Study each other's notes. Decide whose notes are best, and why.

3 Use the notes you have made and write out the store detective's or the policeman's report of the interviews. Before you begin, discuss how the report should be laid out. What sort of language should be used in a formal report such as this? Discuss the difference between direct and indirect speech, and how reported speech should be punctuated in the report.

4 You are a newspaper reporter who has been sent to report on the trial. Reread the playscript, taking notes as you do so. Then, referring only to your notes, and not to the playscript, write your report.

Formal Language and Legal Language

1 Talk about the judge's formal use of language and compare it and the formal language used by the other officials (prosecuting counsel and the policeman) with the informal language used by the witnesses.

2 There are a number of examples in the play of 'legal language'. What is meant by legal language? Collect examples, e.g. hire purchase contracts and insurance policies, and discuss the language used in them. Why is legal language necessary? □

Motor Racing

At times you will use a library for information for an essay or background for a story. You will probably find there are several books on the subject you have chosen. Each book will be different in style and approach, but might give you some information that you could use to make notes for your own piece of writing.

■ Here are three extracts from books on motor racing. Each one covers a different aspect of the subject. The pieces have been chosen to help you complete one of the following assignments. When you have decided which assignment you want to attempt, read the extracts carefully, making a note of all the items of information that you will need. You can then use your notes when planning and writing your own piece.

The Race Write a story which centres on a motor race. The race can form part or all of your story.

Try to add interest by including other characters as well as the driver. The main race scene, for example, could be written from the point of view of any one or more of the following:
the driver's wife or girlfriend watching from the stand;
the driver's parents, listening to a commentary on the radio;
a team manager or mechanic working in the pits;
a television or radio commentator;
. . . or the driver himself or herself.

Write an article on motor racing, giving information about the sport, showing its dangers and excitements.

Either write a rather sensational piece for a teenage magazine, or write a short entry suitable for *The Young Person's Encyclopedia Of Sport*. □

How the Pits Pass on Secrets

Out there on the track each driver is on his own, but back in the pits a complex organization is supporting him.

Boss of the race tactics is the team manager. It is usually he who keeps the all-important lap chart, recording not only the times and positions of his own drivers but of rivals too.

Each car has two mechanics, ready to give it split-second attention if at any time it has to be called in.

Under the team manager the chief mechanic usually directs the signalling of information to the team's drivers.

Each team has its own secret methods of signalling to give the driver all the information he needs — who has dropped out of the race, who has done what speeds, his own position, and so on.

It is a seemingly casual but actually highly organized affair.

Passing the pits at speed the driver has them in view for less than five seconds. He must be able to recognize and take in his own signals at a glance.

Official signals are also given either from the pits or from various parts of the track.

The starting flag is always the flag of the country where an international race is being held.

A yellow-and-red, striped flag means oil on the track; a black one, with a particular driver's number, is an order for him to slow down and call at his pit at the end of the lap.

A blue flag, held stationary, warns a driver that he is being closely followed. Waved, it means that the driver behind is trying to pass.

A yellow flag signifies an obstruction. Drivers seeing it must be prepared to slow down and stop if necessary.

A white flag appearing simultaneously round the course means that a service vehicle is on the track, and a red flag, used only under the direct instructions of the clerk of the course, is a warning to all drivers to stop immediately.

Charles Darby, from *The International Grand Prix Book of Motor Racing*, ed. Leslie Frewin (1965)

Driving at Speed

. . . I am often asked what it is like driving a very fast car round a circuit, and how I feel at speed. To a family man driving his car along a road at 70 m.p.h., speed is relative to the traffic he is passing. He feels as though he is driving quickly and in that context, maybe he is. But to ask a racing driver how he feels about driving at 150 m.p.h., is something completely different. One of the integral parts of racing is being able to feel at home at high speeds. Now this may appear to be a very naive statement to make but think about it for a minute and you will see what I am getting at. On the circuit I find that I am so at home that I never even notice speed. I am too busy watching the dials and thinking that maybe the engine should be turning 300 r.p.m. more at a particular spot on the circuit. The fact that I am travelling at 160 m.p.h. means absolutely nothing. I don't catalogue my laps by thinking that the car should be doing 158 m.p.h. when it is only doing 154 m.p.h. for I am more likely to be asking myself why the car is only showing 9,200 r.p.m. instead of 9,500 r.p.m. If someone asks me about my speed round a given corner, I have to admit that I haven't the faintest idea or else try and work out the speed from the revolutions and the gear ratio. In a race you concentrate so hard that you have to force yourself to forget the inessentials. And one of the inessentials is knowing what speed you are doing. It is far more important to know what the oil pressure or oil temperature is than knowing this purely intrinsic mathematical fact that you are travelling at 160 m.p.h. I could tell you that I come out of a given corner at 7,800 r.p.m. and am doing 9,500 r.p.m. before reaching the braking point for the next. All you are interested in are the instruments, oil pressure and temperature, fuel, water temperature and the number of engine revolutions. Even this becomes very automatic, and when I come into the pits after a race and am asked about the pressures I was getting, all I can say is that the gauges were normal. When I am out in practice I make a point of checking the gauges and can tell the mechanics accurately what each gauge records, but in the race I find that I just flash my eyes across the fascia without really registering anything specific but knowing by the position of the needles that everything is normal. Some drivers turn their revolution counters so that at maximum r.p.m. the needle is vertical in the dial. It is the same thing.

All this is part of getting used to the car. Some drivers take a long time getting into the swing of a new car, or maybe driving a vehicle which has been rebuilt after an accident, or one with a different suspension. They go out and do about twenty or thirty laps and then come in and prepare to go out again and do some really quick laps. I find that if I have been out in the car and then come into the pits and hang about for ten minutes or so I can usually set up a fast time on my third, fourth or fifth laps on going out again. If I don't and a really fast time is needed for a good starting position I then take one slow lap to relax my mind and then have another go for a fast lap. Normally, I never like to stay out for more than about five laps at a time, for this gives me plenty of time to discuss with the mechanics how the car is behaving and carry out any adjustments well within the time of the practising period, apart from the obvious fact of wearing out the car.

from *Jim Clark at the Wheel* by Jim Clark (1964)

Advice to Racers

The First Corner This is probably the most hazardous part of any motor race, partly because everybody is making a forward thrust and naturally because you're all bunched together; experienced with inexperienced and healthy car with unhealthy car. It always seems as though the whole race has got to be decided in that first turn, whether it's a ten-miler or a 200-miler, and we've all seen drivers from the World Champion down come flying off in that first turn.

Apart from the drivers lucky enough to be leading, the first corner is always obscured by the inevitable haze of oil and rubber smoke. Back down the grid visibility is literally awful, the noise is overpowering no matter what ear plugs you're wearing and the fumes are so terrible you often come into that turn with your eyes watering. Under these conditions it's very hard to be fully rational and in command of the situation, and down in the field it is also very easy to be lulled into a false sense of security. There's no speed differential between your car and those around you, and you're liable to be drawn into the corner too fast.

Everybody will be relying on their ability, experience and plain animal instinct in that first corner, and the only advice you can ever give is to take the middle of the road, be sure you have a clear marker on which to brake, and make a nice smooth job of it.

Don't jump on your brakes suddenly, expecting the driver behind to be reading your mind, because you can start off the world's biggest chain reaction. This has all been done before, you wouldn't be pioneering anything, but the prime rule is not to get involved, at all costs. With cool tyres, cool brakes and a car heavy with fuel, any sudden action is liable to end in some kind of disaster, major or minor, and so first corner tactics are a matter of common sense. The unfortunate thing is that it's hard to find common sense under such enormous pressures, and at times under such discomfort.

It's a very good thing to be really familiar with your cockpit, and to practise knocking the ignition off so that it's a conditioned reflex, even under the most extreme pressure of being involved in an accident. If we presume that you're not going to be the man who starts the accident, then there's always the distinct possibility of becoming involved in some-one else's, and so a few thoughts on evasive action might be worth while.

Over the years you learn some kind of

general rules, and really the first one is *'Don't* take evasive action'! You usually learn that by aiming at the spinning car it's just not going to be there when you arrive. It's a kind of funny thing, but it usually seems to spin out of your way. Trying to avoid a spinning car almost invariably lands you in trouble, and through instinctively trying to avoid him you've given yourself a nice accident of your own.

It's easy to say you should do this and that, and it takes experience and a lot of conditioned reflex to make yourself drive delicately in this kind of situation, but the last thing you want is a vicious application of the brakes, because that will impair your steering — your aim — in any case.

So in those points of a second when you have to assess what's happening and take action to avoid it, you have to delicately brush-in your brakes and aim your car at where the accident has started. This will give you around a 90 per cent chance of avoiding disaster, but if you actively take violent evasive action I would say you stand about a 90 per cent chance of joining it.

Racecraft You can have problems in traffic, particularly if you're not very used to it and you had a fairly lonely time during practice. Being in close contact with other cars can be uncomfortable, because you've got their

exhaust notes ringing in your ears, stinking gas blowing back into your face and maybe some buffeting — in a long race it leaves a nasty taste around your lips.

Racing in close contact like this means that things like braking points generally go out of the window, particularly if it's a fast track. It becomes a matter of braking when the driver just ahead brakes, otherwise you're going to climb into his cockpit with him. When you're slipstreaming, say into a 130—140 m.p.h. corner, you have to brake earlier than you would if you have the track to yourself, partly because the other car's slipstream will have sucked you down the straight faster than before, and partly because your brakes won't have had quite the same draught of cooling air they might normally expect — and need.

Added to which, your car will handle differently in the corner, purely due to the aerodynamic disturbance set up by the cars ahead in which it's having to travel. You won't be cornering your car in fresh, clean air, and it won't have that wall of undisturbed air to lean on.

There's no way you're going to become an effective racing driver if you just sit there clutching this wheel and pressing these pedals in the right order, and always at the last possible moment. This is a one-way ticket to disaster. You must get tuned-in to what's happening to the cars just ahead, and don't make the obvious

mistakes like getting so close you run the man over if he so much as misses a gear. You've got to give yourself some escape route.

Knowing where everybody else is in relation to your car is a vital thing, and you really ought to have it all worked out before you enter the corner. You know if you're being slipstreamed and whether your line is going to be blocked by someone storming up inside. Now the onus is on you to position your car correctly before you climb on the brakes, and if you think you need to be on the inside line don't wait for the last minute to swoop across to it, because there's no way you're going to make it every time.

It's all a question of assessing the situation and acting upon that assessment, and with experience you'll find that assessment is usually right. For instance, if you're having a real duel with someone and the cars are really neck and neck, there's no point being desperate to get past him if there's half or maybe two-thirds distance still to go. The driver ahead is always the one in the real hot seat and there's always the chance that your continual pressure will push him into making a mistake, giving you an opening and away you go.

Another point is that if there's been a crash anywhere then the driver ahead of you is going to be the first on the scene. It's funny but however much I become absorbed in my driving I find you get a lot of information from out of the corners of your eyes. You notice a flag marshal suddenly tweaking his flag into action, and several times over the years I've been running a close third or fourth, and I've just had that little extra split-second in which to avoid the accident while those ahead of me have joined it. Marshals' reactions are worth noticing, and so are the crowd's. If you suddenly get an impression of heads turning or people running then you know to expect trouble, and often on a changeable kind of a day you'll spot umbrellas going up in the crowd and know the road's awash round the next corner.

You can study the tyres for this kind of news. A kind of sheen will appear on them as the oil comes down, but some kinds of weather conditions may obscure this effect, as can muck on your visor or goggles. You also get a transition in the colour of a tyre from a wet to a dry track, and if you arrive where there has been a shower you can often see how safe it is to press on by the colour of the tyres.

The race is going to be a thrill a second and there's a lot to take in, interpret and act on, and sometimes you're going to get a race which is a bit more thrills per second than most of them.

adapted from *The Castrol Racing Driver's Manual* by Frank Gardner with Doug Nye (1973)

Two More Racing Drivers

Davina Galica, ex-Olympic skier:

After plunging downhill on impossible surfaces on two planks — and that often scared me — motor racing has never frightened me. But it needs more brains, and that's fun. . . .

I would like to do two or three Formula 1 races a year and to concentrate in the main on other races. I know all about the pressures of top level grand prix competition, because I experienced them myself in the skiing world, and frankly I don't think that this sort of motor racing is quite for me. It will be sufficient for me to be able to race against top grand prix drivers on more or less level terms. If I can prove I can do that it will give me a great feeling of satisfaction and accomplishment.

Ann Moore, former show-jumping champion:

Both sports demand concentration, co-ordination, judgement of speed and distance, precision and a delicate feel for balance.

The Times, 9 July 1976 and 24 Feb. 1976

Davina Galica

The Northfield Robbery

The following is an account of a robbery carried out by the Jesse James gang and the Cole Younger gang. Read it through once, without taking notes, in order to get a general idea of what happened.

Then study the account and make notes on it under the following headings: The plan; The robbery; Why the robbery went wrong.

The town drowsed in the autumn sun as Bill Chadwell and Cole Younger rode in to reconnoitre. They crossed a small iron bridge over the Cannon River, which divided the town into two, and drew rein in the small square beyond. They looked around.

On the right-hand side of the square were two buildings, a small one which housed the town's two hardware stores owned by J.A. Allen and A.E. Manning, and then, separated from the hardware stores by a narrow alley, the big, stone-built Scriver building. This was a two-storey block with imposing arched windows and it stretched down to the far corner of the square. Round the corner of the Scriver block, in Division Street, an iron staircase ran up the outside of the building to the offices on the second floor. Beyond the staircase was the entrance to the First National Bank. Its offices ran back through the Scriver Block to a small door opening on to the narrow alley. Facing the bank, on the other side of Division Street, was Wheeler & Blackman's drugstore and, next to it, a small hotel, The Dampier House. All were to play an important part in what followed the next day. . . .

7 September 1876 looked as if it was going to be just another day for the inhabitants of Northfield. Upstream, the flourmill was working full blast. In the First National Bank, Joe Heywood, the cashier, was talking to his two tellers, Frank Wilcox and A.E. Bunker. Manning and Allen were busy in their respective stores. Over on Division Street, Henry Wheeler, a young medical student home on holiday, was helping his father in the drugstore. There were other citizens about, too. Nicholas Gustavson, a Norwegian emigrant who didn't understand much English, and a man called Elias Stacey. These were just some of the people who were going to prove Bill Chadwell very wrong in his opinions of country-folk.

Just before noon, three men clad in linen dusters clattered across the iron bridge and dismounted before the Scriver block. Tethering their horses, they asked for a good place to eat. The church clock up on the hill was chiming twelve as they walked into Jeft's Restaurant and ordered a meal. They didn't take off their dusters as they were pretty heavily armed underneath. But they aroused no suspicion, and shortly before one o'clock they strolled back to the square and sat on some packing cases in front of Manning's hardware store.

Then the church clock struck one and, leisurely, the three men got up and strolled to the corner of the Scriver block. For a moment they inspected their horses. That moment, as the echoes of the bell died away, was the last moment of peace Northfield was to know for some time. From over the river came a sudden outburst of noise, the staccato crack of sixguns, the screaming of guerrilla yells. Over the bridge into the square thundered Bob Younger, Bill Chadwell and Clell Miller, linen dusters flapping in the wind, hats pulled low and revolvers blazing.

At the same moment, Cole and Jim Younger swept into the square from the other side, Cole swinging down from his horse in the middle of Division Street. With a pistol in each hand, he began shooting and, at the same time, Jesse, Frank and Charlie Pitts, the 'inside men', ran from the horses and burst through the doors of the bank.

All around the square, people were running for cover as the bandits raced up and down raising the dust and shouting orders. Gustavson, who couldn't understand what was being said, tried to cross the street. Cole Younger felled him with one bullet. For those first few moments it looked as if the old 'hurrahing' tactics were going to succeed again. But the Minnesotans lived deep in deer country: they were hunters, and many of them were veterans of the Civil War. They were not going to be cowed that easily. Almost simultaneously the movement to strike back at the bandits began.

From the drugstore opposite the bank, young Henry Wheeler saw the three men run in with drawn revolvers and knew that the bank was being robbed. There were no guns in the drugstore but he remembered that in the hotel next door was a Sharps carbine. Ignoring the ricocheting bullets and the shouting outlaws, he made a dash for the doors of The Dampier House, grabbed the gun and some ammunition from its case and raced upstairs to a front window.

In the hardware stores, Manning and Allen had unlocked their gun racks and were loading everything that came to hand and yelling for men to come and get them. . . .

Cole had remounted and was thundering up and down Division Street with the rest of them. Dust and powder smoke rose in the afternoon sunlight. The crash of glass was added to the noise as windows began to go. When young Wheeler appeared at the upstairs window of The Dampier House with the Sharps carbine, Clell Miller spun his horse and took a quick shot at him. Wheeler calmly levelled the carbine and knocked Miller out of the saddle.

From the top of the iron staircase on the opposite side of the road, Stacey began to blast away with his shotgun. The pellets were not lethal but they hurt. Bill Chadwell was half blinded by a burst and two of the Youngers were hit.

Now Manning decided to take a hand. Stepping out of his store, he ran along the front of the Scriver building with a loaded rifle in his hands. Cole Younger saw him and turned to charge. Manning straightened and coolly put a bullet through the bandit's shoulder. Still Cole came on. At that moment, a shot from Wheeler's carbine took Cole's hat off and the outlaw lurched round and disappeared into the dust of Division Street. Bill Chadwell came weaving drunkenly into the square, his face bloodied by Stacey's bird-shot. Manning brought him down with a bullet through his chest.

Inside the bank things were not going well either. Heywood had refused to open the inner door of the vault and had been pistol-whipped by Charlie Pitts; he lay senseless and bleeding on the floor. Bunker had made a dash for the back door, hit it with his shoulder and burst through. As he ran out of the alley, Jim Younger came out of the melee in Division Street and hit him with a snap shot. Nevertheless, Bunker crawled to the safety of the hardware building.

By now, the 'inside' men could hear the rifles booming above the sixguns in the street. Leaving the vault, they scooped up money from the tills and stuffed it into their pockets. As they made for the door Jesse turned and saw Heywood pulling himself up by the counter. The outlaw chief shot the cashier in the head, killing him instantly. At that moment Cole rode up to the bank doors and yelled: 'Come on. They're killing us out here!'

There was shooting on all sides now as Jesse stepped into the street and took in the scene. Clell Miller and Bill Chadwell lay dead in the dirt. Bob Younger's horse was down and Bob himself crouched under the iron staircase, trying to fire effectively with his left hand because his right hung uselessly at his side. Cole Younger had his face pitted with birdshot as well as the wound in his shoulder and brother Jim's jaw was partially shot away. And still the remorseless shooting continued. As Frank James ran for his horse a bullet went into his thigh. Bob Younger limped out from under the stairs and Cole, despite his wounds, hauled him up across his saddle horn . . . Somehow, the gang got over the bridge and headed west. . . .

From his office in Northfield, the telegraph operator immediately began putting news of the raid on the wire to the entire state.

from *The Outlaws* by Kenneth Ulyatt

■ 1 You have been asked to write an article of 500 words on The Northfield Robbery for a book entitled *Great Robberies*. Remember that you are restricted to 500 words. You must concentrate on the main points and leave out many minor details.

2 Use your notes to write a report that might have appeared in a Northfield newspaper on 8 September 1876. Start with the headline.

3 From the account, draw a plan of the Northfield town square. Imagine you were an eye-witness. Decide where you were and what you would have seen. Improvise a scene in which you are interviewed by a newspaper reporter about what you saw, and then write an eye-witness account of the robbery.

4 Write the message that the telegraph operator might have sent.

5 Write the copy for a wanted poster, using only the information in the account.

6 Make notes on the part that each member of the gang played in the robbery. Discuss your notes, then choose one of the outlaws and write a paragraph about his part in the robbery. □

The Intruder

In the trial, the same story was told from different points of view. In the extract below from *The Intruder* by John Rowe Townsend, a fight takes place between the main character, Arnold Haithwaite, and a mysterious stranger called Sonny. Later, Sonny gives his version of what happened.

■ 1 Read up to the end of the fight ('But Sonny had won . . .') and try to decide what you think is happening:
(a) Who do you think Sonny really is?
(b) What is he doing in the Haithwaites' house?
(c) What sort of man is he?
(d) What influence does he have over Ernest Haithwaite? Why?
(e) Why is Arnold so angry with him?
(f) Why does Arnold want him to go?
(g) What do you think is the relationship between the three characters?

2 Read the second part of the extract and note down any new clues you find about the incident and the characters.

Each of the three people involved would have different feelings about the fight and would describe it in different ways according to their points of view. When you have worked out what you think is going on, write three short descriptions of the incident, writing as though you were first Arnold, then Sonny, then Ernest. Remember that each of them would emphasise different aspects of what happened.

3 The policeman tries to discover what happened by interviewing the people involved. He listens to Sonny and Ernest but he doesn't give Arnold a chance to explain his side of the story. If he interviewed Arnold on his own, what questions would he ask? What would Arnold say to explain what had happened and why he behaved as he did?

Write a conversation between Arnold and the policeman in which Arnold gives his account of the fight with Sonny.

4 The policeman has to piece together all the various bits of information and to take account of the fact that what people tell him may be biased. Bearing this in mind, write the policeman's report on the incident to be submitted to his sergeant at the police station. □

'I'm looking after you now, aren't I, Uncle?' said Sonny. 'Aren't I, Uncle?'

The old man nodded.

'But, Dad, you told me . . .' Arnold began.

Ernest Haithwaite couldn't meet his eyes.

'Aye, lad, Sonny's looking after me,' he said. 'He reckons I'll have to stay in bed. Been over-tiring myself, like.'

'Get out!' said Arnold to the stranger for the third time.

At last Sonny spoke to him.

'Listen here, young man,' he said. 'You and me's going to have to come to an understanding.'

'Understanding nothing!' Arnold said, and hit him in the face.

. . . The stranger stood still. He raised a hand to his cheek, stroked it thoughtfully. A red patch was appearing on it.

'You don't know the risk you're taking,' he said.

The man was calm today. There was no twisting of his fingers. His voice stayed level and under control.

'Go to your own room,' he said quietly.

For a moment, and for the first time, Arnold felt the force of command, almost hypnotic. He turned, on the point of doing as he was told. But the spell was brief. It snapped. Arnold moved in, grabbed the man round the body, tried to throw him.

Then they were on the floor, struggling. . . . He didn't hit Arnold, didn't do anything to make a mark but in half a minute was on top, was propelling Arnold, on a hand and a knee, out of the room, across the landing, through his own door.

The door slammed behind him. He jumped up, opened it, threw himself at the stranger again. But Sonny had won . . . .

The policeman stood by Ernest Haithwaite's bedside.

'So this gentleman is your nephew, Mr Haithwaite? . . .

'And you've invited him into your house to stay with you?'

'Aye,' said Ernest. He didn't sound too certain. After a moment he went on, as if he felt an excuse was called for, 'I'm getting old, you know. Not so strong as I was. I need somebody to look after the house and shop and keep an eye on young Arnold here.'

'And what's all this about a fight?' . . .

'The lad attacked me,' the stranger said.

'Is that right, Mr Haithwaite?' Fred Bateman asked.

The old man nodded, though he didn't look happy about it.

'He's a good lad at heart, Fred,' he said.

'But he hit your nephew. Was anything said or done to provoke him?'

Ernest Haithwaite thought for a while. He looked worried, as if there was something in his mind that he hadn't got words for. Then he said, hesitantly:

'No, nothing.'

'He shouted at me three times to get out,' the stranger said. 'Then he hit me without warning. That's right, isn't it, Uncle?'

'That's right,' said Ernest Haithwaite.

'And you used force to defend yourself?' the policeman asked.

'I used the least force I could,' the stranger said. 'You can see that. Who would you think had won, from looking at us?'

'And the lad hasn't been thrown out?' asked Fred.

'I never said I was,' Arnold interrupted.

'You wait till you're spoken to!' The policeman said. There was no sympathy in his voice.

'Thrown out? Not a bit of it,' the stranger said. 'I've told the lad time and again, there's a home for him here as long as he cares to stay, if only he'll behave himself. . . .'

adapted from *The Intruder* by John Rowe Townsend

Unit 8   Comedy Writing

Douglas Adams was hitch-hiking round Europe with a copy of a book called *The Hitch-Hiker's Guide to Europe* in his rucksack. One night, staring up at the stars, he thought that the idea of hitch-hiking round outer space could provide the basis for a new science-fiction story.

'There really is no reason why we should have to wait until we can build our own long-distance spacecraft before being able to travel around the universe,' he says. 'I rather like the idea of being able to hitch a ride on somebody else's.'

His idea eventually turned into a popular radio serial called *The Hitch-Hiker's Guide to the Galaxy.* This extract is from the first episode.

One of the characters is 'a human from the planet Earth' who 'no more knows his destiny than a tea leaf knows the history of the East India Company. His name is Arthur Dent, . . . a six-foot-tall ape descendant, and someone is trying to drive a bypass through his home.'

It turns out, in fact, that on the very day that Arthur Dent's house is demolished, the whole planet Earth is to be destroyed — to make way for a hyperspace express route.

Arthur manages to escape with the help of his friend Ford Prefect, who, he thought, came from Guildford. Actually, he discovers, Ford Prefect comes from a small planet somewhere in the vicinity of the star Betelgeuse.

ARTHUR: What the Hell's that?

AN UNEARTHLY SCREAM OF JETS THUNDERS ACROSS THE SKY. MASS PANDEMONIUM BREAKS OUT WITH PEOPLE RUNNING, SHOUTING IN EVERY DIRECTION.

FORD: Arthur! Quick, over here!

ARTHUR: What the Hell is it?

FORD: It's a fleet of flying saucers, what do you think it is? Quick, you've got to get hold of this rod!

ARTHUR: What do you mean, flying saucers?

FORD: Just that, it's a Vogon constructor fleet.

ARTHUR: A what?.

FORD: A Vogon constructor fleet. I picked up news of their arrival a few hours ago on my subether radio.

ARTHUR: (STILL YELLING TO BE HEARD OVER DIN) Ford, I don't think I can cope with any more of this. I think I'll just go and have a little lie down somewhere.

FORD: No! Just stay here! Keep calm...and just take hold of....(LOST IN DIN)

             CLICK OF A P.A. CHANNEL OPENING.
             ALIEN VOICE REVERBERATES ACROSS THE LAND:

ALIEN   People of Earth, your attention please. This is Prostetnic Vogon Jeltz of the Galactic Hyperspace Planning Council. As you will no doubt be aware, the plans for the development of the outlying regions of the Western Spiral arm of the Galaxy require the building of a hyperspace express route through your star system and, regrettably, your planet is one of those scheduled for demolition. The process will take slightly less than two of your Earth minutes. Thank you very much.

CLICK OF CHANNEL TURNING OFF AGAIN.
WILD HUBBUB OF PROTEST AS PANIC BREAKS OUT.
CLICK AS CHANNEL OPENS AGAIN.

ALIEN: There's no point in acting all surprised about it. All the planning charts and demolition orders have been on display at your local planning department in Alpha Centauri for fifty of your Earth years, so you've had plenty of time to lodge any formal complaints, and it's far too late to start making a fuss about it now.

MORE PROTESTING HUBBUB

ALIEN: What do you mean you've never been to Alpha Centauri? Oh for heaven's sake mankind it's only four light years away you know. I'm sorry, but if you can't be bothered to take an interest in local affairs that's your own lookout. Energise the demolition beams. (TO HIMSELF) God, I don't know, apathetic bloody planet, I've no sympathy at all....

A LOW THROBBING HUM WHICH BUILDS QUICKLY IN INTENSITY AND PITCH. WIND & THUNDER, RENDING, GRINDING CRASHES ALL THE NIGGLING LITTLE FRUSTRATIONS THAT THE BBC SOUND EFFECTS ENGINEERS HAVE EVER HAD CAN ALL COME OUT IN A FINAL DEVASTATING EXPLOSION WHICH THEN DIES AWAY INTO SILENCE.

LONGISH PAUSH. THEN A FAINT BUT CLEAR BACKGROUND HUM STARTS UP. VARIOUS QUIET ELECTRONIC MECHANISMS. A FEW VAGUE RUSTLES OF MOVEMENT. SOME SOFTLY PADDING FOOTSTEPS. A PAUSE.   (JUST LONG ENOUGH TO BUILD UP THE SUSPENSE) THEN:

FORD: I bought some peanuts.

ARTHUR: Whhhrrr?

(THIS CONVERSATION MOSTLY IN HUSHED TONES)

FORD: If you've never been through a matter transference beam before you've probably lost some salt and protein. The beer you had should have cushioned your system a bit. How are you feeling?

ARTHUR: Like a military academy - bits of me keep passing out. If I asked you where the hell we were would I regret it?

FORD: We're safe.

ARTHUR: Good.

FORD: We're in a small galley cabin in one of the spaceships of the Vogon Constructor Fleet.

ARTHUR: Ah, this is obviously some strange usage of the word safe that I wasn't previously aware of.

FORD: I'll have a look for the light.

ARTHUR: All right. How did we get here?

FORD: We hitched a lift.

ARTHUR: Excuse me, are you trying to tell me that we just stuck out our thumbs and some bug-eyed monster stuck his head out and said 'Hi, fellas, hop right in, I can take you as far as the Basingstoke roundabout"?

FORD: Well, the thumb's an electronic sub-ether device, the roundabout's at Barnard's Star six light years away, but otherwise that's more or less right.

ARTHUR: And the bug-eyed monster?

FORD: Is green yes.

ARTHUR: Fine. When can I go home?

FORD: You can't. Ah, I've found the light.

THE SOUND OF LIGHT GOING ON IN A VOGON SPACESHIP

ARTHUR: (WONDERMENT) Good grief! Is this really the interior of a flying saucer?

FORD: It certainly is. What do you think?

ARTHUR: It's a bit squalid, isn't it?

FORD: What did you expect?

ARTHUR: Well I don't know. Gleaming control panels, flashing lights, computer screens. Not old mattresses.

FORD: Here, have a look at this.

ARTHUR: What is it?

FORD: The Hitch-Hiker's Guide to the Galaxy. It's a sort of electronic book. It'll tell you everything you want to know. That's its job.

ARTHUR: I like the cover. "Don't Panic". It's the first helpful or intelligible thing anybody's said to me all day.

FORD: That's why it sells so well. Here, press this button and the screen will give you the index, several million entries. Fast wind through the index to "V". There you are, Vogon Constructor Fleets. Enter that code on the tabulator and read what it says.

NARRATOR: Vogon Constructor Fleets. Here is what to do if you want to get a lift from a Vogon: Forget it. They are one of the most unpleasant races in the Galaxy - not actually evil, but bad-tempered, bureaucratic, officious and callous. They wouldn't even lift a finger to save their own grandmother from the Ravenous Bugblatter Beast of Traal without orders signed in triplicate, sent in, sent back, queried, lost, found, subjected to public inquiry, lost again and finally buried in soft peat for three months and recycled as fire lighters. The best way to get a drink out of a Vogon is to stick your finger down his throat, and the best way to irritate him is to feed his grandmother to the Ravenous Bugblatter Beast of Traal.

ARTHUR: What a strange book. How did we get a lift then?

FORD: The Dentrassi let us on board.

ARTHUR: I thought you said they were called Bogons...

FORD: Vogons.

ARTHUR: Not Dentrassi.

FORD: No, the Dentrassi are the in-flight caterers. Great guys. The best cooks and the best drinks mixers, and they don't give a wet slap about anything else. And they will always help hitch-hikers, partly because they like the company, but mostly because it annoys the Vogons. Which is exactly the sort of thing you need to know if you're a penniless hitch-hiker trying to see the marvels of the Galaxy for less than thirty Altairian dollars a day.

ARTHUR: But the book doesn't mention them.

FORD: It's not very accurate. I'm researching the new edition. That's my job. Fun, isn't it?

ARTHUR: It's amazing.

FORD: Unfortunately I got stuck on the Earth for rather longer than I intended. I came for a week and was stranded for fifteen years.

ARTHUR: But how did you get there in the first place?

FORD: Easy, I got a lift with a teaser. You don't know what a teaser is, I'll tell you. Teasers are usually rich kids with nothing to do. They cruise around looking for planets which haven't made interstellar contact yet, and buzz them.

ARTHUR: Buzz them?

FORD: Yes. They find some isolated spot with very few people around, then land right by some poor unsuspecting soul whom no one's ever going to believe and then strut up and down in front of him wearing silly antennae on their heads and making beep beep noises. Rather childish really.

1 What features of this extract do you find amusing? In particular, discuss the following:
the use of unusual names;
amusing comparisons and puns;
understatement;
the imaginative use of scientific facts;
comic references to things that do often occur in science-fiction stories.

2 The Hitch-Hiker's Guide to the Galaxy is an electronic book that contains information about everything and every place in the Universe. You have heard what it has to say about Vogon Constructor Fleets.

What do you think it has to say about Earth?

Write some more short entries in the book about parts of the Universe as you imagine them to be.

3 Continue the adventures of Ford and Arthur. How do they escape from the clutches of the Vogons? What dangers do they find themselves facing after that? □

Gunfight at the OK Grill Room

High meat prices have made rustling highly lucrative, and it is increasing, says the National Farmers' Union. Livestock worth £30,000 was stolen last year. The NFU said another worrying development was that groups of townsmen were going out with .22 rifles to "kill themselves a sheep". Guardian

He came over the ridge at sun-up, riding hard. He was tall in the saddle, and lean, and he was the law. He was grey with dust, and the grey was streaked with sweat, like a dry gulch veined briefly with morning dew before it burns off, cracking the parched soil again. It was a long ride out from town. At the top of the ridge, he dismounted, and took off his cycle-clips.

''Allo,' he said, ''allo, 'allo.'

He was a man of few words. But he moved quickly, for a big man.

'Woss,' he said, 'all this, then?'

The two men crouching over the terrible remains looked up. He knew them. They farmed the area. They didn't say anything. They didn't need to. Not with what one of them was holding in his hands.

'That's a sheep's head,' said the lawman.

'That's right,' said the elder farmer.

'Very nice, boiled,' said the lawman. 'With a drop of vinegar.'

'It's the rest of the sheep we're worried about,' said the farmer's son.

'I'd roast that, personally,' said the lawman. 'Saddle, neck, best end, scrag—.'

'It's gone,' said the farmer. 'Nothing left but the feet.'

'Ah,' said the lawman. His grey eyes narrowed to slits, and he stared at the bright horizon, thinking hard. 'Soup,' he said, at last.

'What?'

'From the feet. Course, you'll have to watch for ticks. Mind you they tend to float out when it boils.'

The farmer stood up. His jaw was set.

'We want the man,' he said, 'who stole the carcase.'

The lawman took off his helmet, and squinted at the sun, and wiped the sweat from his forehead.

'I understand,' he said. 'There must have been a good forty dinners there.'

And, leaving them to ponder upon these telling words, the tall man threw a long leg over his saddle and rode back towards town.

The saloon fell quiet as his shadow slipped across the floor. Only the consumptive coughing of the hawkfaced doctor slumped at the cribbage-board punctuated the silence, as the sheepmen watched the man in blue walk to the bar, slow and easy.

'Stone's Ginger Wine,' he said.

The blonde bar maid piled her ravishing bust loosely upon the bar, and the thump of her golden heart rattled the glasses on the shelf behind her.

'That's five sheep gone this week, then,' she said.

'In a manner,' said the lawman, 'of speaking.'

'Why is it always bleeding sheep?' cried an embittered old solicitor from a far corner of the room, who had watched rustlers

make nonsense of his subsidy from his far Holborn chamber, and had taken the unprecedented step of visiting his property only to find his flock was a bucket of tails and an old ewe wit croup.

'He's right!' exclaimed a young don, whose face was know to millions of TV fans and whose weekend cottage was now mockery following the theft of the photogenic little lamb tha had stood outside it in countless colour supplements. 'Why d they never steal cattle?'

The lawman turned, real slow, and fixed them all with h steely eye.

'What do you think, Doctor?' he said.

The hawkfaced man beat his heaving chest. Ash fell from h cigarette. Liquor spilled from his glass. Cards flew from h sleeves.

'There's a lot of it about,' he wheezed at last. 'Take two—wurrgh!—take two aspirins and go to—aaaargh!—bed, and if it no better, give me a—arf! arf!—ring in the morning.'

They all nodded. It was a small community. They owed hir a lot.

'Never steal beef, do they?' said an ex-shepherd, forced no to open a discotheque. 'What kind of rustlers steals only sheep.

They were still deliberating upon this, when the bar-door flew suddenly open, and a distraught and trail-stained farm worker hurled himself among them. His eyes were wild, an his trembling finger jabbed behind him.

'Come quick!' he croaked, and ran out again.

The lawman rushed after him, pausing only to fix his clip sharpen his pencil, adjust his chinstrap, tune his whistle, an telephone the greengrocer. Within minutes, he was riding afte the vanishing dot.

He caught him on the outskirts of town. The man was hidin behind a tree and pointing across open country to a cloud o moving dust.

'Rustlers!' he cried, as the lawman dismounted and bega oiling his chain. He put his ear to the ground.

'Not making much noise,' said the lawman. 'You'd expect th thunder of hooves.'

'Not with chickens,' said the farm-worker.

The lawman looked again. It was true. A vast herd of Leghorn was galloping into the distance. Dimly, through the rising dus they could make out the figure of a man on a moped, waving a umbrella to urge them on.

'Come on!' cried the farm-worker.

The lawman sucked his lip, thumb in his belt, eye on the sur He put up a wet finger, testing the wind.

'We'd best be off home, now,' he said. 'You can't never te with chickens. Get in among that lot, you'd be pecked to ribbon before you knew it. It'll all be in my report, after my elevenses

'Chickens now,' said his wife. 'First sheep, now chickens. N beef.' She wrung out the tea-bag and put it back in its jar. Time were hard. Dripping hardly stained the bread, these days. ' know!' she said suddenly. 'It's someone selling to the Indians

The lawman went upstairs, not speaking, and had a bath. H came down again. It was nearly noon.

'There's a thought,' he said.

He knew Indians and Indian territory like the back of his hand He had known it in the days when it was Ye Olde Kopper Kettle He took his helmet off, and went in. His serge arm rasped on th flock wallpaper, and an Indian slid out of nowhere at the sounc

'I am saying good day to you, what incredibly magnificen

weather we are having, my goodness,' said the lawman, who had studied their ways and knew their tongues. 'Is it possible for you to be telling me what it is you are offering on the Businessman's Special this fine day?'

'Lamb curry,' grunted the Indian, 'tandoori chicken, mutton Madras.'

'Would it be possible for you to be giving me the incredibly necessary information concerning where you are purchasing this meat, by Jove?' said the lawman.

'Bloke comes Wednesdays,' said the Indian. 'Does me first, then he's off down the OK Grill-Room, isn't he? Probably catch him there now, if you're quick.'

'It has been an indescribable pleasure talking to you, oh my word, yes,' said the lawman, and backed out, bowing.

The sun glared fierce in the street. It hung overhead, like a great brass gong. It was noon. There was no one else about. He thought of getting the Doc, but this was the time he took his punctus. He thought of asking some of the other citizens, but he knew what their reaction would be. They'd tell him to do something.

He was about to tiptoe, with his slow, easy, loping tiptoe past the OK Grill-Room, when the door opened, and a man came out. He wore a black jacket, waistcoat and striped trousers, and a bowler hat. In one hand he carried an umbrella, in the other a rifle. He looked at the lawman.

'Oh, I say!' he said. 'Haw, haw, haw! Well I jolly old never! A jolly old harry coppers!'

The lawman looked at the gun, and he looked at the man, and his throat was dry. But a man had to do what a man had to do. The lawman jerked his head towards a Jaguar parked at the kerb. A sheep's head was sticking out of the boot, dripping on the pullets tied to the rear bumper.

'Is this your car?' said the lawman.

'Jolly old is, I'm afraid, haw, haw, haw!' said the man with the gun.

The lawman drew in his breath.

'Can't leave it there,' he said. 'That's a double yellow line.'

Alan Coren, from *Golfing for Cats*

Alan Coren

Is this story a western?

Alan Coren has used some of the features we associate with westerns as the framework for his story. But the subject and some of the characters seem out of place in a western and it is from this that the humour comes. The story is a parody; it is the written equivalent of what an impressionist such as Mike Yarwood does in his act.

■ Choose a kind of story you are familiar with, such as:
a romance;
a horror story;
a gangster story;
a science-fiction story;
a detective story.
Work out the features usually associated with the kind of story:
the main characters;
the way they talk;
typical scenes and incidents;
the setting;
the ending.
Then write a parody of the type of story you have chosen. □

More Parodies

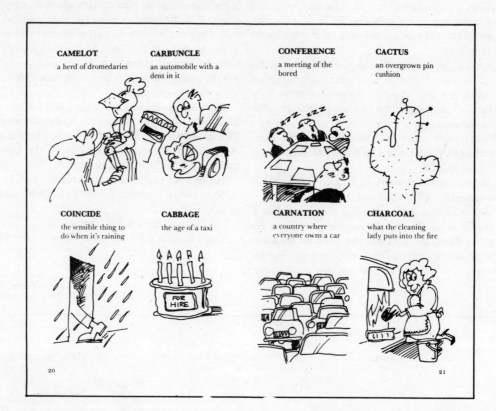

CAMELOT
a herd of dromedaries

CARBUNCLE
an automobile with a dent in it

CONFERENCE
a meeting of the bored

CACTUS
an overgrown pin cushion

COINCIDE
the sensible thing to do when it's raining

CABBAGE
the age of a taxi

CARNATION
a country where everyone owns a car

CHARCOAL
what the cleaning lady puts into the fire

20

21

Advice to foreign tourists in Britain

At a request bus stop, you can signal the driver to pull up by facing away from the road and whistling a popular tune.

Have you tried the famous echo in the reading room of the British Museum?

On British Rail trains, second-class tickets entitle you to sit anywhere; inspectors are there to ensure your satisfaction with the coffee.

On entering a railway compartment make sure to shake hands with all the passengers.

DO HER EARS FLAP?

Girls with large, haphazard ears need that little something which will keep these important features to their moorings. No man wants to dance with a girl whose ears flap like broken shutters. Ear-poise is now more important than ever. In these days of stress restful ears are what men want, not the ears that break the windows on each side of an alley on windy days, nor the ears that create a breeze like the flippers of a great fish. Consult Mme Zaphroma, who will tell you the secrets of the ages. Many a marriage has been wrecked by incessant ear-movements in the home. How often has the tired City man, craving peace by the fireside, been driven to despair and madness by the restless ears of his mate. Bicycle clips, hat guards, strong leather bags have all been tried in vain. The smart girl goes to Mme Zaphroma for the fifty-guinea course of ear-control. Tackle those ears now!

from Beachcomber edited
by Richard Ingrams

Three Men

If you look closely at the players as they come out of the tunnel and on to the pitch before the start of a game you will notice that amongst them are three men, who, try as they may, cannot run quite as fast as the rest of the lads.

On closer inspection you will see that these three rather elderly gentlemen are wearing black rig-outs with dinky white collars and cuffs. Because of this strange clothing it is possible that you will mistake them for tea-shop waitresses, but a little reflection will confirm your suspicions that they are nothing of the kind (unless your team happens to be playing a friendly game against Lyons' Corner House).

These three gentlemen are the match officials, the referee and his two accomplice linesmen, specially selected and appointed by the Football Association to ensure that your lads stand the least possible chance of gaining a couple of points. There are thousands of appointed referees and linesmen up and down the country and, with growing conviction week by week, you will come to realise that each and every one of them has been recruited by the FA primarily because he bears a personal grudge against your side.

Match days apart, many referees are quite sane and responsible citizens, quite a number of them hold down respectable jobs — but not one of them is willing to declare to the public his biased interest in the game. Only on Saturday afternoons and at evening floodlit matches do these men reveal themselves in their true colours and announce to the spectators what a rotten, ignorant pig-headed lot they really are. In order that you should not recognise them during their non-refereeing hours all referees adopt a simple disguise tactic during the match: they take off their glasses.

'PUT YOUR GLASSES ON, REF!' is a cry which you will hear again and again during the course of a single season. Whenever this heart-rending appeal deafens your ear on the terraces you will know that yet another referee has had his disguise penetrated by one of his workmates or neighbours.

from The A-Z of Soccer
by Michael Parkinson and Willis Hall

Today's News

Orang-Outang Kisses Plumber
Dead Fish in Mayor's Wardrobe
Egg-Throwing Baronet Detained

Bubbles from Meat are Invisible
says Gas Man's Daughter

Shot a Fungus Off Own Nose
— Chemist's Mad Feat

from *Beachcomber* edited by Richard Ingrams

More Parodies
On these pages there is a collection of short parodies: the writers have taken a familiar idea and imitated it in a humorous way. They use the language of the original form but the content is not what we would expect. Try writing your own parodies in the same form:
(i) *Definitions* Compile a series of dictionary definitions for words connected in meaning; for example you could use the words teachers use for the kinds of work you have to do in school: assignment, project, essay, worksheet, topic and so on.
(ii) *Misleading advice* Write your own guide which would get people into trouble; for example you could offer advice to newcomers to your school.
(iii) *Problem page* Work in pairs. Write a letter from someone with an improbable problem, then change letters with your partner. Write the answer to your partner's letter, offering some funny advice.
(iv) *Advertisements* Design an advertisement for an unlikely product, such as nose plugs to keep out nasty smells, or spray-on anti-squeak shoe lotion. Look at **Unit 2: Advertising** in this book for some examples of real advertisements whose style you could use.
(v) *'Three Men'* Write a similar explanation of another person in the public eye, for example a traffic warden, a dentist, a disc jockey.
(vi) *Headlines* As well as thinking up some more odd headlines, you could try writing a far-fetched news story to go with them, using the style of newspaper reporting.

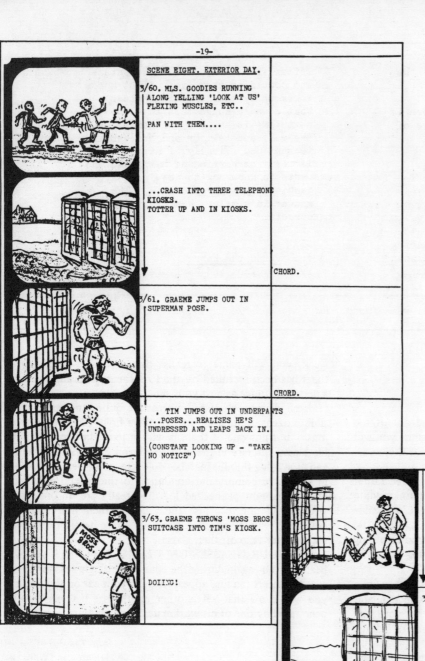

-19-

SCENE EIGHT. EXTERIOR DAY.

3/60. MLS. GOODIES RUNNING ALONG YELLING 'LOOK AT US' FLEXING MUSCLES, ETC..

PAN WITH THEM....

...CRASH INTO THREE TELEPHONE KIOSKS.
TOTTER UP AND IN KIOSKS.

CHORD.

3/61. GRAEME JUMPS OUT IN SUPERMAN POSE.

CHORD.

. TIM JUMPS OUT IN UNDERPANTS ...POSES...REALISES HE'S UNDRESSED AND LEAPS BACK IN.

(CONSTANT LOOKING UP - "TAKE NO NOTICE")

3/63. GRAEME THROWS 'MOSS BROS' SUITCASE INTO TIM'S KIOSK.

DOIING!

Visual Comedy

In radio programmes, the scriptwriter has to rely entirely on words and sound effects. In television and film comedies, the humour is often visual. For television comedy programmes, like *The Goodies*, in which much of the humour is based on the characters' actions and on special visual effects, a storyboard shooting script is produced.

The extracts shown on these two pages are from the storyboard shooting script of a *Goodies* programme entitled *U Friend or UFO?* A number of trombonists have mysteriously disappeared. The Goodies have discovered that the trombonists have been kidnapped by a UFO. In scene 8, the Goodies — Tim, Bill and Graeme — decide to rescue them. They rush off to find a telephone box each, so that they can change into their Superman costumes.

-20-

....TIM FALLS OUT.

GRAEME BUNDLES HIM BACK.

3/64. BILL'S KIOSK.

CHORD.

NOTHING.

3/65. TIM'S KIOSK.

CHORD.

TIM LEAPS OUT AS SUPERMAN, WITH TOP HAT ON.

3/66. BILL'S KIOSK.

CHORD.

KNOCKING

..GRAEME OPENS DOOR. BILL STUCK INSIDE WITH HUGE INFLATED MUSCLES

BALLOON NOISES.

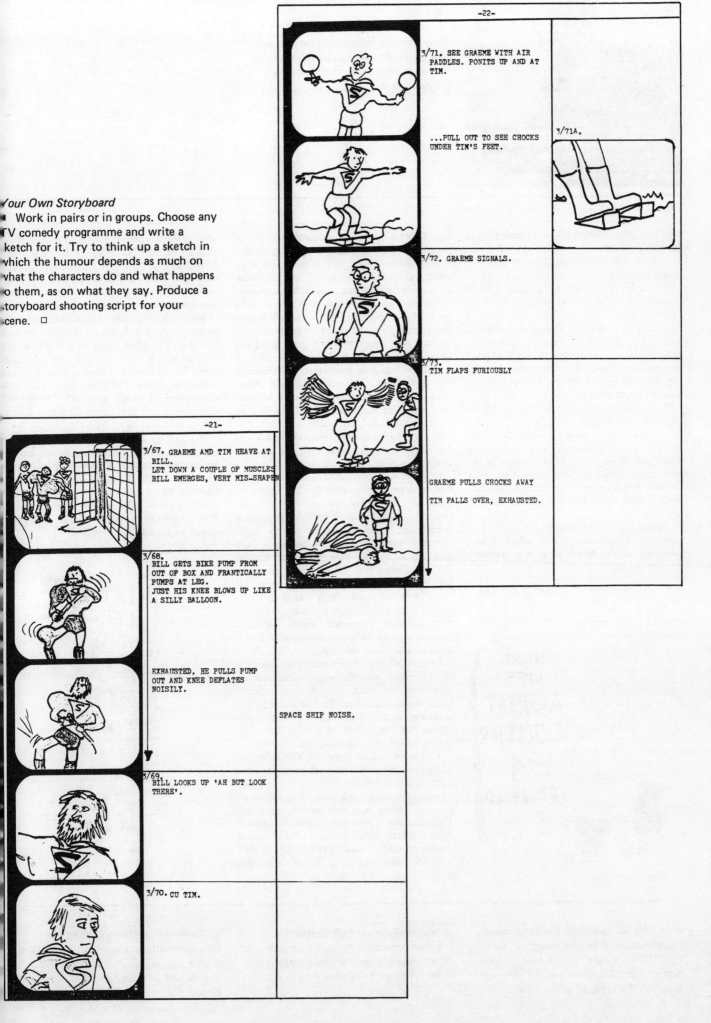

Your Own Storyboard
■ Work in pairs or in groups. Choose any TV comedy programme and write a sketch for it. Try to think up a sketch in which the humour depends as much on what the characters do and what happens to them, as on what they say. Produce a storyboard shooting script for your scene. □

Cartoons

Tony Cox is a freelance journalist and cartoonist. At present, he spends more time on the journalism than he does on the cartooning.

It's not easy to establish yourself as a full-time cartoonist. But I have an ambition that eventually I could earn my living from it.

I find it very hard to explain how I arrived at the point of wanting to be a cartoonist more than anything else. I started as a journalist when I was sixteen. In my last year at school, the art teacher refused to put me in for the GCE O-level Art exam, saying that my style of drawing was far too cartoony. He even wrote that on my report!

But it never occurred to me to try to become a cartoonist. I became a journalist for a good many years, eventually working on the *Daily Express* and the *Evening Standard*. Then, I decided I'd like to do something different with my life, so I trained as a teacher. I worked as a teacher for a while, but I found I missed journalism.

I think the point at which I started to work as a cartoonist was when I was working on the Art desk of a newspaper and I actually saw cartoons, and I was amazed at how casually they were drawn. I had always had the impression they were substantial pieces of art in themselves. But that's not true. Many cartoons are drawn on flimsy paper — I draw mine on typing paper, and most cartoonists do the same. They come with holes in, tea stains on, fingerprints and goodness knows what else. So I realised that it would be possible for me to do drawings of this kind, especially as I'd been accused of being a cartoonist on at least two previous occasions. So I decided to try my hand and, fortunately for me, the very first cartoon I submitted, which was to *Private Eye*, was accepted, and printed, and that was the starting point.

If you want to be a cartoonist, you have got to be prepared for the fact that most of your work will be rejected. The rejection rate for any cartoonist who is submitting work speculatively is high, and my rejection rate is between 90% and 100% — and that means of course that you send out 10 cartoons and you get 9 back. Those 9 you can send out again, and one sends them round and round. One memorable week my rejection rate actually exceeded 100%, when a previous acceptance was returned, because the magazine was folding.

I think what is fine about cartooning is that it makes people laugh at themselves. The most difficult part of a cartoonist's work is getting ideas. The actual drawing is far less important, though the communication of the idea depends upon its presentation in an appropriate drawing.

You have got to have the ability to see a cartoon in life around you, in your everyday experiences. Every experience can be rich in cartoon potential, riding on a train, eating in a restaurant, anything. For example, I was walking down Oxford Street quite recently and there was a doorway and it said FIRE EXIT KEEP CLEAR and standing in it was this wretched old tramp selling matches. Now that's straight off the street. But I wonder how many people saw it. Another time, I was on a train. I like reading on the train and I am infuriated by people getting into my empty carriage and having this long boring conversation about their nephew in South Africa. I was so annoyed by this one day, I was brooding on it and wanting to commit murder on the two old baggages in the corner. Then, suddenly, I had a cartoon. There I was, sitting in a railway compartment with the NO SMOKING sign stuck on the window. But what in fact it said was NO TALKING.

If I get an idea, I always put it in my notebook. Then, later on at home, I draw the actual cartoon. You don't need much drawing ability to be a cartoonist. You have got to be able to draw, of course, but drawing skills will improve with practice. What matters most is ideas, and your desire to communicate them.

Tony Cox

■ 1 Work in a group. Collect cartoons from as many different sources as you can. Make a note of where each cartoon comes from. Are there any differences between the types of cartoons that appear in different publications?

Either produce a folder of cartoons, or select your top ten cartoons and mount them on paper to display on the wall.

2 Organise a cartoon competition. Entries could be restricted to a particular theme, e.g. pollution, or to anything topical within your school or neighbourhood. □

Peter Maddocks is a Fleet Street cartoonist. Often, a newspaper editor will telephone him to ask him to draw a cartoon to accompany a particular news story. The story opposite appeared in the *Daily Mail* on Monday, 17 September 1979. Below is the cartoon which Peter Maddocks drew to go with this news story.

YOU SHOULD HAVE SPENT A PFENNIG BEFORE WE LEFT THE GROUND!

-MADDOCKS-

Up, Up and Away to Freedom

FROM COLIN LAWSON IN BONN

Two young families yesterday brought off the most fantastic defection of all — over the East-West German border at 1,500 ft in a home-made hot-air balloon.

Four adults and four children, the youngest only two years old, made a 30-minute flight to freedom clinging to a wooden platform about 4½ ft square.

Above them was the balloon envelope, 137 ft high and 114 ft across, patched together by the two wives from nylon sheets and curtains.

The platform had a single safety precaution — a clothes line wound round four corner stanchions. The children were at the corners, one on each side.

The adults hung on to a flimsy cage in the middle which contained four large cylinders of butane gas to provide crude hot air burners.

This was the extraordinary sight that rose into the night sky at 2.40 a.m. from a remote field outside the East German village of Poessnek, in the province of Thuringia. Six miles to the south lay the border, Bavaria — and freedom. It had been a nail-biting hour to inflate the balloon.

It was a clear, starlit night and the wind was right. But it had been bitterly cold and they were terrified.

At one awful moment during the flight, a searchlight, presumably manned by Communist border guards, actually caught the balloon. The escapers waited for the shooting to start — but, inexplicably, nothing happened.

They were the more astonished because on a previous attempt in July their balloon had come down 200 yards short of the border. They managed to get away, but the wreckage was found by border guards.

The pilot, and the man who designed the balloon, was 37-year-old aircraft mechanic Hans-Peter Strelzik. His friend Gunther Wetzel, a 24-year-old bricklayer, and Strelzik's sons Frank, 15, and Andreas, 11, helped him to build it while the wives sewed. They bought the material bit by bit in different places so as not to attract attention and hid it in a cellar.

They did it, Strelzik said, not because either family was badly off in material terms — 'things were pretty good for us over there by East German standards. We each had a house and a car.

'But it was no longer possible for us to lie to our children and put up with the political conditions.'

Daily Mail, 17 Sept. 1979

■ 1 Collect examples of topical cartoons from newspapers and magazines. Compare different cartoons based on the same news item. Decide which is the most successful and why.

2 Work in a group. Study your local newspaper. Choose one of the items and discuss ideas for a cartoon based on that item. One of the members of the group could then draw the cartoon.

3 Design and produce a picture-strip, which aims to tell visitors about places to go and things to do in your area. □

Cartoonists are sometimes asked to draw a picture-strip, giving instructions or offering advice.[1] Peter Maddocks drew this picture-strip, which offers advice on jogging, for a Health Education Council pamphlet called *Look After Yourself*.

[1] Look on page 28 where you will find a picture strip recipe drawn by Peter Maddocks.

Masculine Protest

For months things had been getting difficult between Mother and me. At the time we were living in Boharna, a small town twenty miles from the city — Father, Mother, Martha, and I. I had managed to put up with it by kidding myself that one day Mother would understand; one day she'd wake up and see that the affection of Dad and Martha was insincere, that the two had long ago ganged up against her, and that I, the black sheep, the clumsy, stupid Denis, was the only one who really loved her.

The revelation was due to take place in rather unusual circumstances. We were all to be stranded in some dangerous desert, and Mother, with her ankle broken, would tell us to leave her, with only a pretence of concern. I could even imagine how Dad would look back regretfully, with his eyebrows raised, and shrug his shoulders, as much as to say that there was nothing he could do. But I, in my casual way, would simply fold my hands about my knees and ask listlessly, 'What use is life to me without you? It's all very well for Dad and Martha; they have one another, but I have only you.' Not a word more! I was determined on not having any false drama, any raising of the voice. I was never one for high flown expressions; the lift of the shoulder, the way I pulled a grass-blade to chew (it needn't be a desert), and Mother would realize that though I was not demonstrative — just a plain, rough, willing chap — I had a heart of gold.

But Mother had a genius for subjecting hearts of gold to intolerable strain. It was the same as with Flossie, our dog. We had been brought up with Flossie, but when Dad had to go on a long trip and Mother wanted to accompany him, Flossie got in the way. She was sent to the vet, and I wept for hours over her.

It wasn't that Mother was actively unkind, for she thought far too much of the impression she wanted to make to give one of unkindness. It was just that she didn't care; she was more and more away from home. She visited friends in Dublin and Galway, Birr and Athlone; I never met a woman with so many friends or one so fond of them. All we saw of her was the flurry between one foray and the next as she packed and unpacked. Dad was absorbed in his work, but that was different. He never gave you the same impression of invulnerability as Mother. He came in while she packed, looking like an overgrown schoolboy, in spite of his moustache, and stood with his hands in his trouser pockets and his long neck out, making jokes at her in a mock-vulgar accent. Then, when she grew serious, he put on a blank face and shrugged his shoulders while his thin voice grew squeaky with anxiety — a bit of a nonentity, really, as you could see from the way she took him.

But I who loved her realized that she expected me to be a nonentity, too. She thought Dad made too many demands on her, which you could understand, but she thought the same of me, and sometimes I thought this was also how she must have felt about poor old Flossie.

Things came to a head when she told me she couldn't be at home for my twelfth birthday. There was no particular reason why I should have gone off the handle about that more than anything else, but I did. The trouble was that the moment I did so, I seemed to have no reasons on my side. I could only sob and stamp and say she hadn't done it to Martha. She looked at me coldly and said I was a pretty picture, that I had no manliness.

'And you did the same to Flossie!' I shouted, stung to madness by her taunt.

I thought she'd hit me, but she only drew herself up, looking twice as noble and beautiful, and her lip curled. 'That is a contemptible remark, Denis,' she said, 'and one I'd expect only from you.'

Then she went off for the evening with the Clarkes, leaving Martha and me alone. Father was still at the office. Martha looked at me half in pity, half in amusement. She was never really very disappointed in Mother, because she expected less of her.

'What did I tell you?' she said.

I went up to my room and cried like a kid. It was the taunt about my lack of manliness that stung me most. I simply felt I couldn't live in the same house any longer with a woman who had said such a thing. I took out my Post Office savings book. I had four pounds fifteen — enough to keep me for a month or more till I found some corner where people wanted me, a plain, rough-spoken chap who only needed a little affection. If the worst came to the worst I could always make for Dublin, where Auntie May and my father's father lived. I knew they'd be glad to help me, because they had never even pretended to like Mother, and though I had resented this in them, I now saw they might have been right. It would be something just to reach their door and say to Auntie May in my plain, straightforward way, 'I see now I was wrong.' Then I dried my eyes, went downstairs, and took out my bicycle. It was equipped with dynamo lamp and everything — a smasher!

'Where are you off to?' Martha asked.

'You'll soon see,' I said darkly, and cycled off.

Then I had my first shock, because as I cycled into Main Street I saw that all the shops were shuttered for the weekly half-day and knew that the post office, too, would be closed. Apart from what I had in the bank I had nothing, and I knew I couldn't get far without money — certainly not as far as I hoped to get, for I intended not to come back.

I stood for ten minutes outside the post office, wondering wildly if one of the clerks would turn up. I felt that I simply couldn't return home. And then the idea struck me that the city was only twenty miles away, and that the post office there was bound to be open. I had been to the city a couple of times with Mother, so there was nothing very unfamiliar or frightening in the idea of it. When I got my money I could either stay the night at a hotel or cycle on through the dark. I was attracted by the latter idea. It would be good fun to cycle through the sleeping villages and towns, and see the dawn break over Dublin, and arrive at Auntie May's door, in the Shelbourne Road, while she

was lighting the fire. I could imagine how she would greet me — 'Child of Grace, where did you come from?' 'Ah, just cycled,' I would reply, without any fuss.

It was very pleasant, but it wasn't enough. I cycled slowly and undecidedly out the familiar main road where we walked on Sunday, past the seminary and the little suburban houses. I was still uncertain that I should go on. Then something happened. Suddenly the countryside struck me as strange. I got off my bicycle and looked round. The town had sunk back into its black, bushy hills, with little showing of it but the spire of the church and the ruined tower of the abbey. It was as though it had accompanied me so far and then silently left me and returned. I found myself in new country, with a little, painted town sprawled across a river and, beyond it, bigger, smoother, greener hills. It was a curious sensation, rather like the moment when you find yourself out of your depth and two inclinations struggle in you — one to turn back in panic to the shallows, the other to strike out boldly for the other side.

The mere analogy was enough for me. It was like a challenge, and that moment of panic gave new energy to my cycling. The little town, the big red-brick mansion at the end of a beech avenue, the hexagonal brown building on top of the smooth hill before me, and the glimpses I caught of the river were both fascinating and frightening. I was aware of great distances, of big cloud masses on the horizon, of the fragility of my tyres compared with the rough surface of the road, and everything disappeared in the urgent need to get to the city, to draw out my money, to find myself food and a bed for the night.

For the last ten miles I hadn't even the temptation to look at my surroundings. Things just happened to me: the road bent away under me; wide green rivers rose up and slipped away again under my tyres; castles soared from the roadside with great arches blocked out in masses of shadow. I was lightheaded with hunger. I had been cycling with such savagery that I had exhausted myself, and the spires of the city sticking up from the fields ahead merely presented a fresh problem — whether or not the post office would be open.

Though that is not altogether true. There was one blessed brief spell when the rocky fields closed behind me like a book, and the electric-light poles escorted me up the last hill and gently down between comfortable villas and long gardens to the bridge. The city was stretched out along the other side of the river — a castle by the bridge, a cathedral tower above it, a row of warehouses, a terrace of crumbling Georgian houses — and I felt my heart rise at the thought that whatever happened I had proved I was a man.

But now emerged the greater problem of remaining one.

Beyond the bridge the road climbed to the main street, two long facades of red-brick houses broken by the limestone front of a church. As I passed, I promised God to come in and thank Him if the post office was open. But as I crossed its threshold I knew my luck was out. Only the stamp counter was open, everything else was shut. At the stamp counter they told me I must come back next morning. They might as well have told me to come back next year.

Stunned and miserable, I pushed my bike back up to the main street and looked up and down. It was long and wide and lonesome, and I didn't know a soul I could turn to. I knew that without a meal and a rest I couldn't set out for Dublin. I was whacked. I had proved to myself that I was manly, but what good was manliness when Irish post offices wouldn't remain open after five o'clock?

It was just because I was so tired that I went to sit in the church — not out of any confidence in God, who was very much in my black books. I sat in the last row, at the end of the church. It was quiet and dark, with a red light showing far away in the sanctuary. And it was then that the thought of Dad came to me. It was funny that I hadn't thought of him before, even when thinking of Grandfather and Auntie May. I had thought of them as allies in my campaign against Mother. Dad seemed so ineffectual that I hadn't thought of him at all. Now, as I began to imagine him, with his long neck and weak face, his bowler hat and his moustache, which made you think of a fellow dressed up in a school show, his puerile jokes in his vulgar accent, everything about him seemed attractive. And I swear it wasn't only the hunger and panic. It was something new for me; it was almost love. Full of new energy, I knelt and prayed, 'Almighty God, grant I can talk to Dad on the phone!' The sanctuary lamp twinkled conspiratorially, like a signal, and I felt encouraged.

It wasn't as easy as that, though. The first place I asked permission to telephone they just hooshed me out, and the feeling that I was obeying an injunction of Heaven gave place to indignation. The sanctuary lamp had no business making signals unless it could arrange things better. I dawdled hopelessly along the main street, leaving my bike by the kerb and gazing in shop windows. In one I found a mirror where I could see myself fulllength. I looked old and heartbroken. It was like a picture. The title 'Homeless' suggested itself to me and I blinked away my tears. There were nice model trains in the window, though — electric ones.

Then, as I passed a public-house, I saw a tall man in shirtsleeves by the door. I had a feeling that he had been watching me for a good while. He winked, and I winked back.

'Is it a pint you're looking for?' he asked in a loud, jovial tone, and I was disappointed, because it struck me that he might be only looking for trade.

'No,' I said, though I shouldn't have said it if he had asked me whether I was looking for lemonade.

'I'm sorry,' he said. 'I thought you might be a customer. Are you from these parts?'

'No,' I said modestly, conscious that I had travelled a long distance, but not wishing to boast, 'I'm from Boharna.'

'Boharna, begod!' he exclaimed, with new interest. 'And what are you doing in town?'

'I ran away from home,' I said, feeling I might as well get that in, in case he could help me.

'You couldn't do better,' he said with enthusiasm. 'I did it myself.'

'Did you?' I asked eagerly. This seemed the very sort of man I wanted to meet. 'When was this?'

'When I was fourteen.'

'I'm only twelve,' I said.

'There's nothing like beginning young,' he said. 'I did it three times in all before I got away with it. They were fed up with me then. You have to keep plugging away at it. Is it your old fellow?'

'No,' I said, surrendering myself to his experience and even adopting his broad way of speech. 'My old one.'

'Ah, cripes, that's tough,' he said. ''Tis bad enough having the old man on your back, but 'tis the devil entirely when you haven't the old woman behind you. And where are you off to now?'

'I don't know,' I admitted. 'I wanted to go to Dublin, but I can't.'

'Why not?'

'All my money is in the savings bank and I can't get it till tomorrow.'

'That's bad management, you know,' he said, shaking his head. 'You should have it with you.'

'I know,' I said, 'but I only made up my mind today.'

'Ah, cripes,' he said, 'you should have a thing like that planned for months ahead. 'Tis easy seen you're not used to it. It looks as if you might have to go back.'

'I can't go back,' I said despondently. ''Tis twenty miles. If I could only talk to Dad on the phone, he'd tell me what to do.'

'Who is your dad?' he asked, and I told him. 'Ah, we might be able to manage that for you. Come in.'

There was a phone in the corner, and he beckoned me to fire ahead. After a few minutes I heard Dad's voice, faint and squeaky with surprise, and I almost wept with delight.

'Hullo, son,' he said. 'Where on earth are you?'

'In Asragh, Daddy,' I said lightly. Even then I couldn't make a lot of it, the way another fellow would.

'Asragh?' Dad said, and I could almost see how his eyebrows worked up his forehead. 'What took you there?'

'I just ran away from home, Dad,' I said, trying to make it sound casual.

'Oh!' he said, and he paused for a moment, but his voice didn't change either. 'How did you get there?'

'On the bike, Dad.'

'The whole way?'

'The whole way.'

'Are you dead?' he asked with a laugh.

'Ah, just a bit,' I said modestly.

'Have you had anything to eat?'

'No, Dad.'

'Why not? Didn't you bring any money with you?'

'Only my savings-bank book, but the post office is shut.'

'Oh, hard luck!' he said. 'And what are you going to do now?'

'I don't know, Dad. I thought you might tell me.'

'Well, what about coming home?'

'I don't mind, Dad. Whatever you say.'

'Hold on a minute now till I see when the next bus is . . . Oh, hullo! You can get one in forty minutes' time — seven-ten. Tell the conductor I'll meet you and pay your fare. Is that all right?'

'That's grand, Dad,' I said, feeling that the world had almost come right again.

'Good! I'll have some supper ready. Mind yourself now.'

When I finished, the barman was waiting for me with his coat on. He had a girl looking after the bar for him.

'Better come and have a cup of tea with me before the bus,' he said. 'We can leave the old bike here.'

The lights were just being switched on. We sat in a brilliantly lit cafe, and I ate cake after cake and drank hot tea while the barman told me how he had run away. You could see he was a real reckless sort. On the first two occasions he had been caught by the police. The first time he had pinched a bicycle and cycled all the way to Dublin, sleeping in barns and deserted cottages. The third time he had joined the Army and not come home for years. It seemed that running away was not so easy as I had thought. On the other hand, it was much more adventurous. I felt the least shade sorry that I hadn't planned more carefully, and resolved to have everything ready if I did it again.

He put me and my bicycle on the bus and insisted on paying my fare. He also made me promise to tell Dad that he had paid my fare and that Dad owed me the money. He said in this world you had to stick up for your rights. He was a rough chap, but you could see he had a heart of gold. It struck me that only rough chaps like us were really that way and I promised to send him a letter.

When the bus drew up before the hotel, Dad was there, with his bowler hat, and with his long neck anxiously craned to find me.

'Well, the gouger!' he chuckled in his commonest accent. 'Who'd think the son of a decent, good-living man like me would turn into a common pedestrian tramp? Did you get an old bone in the doss-house, mate?'

I felt it was only right to keep my promise to the barman, so I told him about the fare, and he laughed like a kid and gave me the money. Then, as he pushed my bike down the main street, I asked the question that had been on my mind since I had heard his voice on the phone. 'Mummy back yet, Dad?' What I really meant, of course, was 'Does she know?' But I couldn't put it like that — not to him.

His face changed at once. It became strained and serious again. 'No, son, not yet,' he said. 'Probably won't be in before ten or eleven.'

I was torn with the desire to ask him not to mention it to her, but it choked me. It would have seemed too much like the very thing I had always blamed Martha for — ganging up against Mother. At the same time I thought that maybe he was thinking the same thing, because he mentioned with careful casualness that he had sent Martha to the pictures. We had supper when we got home, and when we washed up together afterwards, I knew I was right.

Mother came in, and he talked as though nothing had happened, questioned her about her day, shrugged his shoulders over his own, looked blank and nervous. He had never seemed more a nonentity than then, but for the first time I realized how superficial that impression was. It was curious, watching him create understanding between us, understanding in more ways than one, for I realized that, like myself and the barman, Dad, too, had run away from home at some time in the past, and for some reason — perhaps because the bank was shut or because he was hungry, tired, and lonely — he had come back. People mostly came back, but their protest remained to distinguish them from all the others who had never run away. It was the real sign of their manhood.

I never ran away again after that. There was no need for it, because the strands that had bound me so inescapably to my mother seemed to have parted.

Frank O'Connor

■ Discuss the following questions:

1 'I went up to my room and cried like a kid. It was the taunt about my lack of manliness that stung me most.'
What can you find in Denis's daydreams to show why he was so upset by his mother's taunting remark?

2 'It wasn't that Mother was actively unkind . . .'
'Tis bad enough having the old man on your back, but 'tis the devil entirely when you haven't the old woman behind you.'
What was it about Denis's mother that made him want to run away from home?

3 'Martha was never really very disappointed in Mother, because she expected less of her.'
Do you think there are other important reasons why Denis's sister did not get upset by Mother's behaviour?

4 'He had never seemed more a nonentity than then, but for the first time I realized how superficial that impression was.'
Why was Denis now able to think of his father with respect and affection?

5 'He said in this world you had to stick up for your rights.'
Do you think the story confirms what the barman says? □

Principle

Mrs Stringer had a hot meal ready for the table at twenty-five past five when the click of the gate told her of her husband Luther's approach. His bad-tempered imprecation on the dog, which was lying on the doorstep in the evening sun, told her also what frame of mind he was in.

With the oven-cloth protecting her hands she picked up the stewpot and carried it through into the living-room. 'Your father's in one of his moods, Bessie,' she said to her daughter, who had arrived home a few minutes before and was laying the table for the meal. 'For goodness' sake don't get his back up tonight. I've had a splittin' head all day.'

There was the sound of running water as Luther washed his hands under the kitchen tap, and in a few minutes the three of them were sitting together round the table. Luther had not spoken a word since his entrance and he did not break his silence now until Bessie inadvertently went almost to the heart of the trouble when she said casually:

'Did Bob say anything about coming round tonight?'

Luther was a thickset man of a little above medium height. He had a rather magnificent mane of iron-grey hair which

in his youth had been a reddish-blond colour and of which he was still proud. It topped a lean and rather lugubrious face with blue eyes and a thin-lipped mouth which had a tendency to slip easily into disapproval. He loved to argue, for he had opinions on all the topics of the day. But he was also a man who never saw a joke and this, with his baleful, ponderous way of making a point, made him, unconsciously, a source of amusement to the younger of his workmates, among whom he was known as 'Old Misery.'

He chewed in silence and swallowed before attempting to answer Bessie's question. Then he said briefly, 'No, he didn't'.

'Didn't he mention it at all?' Bessie asked.

'I haven't spoken to him all day,' Luther said, and blew hard on a forkful of steaming suet dumpling.

'Well, that's funny,' Bessie said, 'an' him working right next to you. Is there summat up, or what?'

'You might say that.' Luther took a mouthful of water. 'They've sent him to Coventry.'

'They've what?' Bessie said, and her mother, taking a sudden interest in the exchange, said, 'But that's miles away. Will he be home weekends?'

'What d'you mean they've sent him to Coventry?' Bessie said.

'Just what I say.'

'But whatever for?'

Luther put his elbow on the table an' looked grimly along his fork at Bessie. ' didn't work yesterday, did I?'

'No, you didn't. But—'

'I didn't work,' Luther said, 'becaus we had a one-day token strike in suppor o' t'union wage claim. I didn't work an none o' t'other union members worked— bar Bob. He went in as usual.'

'And you mean none of you's talkin to him just because of that?'

'Aye,' Luther said with heavy sarcasm 'Just because of that.'

Bessie drew herself up indignantly 'Well, it's downright childish, that's wha it is. Nobody talking to him because h worked yesterday.'

Luther put down his knife and fork.

'Look here. What do you do wi' a las when you've no room for her?'

'Well, I. . . .'

'Come on,' Luther said. 'Be hones about it.'

'Well, I don't have owt to do with he But—'

'That's right,' Luther said, picking u his knife and fork and resuming eatin now that the point was made for him 'An' when a lot o' men feels that wa about one chap it's called sendin' him t Coventry.'

'You've don't mean to say you've falle in with it, Luther?' Mrs Stringer said.

'I have that,' Luther said, shaking hi head in a slow gesture of determination

'I'm wi' t'men.'

'But Bob's my fiancy,' Bessie wailed.

'Aye, an' my future son-in-law, I'm sorry to say.'

'I must say it does seem a shame 'at you should treat your own daughter's fiancy like that,' said Mrs Stringer, and Luther gave her a look of resigned scorn.

'Now look,' he said, preparing to lay down the law, 'Bob's a member o' t'union. When t'union negotiates a rise in wages Bob gets it. When it gets us an improvement in conditions, Bob gets them an' all. But when t'union strikes for more brass—not just at Whittakers, not just in Cressley, but all over t'country—Bob goes to work as usual. Now I don't like a chap what does a thing like that. An' when I don't like a chap I have no truck with him.'

'I'll bet nobody give him a chance to put his side of it,' Bessie cried.

'He has no side. There's only one side to this for a union member. He should ha' struck wi' t'rest on us.'

'Well, that's a proper mess,' Bessie muttered. But her mind was now on the more immediate problem. 'I don't know whether I've to go and meet him, or if he's coming here. . . .'

'I shouldn't think he'll have t'cheek to show his face in here tonight,' Luther said.

But half an hour later, when the table was cleared and Luther had his feet up with his pipe and the evening paper, and Bessie, now made-up for the evening, was still dithering in distress and confusion, there came a knock on the back door and Bob's voice was heard in the kitchen.

Bessie ran out to meet him and Luther raised his paper so that his face was hidden. To his surprise Bob came right into the living-room as Bessie told him in great detail of her uncertainty about the evening's plans.

'Your dad's told you, then,' Bob said.

'Oh, aye,' Bessie said, 'an' I told him how childish I thought it was. Like a pack o' schoolkids, they all are.'

'A flock o' sheep, more like,' Bob muttered. 'All fallin' in together.'

This brought Luther's paper down to reveal his flashing eyes. 'Aye, all together. How else do you think a union can work?'

'Oh! You'll talk to him now, then?' Bessie said.

'I'm askin' him a question,' Luther said. 'How else does he think a union can work?'

'I don't know an' I don't care,' Bob said. 'I'm fed up o' t'union an' everybody in it.'

'That's a lot o' men, an' there's a fair number on 'em fed up wi' thee, lad. Any-way, happen tha'll not be bothered wi' it for much longer.'

'How d'ye mean?'

'I mean they'll probably call for thi' card afore long.'

'Well, good riddance. I never wanted to join in the first place.'

'Why did you, then?'

'Because I couldn't have t'job unless I did. I was forced into it.'

'An' for why?' Luther said. 'Because we don't want a lot o' scroungers an' wasters gettin' t'benefits while we pay t'subscriptions.'

'Who's callin' me a scrounger?' Bob said, with a first show of heat. 'Don't I do as good a day's work as t'next man—an' better?'

'Well, tha can work,' Luther admitted. 'But tha' hasn't common sense tha wa' born wi'.'

'Sense! I've enough sense to think for meself an' make up me own mind when there isn't an independent man among t'rest of you.'

'That's what I mean,' Luther said blithely. 'All this talk about independence an' making up your own mind. They like it, y'know. It's playin' right into their hands.'

'Whose hands?'

'T'bosses' hands, I mean. They like chaps 'at's independent; fellers 'at don't agree wi' nobody. They can get 'em on their own an' they haven't as much bargaining power as a rabbit wi' a ferret on its tail.'

'Ah, you're fifty year out o' date,' Bob said impatiently. 'Look, here we are with the cost o' livin' goin' up an' up. We've got to stop somewhere. It's up to somebody to call a halt. But what does t'union do but put in for another wage increase. What we want is restraint.'

'Like there is on profits an' dividends, you mean?'

'What do you know about profits an' dividends?'

'That's it!' Luther cried. 'What *do* I know? What do you know? Nowt. We don't see hardly any of it where we are. We have to take t'word of somebody 'at knows, somebody 'at's paid to study these things. T'union leaders, lad, t'union leaders. An' when they say "Look here, lads, these fellers are coalin' in their profits an' dividends and t'cost o' livin's goin' up an' up an' it's time we had a rise," then we listen to 'em. An' when they say "Strike, lads," we strike. At least, some of us does,' he added with a scornful look at Bob.

'Look,' Bob said, 'I believe in a fair day's work for a fair day's pay.'

'No more na me.'

'An' if t'boss is satisfied with me work he gives me fair pay.'

'He does if t'union's made him.'

'He does without that, if he's a fair man. Look at Mr Whittaker.'

'Aye, let's look,' Luther said. 'I've worked for Whittakers now for thirty years. I know Matthew Whittaker and I knew old Dawson afore him. Neither of 'em's ever had cause to grumble about my work an' by an' large I've had no cause to grumble about them. When t'union's put in a wage claim they've chuntered a bit an' then given us it. But they wouldn't if we hadn't been in force, all thinkin' an' actin' together. There's fair bosses an' there's t'other sort—that I'll grant you. But then again, there's bosses an' there's men. Men think about their wages an' bosses think about their profits. It's business, lad. It's life! I'm not blamin' 'em. But you've got to face it: they're on one side an' we're on t'other. An' when we want summat we've got to show 'em we're all together an' we mean to have it. That's what's made us all so mad at thee. We listened to t'union an' tha listened to t'bosses callin' for wage restraint.'

'I don't listen to t'bosses,' Bob said. 'I listen to the telly an' read the papers an' make up me own mind.'

'Well, tha reads t'wrong papers, then,' Luther said. 'Tha'll be tellin' me next tha votes Conservative.'

'I don't. I vote Liberal.'

Luther stared at him, aghast. 'Liberal! Good sainted aunts protect us! An' is this t'chap you're goin' to wed?' he said to Bessie.

'As far as I know,' Bessie said, putting her chin up.

'Well, he'll be a fiancy wi'out a job afore long.'

'Why? He worked, didn't he? It's you lot they should sack, not Bob.'

'But you see,' Luther said with enforced patience, 'they can't sack us because there's too many of us. We've a hundred per cent shop up at Whittakers an' t'men'll not work wi' a chap 'at isn't in t'union. An' your Bob won't be in t'union for much longer, or I'm a Dutchman.'

'Well, if that isn't the limit!' Bessie gasped.

'I do think it's a cryin' shame 'at a young chap should be victimised because of his principles,' said Mrs Stringer.

'You keep your nose out,' Luther said. 'This has nowt to do wi' women.'

'It's summat to do wi' our Bess,' his wife said. 'Your own daughter's young man an' you're doin' this to him.'

'Nay, don't blame me. There's nowt I could do about it if I wanted.'

'Which you don't,' said Bessie, her colour rising.

'I've said what I have to say.' And Luther retired behind his paper again.

'Well, I've summat to say now,' Bessie flashed. 'It doesn't matter what your flamin' union does to Bob. He's headin' for better things than t'shop floor an' bein' bossed about by a pack o' tuppence ha'penny workmen.'

'Shurrup, Bessie,' Bob muttered. 'There's no need to go into all that.'

'I think there is,' Bessie said. 'I think it's time me father wa' told a thing or two. Who does he think he is, anyway? I don't suppose you know,' she said to Luther, who was reading his paper with a studied show of not listening to her, ''at Bob's been takin' a course in accountancy at nights. An' I don't suppose you know that Mr Matthew Whittaker himself has heard about this an' that he's as good as promised Bob a job upstairs in the Costing Office if he does well in his exams. What do you think about that, eh?'

The paper slowly lowered to reveal Luther's face again. 'I'll tell you what I think about it,' he said. 'I think you'd better take that young feller out o' my house an' never bring him back again.' His voice began to rise as his feelings got the better of him. 'So he works because he doesn't agree wi' t'union policy, does he? He thinks we ought to have wage restraint, does he? He stuffs me up wi' that tale an' now you tell me he's anglin' for a job on t'staff. It wasn't his principles 'at made him go in yesterday, it wa' because he wanted to keep on t'right side o' t'management.'

'Calm yourself, Luther,' Mrs Stringer said. 'You'll have a stroke if you get so worked up.'

'I'll have a stroke if ever I see that . . . that blackleg in my house again,' Luther shouted.

'I shall marry him whether you like it or not,' Bessie said.

'Not at my expense, you won't.'

'C'mon Bessie,' Bob said. 'Let's be off.'

'Aye, we'll go,' said Bessie. 'You'd better see if you can control him, Mother. He's yours. This one's mine.'

Bessie and Bob left the house and Mrs Stringer went to wash up, leaving Luther pacing the living-room, muttering to himself. In a few moments he followed her into the kitchen, in search of an audience.

'Wage restraint,' he said. 'Think for yourself. Don't be led off like a flock o' sheep. Oh he knows how to think for himself, that one does. You know, I half admired him for sticking to his principles, even if I did think he was daft in the head. But that one's not daft. Not him. He's crafty. He's not botherin' hisself about wage restraint an' principle. He's wonderin' what Matthew'll think if he strikes wi' t'rest on us. He's wonderin' if Matthew mightn't get his own back by forgettin' that job he promised him. That's what he calls a fair boss. He knows bosses as well as t'rest on us. Principle! He's no more principle than a rattlesnake. . . .'

Mrs Stringer said nothing.

'Well, our Bessie can wed him if she likes. She'll go her own road in the end, an' she's too old to be said by me. But there's no need to plan on bringin' him here to live. They'll have to find some place of their own. . . . An' what's more, I won't have you havin' 'em in the house. when I'm out. You hear what I say, Agnes? You're to have no more to do wi' that young man.'

It was at this point that Mrs Stringer, who had not said a word so far, suddenly uttered a long drawn-out moan as of endurance taxed to its limit. 'O-o-oh! For

heaven's sake, will you shut up!' An' bringing a dinner plate clear of the soap water she lifted it high in both hands an crashed it down on the tap.

Luther's jaw dropped as the piece clattered into the sink. 'Have you gon daft?'

'I shall go daft if I hear you talk much longer.'

'That's a plate from t'best dinner service you've just smashed.'

'I know it is, an' I don't care. You can pay for it out o' that rise your union's gettin' you. As for me, I've had enough. I'm havin' my one-day strike tomorrow. I'm off to our Gertie's first thing an' I shan't be back till late. You can look after yourself. Aye, an' talk to yourself for all I care.'

'You're not feelin' badly, are you?' Luther said. 'What's come over you?'

'Principle,' Mrs Stringer said. 'Twenty-seven year of it, saved up.' And with that she walked out of the kitchen and left him.

Luther went back into the living-room and picked up his paper. He switched on the radio for the news and switched off immediately when he got the amplified roar of a pop group. He tried for some minutes to read the paper, and then threw it down and wandered out into the passage and stood at the foot of the stairs, looking up at the landing as though wondering what his wife was doing. He remained in that attitude for several minutes, and then, as though reaching a decision, or dismissing the problem as not being worth the worry, he reached for his cap and coat and left the house for the pub on the corner where he was sure to find someone who spoke his language.

Stan Barstow

■ 1 'Your father's in one of his moods, Bessie . . . For goodness' sake don't get his back up tonight.'
Why does Luther come home in a mood? What do you learn about the relationship between Luther and a) his wife; b) his daughter from the way he speaks to them?
2 'Well, it's downright childish, that's what it is.'
Why do Bessie and Mrs Stringer take a different view from Luther, when they hear that Bob has been sent to Coventry? Do you agree with their view or Luther's? Explain why.
3 'Sense! I've enough sense to think for meself an' make up me own mind when

there isn't an independent man among t'rest of you.'
What is your opinion of Bob? Do you agree with Luther when he calls Bob 'crafty'?
4 'What's come over you?'
Luther says this to his wife. Why does she smash the dinner-plate? At the end of the story do you sympathise more with Luther or with his wife? Explain why.
5 Discuss why the story is called *Principle,* and briefly explain what you think the author was trying to say in this story. Why is the main character called Luther? □

Writing Your Own Short Story

Use *one* of the following ideas as the basis for a short story of your own.

A story about an event that changes someone's life.
You could write from the point of view of someone looking back on something that happened to them in the past. It could be an important event which marked a stage in the main character's growing up from a child to an adult. Try to show what he or she learnt about him-or herself.

A story in which someone has the courage to face up to a difficult situation.
Your main character may be striking out alone for the first time. He or she copes with difficulties which until now have seemed too frightening to be overcome.

A story which explores a particular character.
Aim to present your main character in depth. Show his or her appearance, personality, way of life, and way of dealing with particular situations. You may well want to base your story on an incident in which the character is involved.

A story which shows the effects of a particular place on people who live there or know the place well.
In this case you will need to concentrate on describing the setting. Choose characters and events that will show how the place influences their behaviour. Possible settings: a small country town; a tower block of flats; a boarding school; an overgrown wood; an empty house.

A story which explores the nature of friendship.
Aim to show why people make friends and what keeps them friends. Show what stresses can be put on friendships and whether these stresses can be resisted. An interesting story would focus on an unusual friendship, between people who might not be expected to get on very well.

A story in which the main event affects different people in different ways.
Choose a happening — tragic or happy — which involves several characters. Aim to show their various attitudes to what happens. Possible events: an accident; a wedding; the demolition of a building; someone starting a new job.

A story set in the future.
Aim to show what the world will be like in the near or far distant future. Don't forget, your view of the future will probably show your opinions of the way the world is now.

A story which centres on some kind of protest.
Your main characters will be involved in a situation which one or several of them think of as a matter of principle. Describe a situation which provokes protest, then show whether the protesters are successful or not.

A story which explores the relationship between adults and children.
You could show a friendship between a child and an adult or you could concentrate on the differences of attitude between a group of adults and some young people. Try to be fair to both sides.

A story which explores relationships within a family.
Aim to go beyond the usual scenes of family arguments and show how the different members of the family really feel about each other. You could show how one member of a family comes to understand the other people's point on a matter of disagreement. □

Before you begin writing, use the following checklist of questions to help you plan your story:

Subject Where will you find your subject matter? From your own experience or from other sources?

Your aims What will your aim be in writing the story? How can you make clear your own point of view?

The readers How will you select your audience? What kinds of audience are there to select from?

The beginning How should the story begin? At the beginning or right in the middle of events? In what order should the events be told?

How much to include How can you avoid having too much happening in your story? How much should be shown and how much simply alluded to?

Time How many ways are there of shifting from one point in time to another? What tense is appropriate?

The setting How is the setting of the story to be described and the mood established? How important are changes from one setting to another?

The characters How will the characters be introduced? Should they be presented from outside only, or should you describe their feelings? What are the advantages of writing in the first or the third person? What are the difficulties involved in writing dialogue?

Language What sort of language will you use for your descriptions? How much detail will you include to bring your story to life?

The climax Where should the climax of your story come? Will it be at the end? Will you have more than one climax?

The ending How many different ways are there of ending a story? How will you tackle the ending of your story?

Two Writers Talk About Short Story Writing

Frank O'Connor, author of 'Masculine Protest'

Frank O'Connor was born in Cork, Ireland in 1903, and he died in 1966. He describes himself as having had 'no education worth mentioning'. He wrote very many short stories in his lifetime. He also gave talks and wrote about the process of short story writing, he studied other short story writers and wrote about them, and ran courses on writing at Harvard, a university in the United States. He was enthusiastic about writing and about stories; this is how he put it in a talk he gave on Writing a Story.

I am dealing here with one man's way of writing a story, and the thing this man likes best in a story is the story itself. A story begins when someone grabs you by the lapel and says: 'The most extraordinary thing happened to me yesterday'. I don't like the sort of story that begins with someone saying: 'I don't know if it's a matter of any interest to you but I'd like to describe my emotions while observing sunset last evening'. I am not saying the second man may not have important things to say, things far more important than those the first has to say, but that particular tone gives me the shivers. I like the feeling that the story-teller has something to communicate, and if he doesn't communicate it he'll bust.

Actually writing a story, though, is hard work, even if you have a good idea what you want to write about. Frank O'Connor describes a number of stages he goes through before he has a story he feels satisfied with.

The Idea
The first thing is the idea for the story. Like many writers, O'Connor wrote about the kind of people and background he knew about — the people and towns of Ireland, especially his home town of Cork. His stories were based on actual events that had happened to him or that he had heard about happening to others. Only rarely would he even go so far as to imagine a possible event. He would make a note of themes in a notebook. But to him a story was more than just a description of events; it had to try to show the meaning of those events. He said:

Sometimes a story leaves you with a question. Sometimes it answers a question that has been in your mind.

The story can be anything from the latest shaggy dog story to an incident so complex that for the rest of your life you will be wondering what the meaning of it was.

Making a plan
He had a method, which he also made his writing students follow, of writing a brief outline of the story in four lines before he began. He found this useful because it made him concentrate on the point or significance of the story. A friend who worked with him at Harvard when he was teaching there wrote:

The central concept was that of the 'theme' — a statement of the complete story boiled down to 'no more than four lines'. Occasionally he relented and allowed six, but anything more than six was bad news and certain to bring forth his displeasure.

The element in a theme that O'Connor stressed most frequently was that of incident. At times he virtually defined a theme as an incident in which the people involved became basically changed. In the last sentence of his famous early story, *Guests of the Nation*, he has the narrator say, 'And anything that happened to me afterwards, I never felt the same again.' When, as a result of the central incident, everything in a man's life is changed, then, in O'Connor's view, the writer has a real story in his grasp.

Even the four-line summary, though, was not enough to start writing. Frank O'Connor would work on the outline before planning the story itself:

Before I start the serious business of writing a story I like to sketch it out in a rough sort of way. I like to block in the general outlines and see how many sections it falls into, which scenes are necessary and which are not, and which characters it lights up most strongly. At this stage it is comparatively easy to change scenes about in order to change the lighting so as to make it fall where you want it.

Starting to write
By this stage he had a fairly clear idea of the shape of the story. Now the problem was to start writing it. He was once asked, 'How do you start a story?' This was his reply. (Maupassant is a famous French short story writer.)

'Get black on white' used to be Maupassant's advice — that's what I always do. I don't give a hoot what the writing's like: I write any sort of rubbish which will cover the main outlines of the story, then I can begin to see it. When I write, when I draft a story, I never think of writing nice sentences, I just write roughly what happened, and then I'm able to see what the construction looks like. It's the design of the story which to me is most important. The thing that tells you there's a bad gap in the narrative here and you really ought to fill that gap in some way or another. I'm always looking at the design of a story, not the treatment.

Rewriting
But of course his writing did not stay as 'any sort of rubbish'. He would work on his stories over and over again before he felt they were finished, beginning on the first version by cutting out bits which were unnecessary for the point he wanted to make.

After that, the rest is rereading and rewriting. The writer should never forget that he is also a reader, though a prejudiced one, and if he cannot read his own work a dozen times he can scarcely expect a reader to look at it twice. Most of my stories have been rewritten a dozen times, a few of them fifty times.

All these stages are important: a first attempt at a story is not a finished product. Frank O'Connor emphasises this point by talking about one of his stories, *First Confession*:

Those of you who know something about my work will realize that even then, when you have taken every precaution against wasting your time, when everything is organized, and, according to the rules, there is nothing left for you to do but produce a perfect story, you often produce nothing of the kind. My own evidence for that comes from a story I once wrote called *First Confession*. It is a story about a little boy who goes to confession for the first time and confesses that he had planned to kill his grandmother. I wrote the story twenty-five years ago, and it was published and I was paid for it. I should have been happy, but I was not. No sooner did I begin to re-read the story than I knew I had missed the point. It was too spread out in time.

Many years later a selection of my stories was being published, and I re-wrote the story, concentrating it into an hour. This again was published, and became so popular that I made more money out of it than I'd ever made out of a story before. You'd think that at least would have satisfied me. It didn't.

Years later, I took that story and re-wrote it in the first person because I realized it was one of those stories where it was more important to say 'I planned to kill my grandmother' than to say 'Jackie planned to kill his grandmother'. And since then, you will be glad to know, whenever I wake up at four in the morning and think of my sins, I do not any longer think of the crime I committed against Jackie in describing his first confession. The story is as finished as it is ever going to be, and, to end on a note of confidence, I would wish you to believe that if you work hard at a story over a period of twenty-five or thirty years, there is a reasonable chance that at last you will get it right.

Stan Barstow, author of 'Principle'.
Stan Barstow was born in Yorkshire in 1928, a coal-miner's son. Most of his short stories are about ordinary people living in a Northern industrial town — people with the same sort of background as he has himself. He writes about what made him become a writer:

It was partly this passion and enormous respect for the written word which daunted me when I first got the idea of trying to write. My circumstances and background didn't seem a very hopeful breeding ground either. There were no writers in my family (there were, in fact, few real readers); I'd enjoyed English at school but I'd done nothing in that line since, and I had no university education to help me. It took me a long time to realise that none of these things mattered, and that talent has a way of springing up in all sorts of apparently unlikely places.

What happened was that at this time in my early twenties—I got an awful feeling that I'd somehow taken a wrong turning in life. I was an engineering draughtsman and had a good job by all the standards I knew; but it was one which left me feeling curiously dissatisfied with my lot and not at all ambitious to advance in that field. This frustration led me to look for a creative hobby and to the daring thought that many of the stories I read in magazines weren't very good and, with a bit of practice, I ought to be able to do as well. I was not really writing for money: it never occurred to me that I had anything serious to say or that anyone might take me seriously. That came later when I found that writing insincerely rarely works, and realised that what I ought to be writing about was the kind of working-class life I knew from my own experience.

Like Frank O'Connor, Stan Barstow emphasises that the events in a story should have some special importance or meaning. The events themselves do not need to be especially out of the ordinary or exciting, but there must be a point to the story, a reason for writing it. So where does the idea for a story come from?

Writers are sometimes asked if they take their stories from 'real life'. Well, the answer is both yes and no. What happens is that many short stories are inspired by some small incident or detail from life; not a complete story but something which makes the writer stop and think, 'How, why? What brought that about? What will be the likely result of it?' One of the stories in my book, *The Little Palace*, was sparked off by someone telling me about a man who, to spite the in-coming tenants, daubed paint on the wall-paper of his house, while his wife wept at the destruction. Nothing more, but just enough to make me ask myself, 'Now how could that be made into a significant

action in two people's lives?' The act of destruction in my story is not the point of the story but a symbol of the wife's feelings about her relationship with her husband. All this I 'made up' and I doubt whether the people in the real-life incident are at all like those in the story.

. . . On the other hand, many stories begin to grow in one's mind without this kind of obvious trigger. They seem to have been lurking among all the memories and experiences stored in the subconscious part of the writer's brain until they are ready to make their presence felt.

Stan Barstow has also written some successful novels (the best-known ones are *Joby* and *A Kind of Loving*). He thinks writing a good short story is just as difficult and that it presents the writer with different problems.

Unlike the novelist, who can lead the reader along through two or three hundred pages, the short story writer must make his effects quickly because his space is limited. He doesn't, as the novelist does, deal with the development of characters —with how people change in accordance with their own nature and the circumstances which affect them—he catches them at a time of crisis or decision, at some turning point in their lives, and he must engage the reader's attention immediately with his opening. And although he cannot, as the novelist can, tell about all the series of events which led up to this crisis, and what comes after as a result of it, he must nevertheless leave the reader with a sense of completeness at the end. It is this instinctive feeling for saying not too much or too little, but just enough, that is the mark of the real short-story writer. One master of the form called it a sense of balance. It is almost like building a structure with matchsticks. One too few and it is not complete; one too many and it all falls down.

Unit 10 Mounting a Campaign

How much say do you have in what happens to you?

Much of our lives is controlled by other people. Many decisions which directly affect the way we live are made by people we have never met and who may not have considered us at all. The governments of foreign countries, our own Members of Parliament, local councillors and civil servants of all kinds have the power to change our lives in small and big ways.

If a change is threatened that we strongly disapprove of, there is little we can do about it directly. If we want to show that we think those who govern us have done something wrong, we have to make a protest of some kind. This may just take the form of a letter to the local council, or if the issue is very important, it may end up as a full-scale publicity campaign. A large campaign is intended to bring facts about the case to as many people as possible, putting forward the reasons why the people in power have made a wrong decision. If enough protesters make their objections clear, the decision might be altered.

■ Discuss what *you* would be prepared to campaign about. Think about:

changes to the appearance of the place you live — knocking down an attractive part of town, building a motorway through peaceful countryside;

changes to the facilities of your area — closing down a cinema or youth club, building on the only football pitch;

changes to the safety of your area — a refusal by the council to build a zebra crossing in a dangerous street, or to put a 30 m.p.h. speed restriction on a main road through a village;

things which you think are wrong — legalising abortion, polluting the environment. □

There are many more issues, local, national and international, that provoke organised campaigns against them.

How a Local Protest Campaign is Organised

1 Local people read in the newspaper that there is a threat to their environment. A few interested people meet to decide what to do and to form an action committee. They decide to hold a public meeting.

2 Leaflets are distributed in the neighbourhood. The leaflets explain what is happening and invite everyone to a public meeting to discuss the threat. At the meeting enough support is given to form an official campaign committee and to decide to fight.

3 Jumble sales and other events are organised to raise funds. A petition is taken around the area and as many signatures as possible are collected. Campaigners are interviewed on radio and for the local papers.

4 The petition is presented to those in power, in this case the local MP.

5 The climax of the campaign is a protest march through the area.

This is the opening paragraph of a booklet published by the Royal Society for the Prevention of Cruelty to Animals:

Once a year, thousands of men armed with clubs descend on the ice floes off the coast of Newfoundland in Canada and slaughter many thousands of baby harp seals for the sake of their soft white pelts. Conservation and animal welfare societies all over the world have protested for several years against this slaughter but the Canadian Government has ignored all pleas to stop the hunt, or even reduce the numbers that are killed each year.

In the autumn of 1979, the RSPCA mounted a large-scale campaign to try and explain to the public exactly what happens to the baby seals born near Newfoundland. They wanted in particular to persuade the British Government to ban the import into Britain of products made from the seals. If no one bought these goods, there would be no profit in killing the animals.

The RSPCA campaign was carefully timed so that it reached its climax in February and March the following year, when the killings take place.

In these pages you can see a few of the ways in which the RSPCA publicised their campaign.

They organised meetings.
They involved Richard Adams, author of *Watership Down* and *The Plague Dogs*. He is famous for his sympathetic views about animals.
They collected signatures for a petition.
They distributed posters and car stickers.
They published leaflets and booklets.
They paid for advertisements in newspapers.

Richard Adams joins plea for seal pups

By Dennis Barker

Mr Richard Adams introduced a new X film to London yesterday and speculated on how he might do for seals what he has already done for rabbits and dogs via his literary imagination.

"There was a woman who fainted on the floor when the film was shown in Birmingham and there was a girl at Torquay who was so hysterically affected that I had trouble with her, too," said the author of Watership Down and The Plague Dogs.

Small wonder. The X film, which has been cut from the RSPCA's already short commercial to be shown in British cinemas from this week, showed seal pups having their skulls smashed in with steel hooks, being dragged across Newfoundland ice wastes by hooks stuck into their heads, and then being skinned while still wriggling and whimpering.

In case the atmosphere was not sufficiently evocative of a charnel house, the RSPCA got one of their beefiest inspectors ("a nice gentle man in real life," explained an organiser), dressed him up in the black mask and jacket of a typical sealer, and supplied him with a club and a pick.

After the RSPCA's showing of the film to journalists, Mr Adams was asked if he would consider humanising seals, as he had already done in his books about rabbits and dogs.

He said: "Such an approach might be sentimental. I think I did sentimentalise rabbits but it was a very unselfconscious book which I wrote for my little girls. The dogs behaved in a much more doggy way.

"If I wrote something about seals I don't think I would make them like humans at all. I would write something rather like Henry Williamson's Tarka the Otter, giving the straightforward life cycle of the seal and then seeing it interrupted and erupting into horror."

The trade in baby seal skins and other by-products, said Mr Adams, was like "smashing the clock" of the creature's life cycle.

"I really don't know what my creative imagination is going to do in the future," he admitted. "But I certainly would like to write something not only about seals but about the whole abuse of the wildlife of the world."

The RSPCA officially launched a campaign to persuade the Government to join the United States and Italy in banning the import of seal products from Canada.

There, 180,000 seals a year, mostly babies, are killed to make what Mr Adams called "useless and trivial and non-essential" items like trimmings for ski jackets.

Sixty MPs are sympathetic to a ban. The RSPCA aims to increase this to over 100, to get the issue debated in Parliament. It then hopes the Government would put pressure on the EEC to follow suit.

"Our attitude to wildlife has got to be different throughout the world," said Mr Adams, after which the RSPCA handed out delicious sandwiches made from smoked and inoffensive salmon.

Guardian 21 Feb. 1980

■ Study carefully the materials produced by the RSPCA.

Design and write similar materials for a conservation campaign of your own. Include:
a poster;
a car sticker or button badge;
a petition;
an advertisement;
a leaflet.
Your campaign could focus on:
an endangered species of animal — the otter, the elephant or the osprey, for example;
wasted resources — such as paper, water, fuel and glass;
other threats to the environment — destruction of hedgerows, the pollution of the atmosphere, the dangers of nuclear waste and so on. □

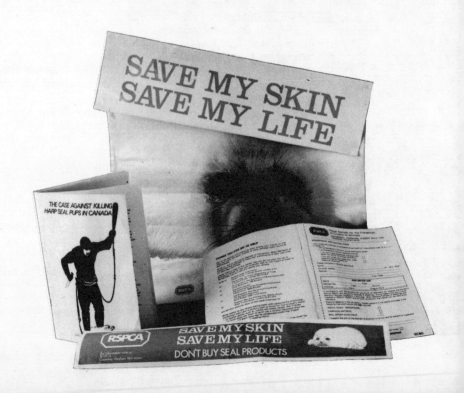

How to stop this bloody massacre

by Richard Adams

Annually, obeying age-old instinct, the harp seal herds migrate from Baffin Bay and Hudson Bay to the Newfoundland ice. Here, in February and March, the cows bear their pups — one each, like other large mammals, including humans. Native to the bitter solitude, they suckle and tend their young.

One day, when the pup is about 3 weeks old, a man approaches. The cow, clumsy and helpless out of water, is driven off and the man batters the pup with a club, turns it over, slits it from throat to anus and strips the pelt, blubber and one flipper. These he drags away leaving the cow sniffing the guts on the ice. Every year, 80,000 to 150,000 pups die in this way—probably about one-third of the number born.

This, says the Canadian Government (which fixes a quota), is a harvest of a natural resource. One Newfoundland Minister has said that it resembles picking a crop of oranges. The principal product is the fur. Since few people nowadays wear sealskin, this is used mostly for trinkets — trimming ski-jackets, purses, car-key rings, and for model seal paper-weights and similar toys.

Some fur is dyed and disguised before sale. The blubber oil, a by-product, is used for margarine and chocolate. The flippers go to restaurants. A pelt's value is about 20 dollars, though the killers get less. The Canadian Government says they average 200 to 300 dollars during the five-week season.

The entire industry does not comprise many people—a few thousand altogether, Canadian and Norwegian. It is not a full-time occupation or anything like the principal livelihood of the sealers. The financial yield represents substantially less than 0.1 per cent of total Newfoundland income. It is a seasonal occupation at a time of year when there is little else to do. It

makes a few dollars. It has done so for the last 300 years.

Sealers fall into three groups. Norwegians, licensed by Canada, kill perhaps 15 per cent of the quota. Licensed Canadian ships kill about 35 per cent. The remaining 50 per cent are killed by 'landsmen' — Newfoundlanders operating on their own initiative. The terrain comprises the 'Front' and the 'Back'. The Front is the Atlantic ice off Newfoundland, reached by ship. The Back, 'hunted' by landsmen, is the Gulf of St Lawrence and the Strait of Belle Isle.

If the slaughter stopped, the human race would be no worse off and no one would be ruined or even much poorer. Why isn't it stopped?

Newfoundland is a bleak country and its people live tough, independent lives, regarding even Canada as alien and not considering themselves Canadian. Values change at different speeds in different places. Great Britain has illegalised steel 'leg-hold' traps. To us the seal-hunt is a nasty anachronism. Newfoundlanders see it differently. There, everyone is either a sealer or descended from a sealer. To them, our indignation is sentimental and we know nothing of true hardship.

In Canada this February, the RSPCA team, of which I was a member, found considerable opposition to the slaughter, in Vancouver, Ottawa and Toronto. But no Government representatives offered to discuss it with us. Why should they? Canadian politics are finely balanced. Neither party can afford to forfeit Newfoundland's support.

How do they defend a business that any dispassionate observer must feel is horribly cruel? (Supervision across the vast ice is impracticable; and how can any 'hunter' guarantee humane slaughter 100,000 times in such conditions? Anyway, what about the suffering to the cows?) The arguments

(now all-too-familiar to the RSPCA) amount to five.
1. It is a traditional part of national culture. The ice is a controlled slaughter-house.
2. It is economically justifiable, since it yields money.
3. The seals eat too many fish.
4. The suffering involved is not as severe as argued.
5. Non-Newfoundlanders have no first-hand experience. They should come and live rough themselves.

Each of these arguments (except No.3) was used 120 years ago to defend slavery in America, and they were all true. Yet slavery *was* abolished, because world opinion felt that its price, in self respect, was too high.

The ice is not a controlled, but an uncontrolled, haphazard, slaughterhouse: and who kills two-week-old lambs and calves by clubbing and then disembowelling them before the mother's eyes? As to fish consumption, the truth is that no one yet knows, accurately, exactly what fish harp seals do eat, or how much. (If anyone has depleted world stocks, it is man. How about the seals diminishing the humans? No, they haven't the power.)

It is axiomatic throughout human society, civilised and primitive, that one does not kill mating, pregnant, nursing or suckling animals. It is against natural law. There is no justification for treating wild animals as non-sentient, expendable objects, like boots or string.

Is immediate stoppage possible? No. The Canadian Government will not consider it. The RSPCA offer two proposals. First, a moratorium, for the matter to be investigated by independent experts. For this the RSPCA would help to pay. Alternatively, phase the slaughter out gradually. Lower the annual quota by 15 per cent per annum and during those seven years create alternative employment

in Newfoundland.

The slaughter is symptomatic of a greater crisis facing today's world. The human race is more numerous and powerful than ever before. We can diminish or destroy any species we like. During the past 300 years, about 300 species have disappeared by slaughter or destruction of habitat. The harp seal, though diminished to 1.3 million from an estimated 10 million 30 years ago, is not yet in danger. But that is not the point.

Have we a responsibility towards other species; or are they the creatures to whom we can do anything we like simply because we have power? Does mere economic gain justify any cruelty? And do our marginal economic interests automatically take precedence over wild creatures' lives? When material gain outweighs moral principle, that is decadence. Only someone who wanted his susceptibilities lulled could credit the Canadian arguments.

One no longer sees leopard-skin coats, or stuffed humming birds in ladies' hats; steel traps, or otter-hunting. We've come a long way. The harp seal slaughter *could* be stopped if everyone felt strongly enough.

There is one effective step Britain can and ought to take, now. The US, France and Italy have banned the import of harp seal products. Why don't we? In the past we led the world in humanity to animals. If every country banned imports, the trade would collapse. It's useless talking to the Canadian Government. But not to our own, who are only waiting for sufficient public pressure to ban imports.

Write to your MP. Write to the Secretary of State for Trade. At least let us all ensure that Great Britain has no further part in this stupid dismal cruelty.

Airport

The number of people travelling by air is increasing. For a long time it has been argued that London should have an extra airport to cope with this increase. Several places have been suggested for the new airport, but many of the people who live in these places are against the idea that *their* towns and villages should be affected.

In 1979, it was announced that Yardley Chase in Northamptonshire was one of the places being considered as a possible site for the new airport. People living in the surrounding villages held meetings to protest about this. They soon decided that they would be more effective in making their case and getting their argu-

ments heard if they banded together, and so the Yardley Airport Resistance Association (YARA) was formed. Sixty-five villages were represented in this association.

Two months after it was first announced that Yardley Chase was being considered, YARA had a network of sixty local action committees in the villages. It had a full-time secretary working for it, and it had produced:

205 000 car stickers;
 19 500 posters;
200 000 maps, information sheets and handouts;
  8600 tee-shirts;
 10 000 badges.

They had set up three sub-committees: the research and information committee,

to look at problems like employment and population, and the effects on the local towns;
the technical committee, to investigate scientific questions like noise and pollution;
the public relations committee, to deal with fund-raising activities, the press, publicity and advertising.

Here is some of the printed material that the campaign produced.
1 Large poster
2 An extract from the newsletter
3 A petition
4 A handout
5 Extract from a glossy brochure showing some of the interesting, historical, or attractive features of the area.
6 Article from the *Guardian*.

Protester goes for plane speaking

Members of an airport resistance group near Yardley Chase, Northamptonshire, one of six areas short-listed as a possible site for London's third airport, are divided over a protest notice painted by the organisation's events manager.

Mr David Jones painted the "Airport sod off," hoarding 12ft by 6ft, and put it by the road at the village of Yardley Hastings nearby but within half an hour it had been pulled down, and the offending word hidden from view.

The sign was erected three times, only to be removed from sight on each occasion. So to foil the phantom sign shifter, Mr Jones, a restorer of vintage cars, towed his message round the county for all to see.

He said yesterday: "Someone is going to a lot of trouble to stop me getting my message across to the authorities. This board must weigh half a ton, and each time I secured it to 3-foot steel posts."

He added: "I have rented an old shooting lodge at Yardley Chase on a long-term lease, and spent my £20,000 life savings restoring it. The lodge is slap-bang in the middle of the proposed runway one. Surely that gives me the right to tell the Department of Trade what I think of their project."

But the Rev. James Davies, vicar of St Andrew's Church, Yardley Hastings, said: "I have got a sign outside my rectory, but it is not crude. It says: 'No Airport Here' – just a simple message.

"His sign has just put a certain number of backs up. It will progress into four-letter words. We ought not be too crude or too modern like this."

Mr Peter Makay, treasurer of the airport resistance group said: "We have had three major disasters in Yardley Hastings since the days of William the Conqueror – the invention of the car, the closing of a village pub, and that hoarding"

But Mr Phil Ives, a farmer, has offered a site for the hoarding in one of his fields, provided that he does not fall foul of the law.

The police said: "We don't think the presence of the sign constitutes any offence, provided there is no question of obstruction or breach of the peace."

Guardian 6 July 1979

Mr David Jones (right) and friends with his protest sign

This is Yardley Chase: the wrong place for London's Third Airport

■ 1 One of the villages in YARA wrote letters to all 635 MPs. Using the information on these pages write a letter to a Member of Parliament trying to persuade him or her to vote against the siting of the airport at Yardley Chase.

2 Reread the item from the newspaper.

(a) Discuss whether the campaigners were right to use the sign, or whether the 'phantom sign-shifter' was right to remove it.

(b) Write a letter to the local Yardley newspaper, giving your views on the controversy.

(c) In groups, work out what might happen at the next meeting of the Resistance Association. Each of you should take the part of one of the people involved. Improvise the discussion of the controversial campaign sign. Try to include some decisions about what actions the campaign should take next, and what the future policy on publicity should be. People at the meeting may make proposals which will need to be discussed and voted on.

You will need some or all of the following characters:

the chairman, who controls the meeting;
the treasurer of the group;
the vicar;
the man who put the sign up;
a representative of the local police;
other members of the group, perhaps including the person who pulled the sign down.

3 The newsletter tells us that another group, in favour of the airport, has been formed. They are called WAY — Wings at Yardley. Discuss the kinds of arguments they might use to put their case, for example:

the effect on jobs and employment prospects;
communications in the area: road and rail;
improved facilities (shops, entertainment and so on) in the towns.
Write and design a campaign handout for the group.

4 YARA argues that if a huge airport were built at Yardley, it would completely change the character of the area. Imagine that there is a proposal for a development in your area which would make equally big changes. (There may be, or have been, a real proposal like this.) For example, there might be a proposal to build:

a motorway;
a new town;
a nuclear power station;
a large factory or industrial estate.

i) You are working for a campaign for *or* against the proposal. Using some of the methods that YARA used, prepare material for the campaign:

(a) a brochure about your area, *either* showing its good features and arguing that it should not be changed, *or* showing how the area would benefit from the new development;

(b) a petition;

(c) a campaigning handout;

(d) a poster.

ii) As a class or group, hold a public meeting to discuss the issue. You will need a chairman to keep order and to ensure that everyone's point of view is heard. Speakers may take the roles of people in the community who would be affected. End the meeting with a vote. □

When the local council announced its plans to close the outdoor swimming pool, as part of its spending cuts, the people of Abingdon in Oxfordshire formed an organisation to oppose the closure. The newspaper cuttings on these two pages tell the story of the fight to save the outdoor pool.

HELP US TO SAVE ABBEY POOL!

Help us save our swimming pool!

That was the plea the **Oxford Star** received this week from four young girls concerned at the planned closure of the Abbey Pool in Abingdon this summer.

by Derek Warren

The Vale of the White Horse District Council recreation and amenities committee has recommended that the open-air pool should remain closed this summer as part of their spending cuts. This will save £18,430, the committee says.

But 14-year-old Karin Lange thinks that rather than closing the pool down, the council should charge more for admission to help meet the costs. Last year they charged only five pence for children on holiday mornings.

Karin wrote to the **Star**, together with her friends Karen and Nikola Morgan, and her sister Juliette. They are worried about the lack of other amenities in Abingdon to keep teenagers occupied during the long summer holidays and think the council should find some other way of saving money.

And the girls are not the only ones concerned at the planned closure of the pool. A member of the Abingdon Swimming Club, Dr Peter Harbour, has formed a local group called Stop — Save The Outdoor Pool.

They are hoping to sink the recommendation to close the pool by showing the district council just how much support there is for a campaign to keep it open. Last week they set up a petition in Abingdon Market Square and collected more than 2,500 signatures in just two days. On the first day they averaged an incredible one signature every 15 seconds, with 1,743 people signing in seven hours.

The petition will be on display in the Market Square again this Friday and Saturday. Information on the Stop campaign is available from Dr Harbour at 2 Spring Terrace, Abingdon, telephone **Abingdon 25793**.

Dr Harbour said the council's claim that the number of people using the pool had dwindled from 90,000 in 1974 to only 24,500 last year was misleading because 1974 was a particularly long and warm summer, whereas 1979 was not a good year. Also, the pool's opening season had been reduced last year.

Dr Harbour also attacked the way the council runs the pool: "Certainly it could be run better than it is at the moment." He said that there were no signs to show anyone where the pool was, and its telephone number cannot be found in Yellow Pages or listed under its name in the ordinary directory.

Two years ago a similar plan by the council toi close the Abbey Pool was abandoned after 6,000 signatures were collected on a petition opposing the closure.

A spokesman for the Vale of White Horse District Council said that it was just not practical for them to run two pools within 800 yards of each other, both at a substantial loss. (The Old Gaol indoor pool is situated just along the river from the Abbey Pool).

He said the admission price for children during the school holidays last year was actually 10 pence and there was no way the council could raise prices enough to pay the running costs of the pool "because no one would then be able to afford to swim there."

Many people wrote letters to the local newspapers to protest about the planned closure. Here is a selection of the letters they wrote.

Tragedy if pool closes

Sir – We were dismayed to learn of the proposed closure of the Abbey Meadow Open Air Swimming Pool.

Our school is situated in the centre of Abingdon and has very little playing area surrounding it.

It has been our custom every year in the summer term to take our children to the shallow learner pool at Abbey Meadow, as we feel that this is a necessary experience, particularly for our children. For some of them it is their only opportunity to bathe.

The pool at the Old Gaol is too deep for young children of this age group.

My staff and I deplore this proposed closure and on behalf of the young children at this school, may I point out that this proposal will deprive them, and many, many under-fives in Abingdon of the opportunity to paddle, splash about and enjoy being in water, which is surely every child's birthright.

E.A.E. Hawes
Headmistress
Carswell County Infant School,
Conduit Road,
Abingdon.

Abingdon Herald 31 Jan.80

Volunteers for pool?

Sir – We were very sorry to see from the Abingdon Herald that the Abbey open air swimming pool will be closed this summer, because it is so expensive to run.

Is there anything that volunteers can do to help in the running of the pool, and so cut costs?

It seems very sad that such a good pool should not be used.

If we have a good summer this year more people will use the pool. Last year was such a poor summer it is no wonder not so many people went there.

We do hope a way may be found to open the pool after all.

Anne Hale
Valerie Hale
Katharine Hale
5 Haywards Road,
Drayton.

Abingdon Herald, 31 Jan.1980

Sir – I have read with the deepest concern of the possibility of the Abbey Meadow pool closing.

In my view this would be a tragic event both for Abingdon and the rest of the Vale of White Horse District, not to mention the numerous holidaymakers – who admittedly do not pay our rates, but find the pool an added attraction of the area.

I understand that it runs at an increasingly large loss. However, school gymnasiums, tennis courts and playing fields would also run at a considerable loss if they had to be accounted for.

In my opinion the pool supplies a similar service for the children of the area, plus a minority of adults.

If the Council must consider increasing the income then perhaps reducing charges and staying open later would have a beneficial effect by increasing the number of users. Another way would be to make it more difficult for people to walk through the exit into the pool area without paying and then change and swim, as I have noticed on many occasions.

The question of whether the outdoor pool is still needed, now we have the Old Gaol pool, is particularly valid with our notorious inconsistent summer weather.

I would answer that, by saying that as long as the outdoor pool is heated, it is preferable by far, except in the most severe weather. I expect that many who have used both pools, as I and my family have for years, find the great advantage of the Abbey pool is the lack of eye irritation and chemical fumes.

Admittedly, goggles can be used, but they are inconvenient, uncomfortable, and reduce the area of vision.

I would add, on a personal basis, that over the last twenty-five years I have swum in many outdoor pools in different areas and I have found the Abbey Pool one of the best with regard to overall comfort in the water, the surrounds, cleanliness and staff supervision.

Stuart Henry
21 Wootton
Boars Hill,
Oxford

Abingdon Herald 7 Feb. 1980

Tragic end?

It is a simple fact, that if Abingdon's open-air swimming pool is closed, some children will meet a tragic end in the river.

At the pool, non-swimmers especially are supervised by trained life savers. What would their fate be if they got out of their depth in the river – where they will surely go to bathe?

Most parents would gladly pay an extra copper or two to know their children would be safe. Give them the chance. Failing that, there must be something else in the town where useless money is being spent.
Mrs. C. Lovegrove, 2 Newland Way, Bostock Road, Abingdon.

Oxford Star 7/8 Feb. 1980

Sir – I write to protest against the proposed closure of the outdoor swimming pool.

The swimming pool is an attractive feature of Abingdon, both for residents and for the summer tourists, including visitors arriving on boats.

It is impossible to assess the value in financial terms, particularly as the use is so dependent on the weather, and the last two summers have been very cold.

If the pool were to shut, money would have to be spent on cleaning, security, etc, whether or not reopening is considered, as the site would surely be an immediate target for vandals. (The nearby children's playground in the Abbey House Grounds has recently been vandalised.)

Furthermore, I imagine that the children's paddling pool in the Abbey Meadow is run by the swimming pool authorities, so would this close as well?

As well as delighting young children in the summer, this pool is a meeting point for mothers and a nice spot for a picnic.

If the Abbey Meadow contained, next to the main car park, a dirty smashed-up derelict building which had once been a swimming pool, and an empty paddling pool, it would not be at all surprising if the number of visitors to Abingdon decreased dramatically and immediately.

Dr Felicity Jenkins
1 Bridges Close,
Abingdon

Abingdon Herald 14 Feb. 1980

■ 1 What reasons do the writers give to support their arguments that the pool should be kept open?
2 In which of the letters does the writer try to counter the arguments given for closing the pool? How does the writer try to counter them?
3 Which of the letters do you think argues most successfully for the pool to be kept open?

4 Find out about any local issues that are currently being debated in your area, and about any local campaigns. Make a wall display of newspaper cuttings and letters to newspapers about a particular local issue.
5 You could invite a local campaign organiser to talk to your group and to explain why the protest was organised and what it is hoped will be achieved by it. If

it is appropriate, you could ask a council representative to give the council's view.
6 Write a letter to your local newspaper expressing your views on a local issue. ▢

YOUR HELP SAVES

ABBEY POOL!

The Abbey Pool will open this summer!

Abingdon's open air pool was given the kiss of life by the Vale of White Horse District Council this week. The councillors agreed to try to reduce the projected deficit of £13,000 and to keep the pool open this summer while its long-term future was decided.

Aided by an offer of £5,000 from Abingdon Town Council, the Vale hoped to save £3,000 by cutting costs at the pool and to absorb the out-

by Derek Warren

standing £5,000 within its budget.

Before the council meeting, the Vale leader, Councillor John Jones, received a petition from Dr Peter Harbour, the organiser of the Save The Outdoor Pool (S.T.O.P.) campaign, and four young girls who wrote to the *Oxford Star* a fortnight ago protesting at the proposed closure of the pool.

Karen and Nikola Morgan, from Abingdon, and Karin and Juliette Lange, from Kidlington, wrote pleading for the pool to be kept open and asking the council to make their cuts elsewhere.

A flood of signatures on the S.T.O.P. petition in Abingdon Market Place followed publicity given to the girls' plea in the *Star* on January 31, swelling the petition total to more than 8,000 names.

A letter from Dr Harbour to Councillor Jones accompanied the petition, outlining the reasons why the campaigners felt the pool should be kept open and offering suggestions for reducing the deficit. Their suggestions included more flexible use of part-time staff and better promotional methods to attract people to the pool.

Two years ago, the Vale council recommended the closure of the Abbey Pool, but backed down after a petition was presented opposing the plan. This time there was a 30-per-cent increase in the number of signatures on the petition and Dr Harbour said he hoped that this would encourage the council to determine a permanent future for the pool.

The leader of the Vale of the White Horse District Council, Councillor John Jones (left) receives the S.T.O.P. petition from Dr Peter Harbour, watched by young campaigners Karen and Nikola Morgan and Karin and Juliette Lange, who wrote to the *Star* to help to save Abbey Pool.

After the council decision Dr Harbour said he was pleased at the town council's £5,000 offer, and that the Vale had decided to accept it.

"The people of Abingdon and District have demonstrated that they want the Abbey Pool to be available and it is extremely pleasing to see the council taking note of their wishes."

He said he was concerned at suggestions that costs at the pool could be cut by reducing heating because he thought attendance would then drop, so money would be lost rather than saved. Councillor Jones said heating expenditure was just one of the areas that the recreation and

amenities committee would be looking at in attempts to cut the running costs.

Another money-saving proposal by the Vale council was a cut in opening hours at the Old Gaol Pool. A second petition was presented to councillors at Tuesday's meeting objecting to this proposal. Containing 370 signatures, it was compiled by a group calling itself FROGS — Friends of Old Gaol Swimmers.

The finance committee chairman, Mr Ray Bond, accepted the petition and said that ways might be found to amend the closure proposals to that public swimming would be available on at least one lunchtime each week.

Flashback to the *Star* of January 31, 1980

Acknowledgements

The authors and publishers wish to thank the following who have kindly given permission for the use of copyright material:

Associated Newspapers Group Limited for the front page of the *Daily Mail*, 17 September 1979;
Arthur Barker Limited for an extract from *Jim Clark at the Wheel* by Jim Clark;
The Boase Massimi Pollit Univas Partnership Limited for the script of a television commercial;
Campaign for Nuclear Disarmament for extracts from a CND pamphlet by David Griffiths and Dan Smith;
Jonathan Cape limited for an extract from *Slaughterhouse Five* by Kurt Vonnegut Jr, and a poem 'Open Day at Porton' by Adrian Mitchell from *Ride The Nightmare*;
The Daily Telegraph Limited for the article 'Heart Man Sits by Bed' from *The Daily Telegraph*, 21 August 1979;
Max Factor & Company for an advertisement for a beauty product;
John Farquharson Limited on behalf of Stan Barstow for 'Principle' from *A Season With Eros*;
Guardian Newspapers Limited for two extracts from *The Guardian* 6 June 1979 and 21 February 1980;
Mrs Valerie Hale for her letter to the *Abingdon Herald*, 31 January 1980;
Hamish Hamilton Limited for four poems from *The Fern On The Rock* by Paul Dehn, copyright © Dehn Enterprises Limited 1956, 1976;
The Hamlyn Publishing Group Limited for a recipe from *Marguerite Patten's International Cookery in Colour*;
Mrs Enid Hawes for her letter to the *Abingdon Herald*, 31 January 1980;
H. J. Heinz Company Limited for their advertising slogan 'It's a Heinz Souperday';
Mr Stuart Henry for his letter to the *Abingdon Herald*, 7 February 1980;
Dr Felicity Jenkins for her letter to the *Abingdon Herald*, 14 February 1980;
Inner London Education Authority for an extract from *Language and Learning* by James Britton; Michael Joseph Limited for an extract from *Kes* by Barry Hines;
James Kirkup for an extract from his poem 'No More Hiroshimas';
London Express News and Feature Services for 'Catwoman' from *Daily Star*, 16 June 1979; 'Heart Man Enjoys his Football' from *Sunday Express*, 11 November 1979 and 'Heart Man's Progress' from *Evening Standard*, 5 October 1979;
London Weekend Television Limited for an extract from *What's New at London Weekend TV*, No. 7, Spring 1979 by Brian Walden;
Longman Group Limited for extracts from

The Human Element by Stan Barstow;
Mrs C. Lovegrove for her letter to the *Oxford Star*, 7/8 February 1980;
Edwin Morgan for his poem 'Bradford June 1972' from *Instamatic Poems* published by Ian McKelvie;
Frederick Muller Limited for extracts from *Beachcomber* edited by Richard Ingrams;
The Observer Limited for an article by Richard Adams in *The Observer*, February 1980;
Oxford University Press for extracts from *The Intruder* by John Rowe Townsend;
Pelham Books Limited for an extract from *The A—Z of Soccer* by Michael Parkinson and Willis Hall;
Penguin Books Limited for an extract from *The Outlaws* by Kenneth Ulyatt, copyright © Kenneth Ulyatt, 1976;
A. D. Peters & Co. Ltd. on behalf of Frank O'Connor for the story *Masculine Protest* and extracts from 'Writing a Story', and on behalf of Ray Bradbury for an article 'Embroidery' from *The Golden Apples of the Sun*;
Margaret Ramsay Limited on behalf of Alan Plater for an extract from *The Mating Season*;
Robson Books Limited for 'Gunfight at the OK Grill Room' from *Golfing for Cats* by Alan Coren;
Deborah Rogers Limited on behalf of Adrian Henri for 'Bomb Commercial';
Royal Society for the Prevention of Cruelty to Animals for an extract from an RSPCA leaflet on seal-hunting;
Saatchi & Saatchi Garland-Compton Limited for a script for the Health Education Council television advertisement;
Shepheard-Walwyn (publishers) Limited for an extract from *Summer's End* by Archie Hill;
Patrick Stephens Limited for an extract 'The First Corner/Racecraft' by Frank Gardner from *The Castrol Racing Driver's Manual*;
Times Newspapers Limited for articles on Davina Galica from *The Times*, 24 February 1976 and Ann Moore from *The Times*, 8 July 1976;
A. P. Watt Limited on behalf of Robert Graves for his poems 'Welsh Incident' from *Selected Poems* and 'The Alice Jean' from *The Penny Fiddle*;
Yardley Airport Resistance Association for an extract from YARA news sheet No. 2 and petition form;
H.O. Zimman Inc. for an extract from the *Colgate Media Guide to Women's Tennis* 1979

The authors and publishers wish to acknowledge the following photograph sources.

Advertising Standards Authority p 19
BBC Copyright Photo pp 10, 20, 21, 23, 36, 38, 40, 75, 76, 77, 84/85

BBC Hulton Picture Limited p 78
British Leyland pp 13, 16 top left, bottom right and right
Jim Brownbill pp 26 bottom, 27 top, 33 top right insert, 34
Camera Press p 7 centre
J. Allan Cash p 26 top
Ron Chapman p 26 centre top and bottom
Chrysler UK Limited p 16 top right
CND p 53 left
Colorsport p 2 bottom
Corgi Carousel, published by Transworld Publishers p 68
Tony Cox, p 72 bottom left and right
Daily Star p 2 top
Dartington Glass Works p 30
Ford of Britain p 16 centre top left
Film from GTO p 7 top
Richard and Sally Greenhill p 8
Guardian Newspapers Ltd p 89 top
Harvey, Unns and Stephen Durbridge Limited p 83
Hitachi p 12 right
Horizon p 14
Intercontinental Book Publishers p 29
Jaguar, Rover, Triumph Limited p 16 centre bottom left
Keystone Press Agency Limited pp 27 centre left, 45, 52
Klorane Limited, p 17 left
LAT Photographic pp 58, 59, 60, 61
Gemma Levine p 67
Longman Group Limited pp 32, 33
Look Now p 9
Lotus Cars Ltd p 16 centre top right
Peter Maddocks p 73 centre left
Mansell Collection p 25
Jim Meads pp 27 top, centre right and bottom
NASA p 64
Oxford Mail and Times pp 90, 92
Quaker Peace and Service p 53 right
RCA Records p 7 bottom
Ian Reid p 73 bottom
Reproduced by kind permission of the Health Education Council, London, pp 17 right, 18, 35
RSPCA p 86
Harriet Sheehy p 82
Solid Fuel Advisory Service p 12 left
Suzy Cookstrip by Suzy Benghiat and Peter Maddocks published by Penguin Books Ltd p 28
Vauxhall p 16 centre bottom right
C. Fiddes — YARA p 88 top right
YARA pp 88 bottom right and bottom, 89 bottom

The publishers have made every effort to trace the copyright holders, but if they have inadvertently overlooked any, they will be pleased to make the necessary arrangements at the earliest opportunity.